A HANDBOOK TO APPALACHIA

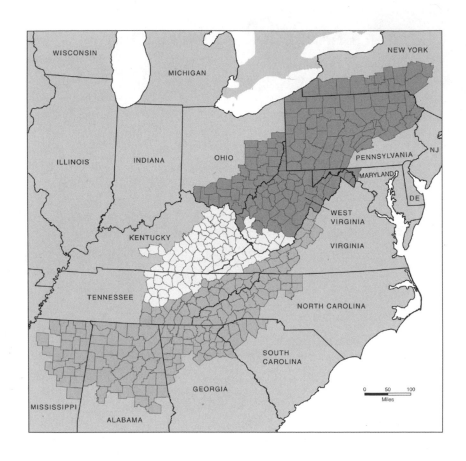

A HANDBOOK TO APPALACHIA

An Introduction to the Region

EDITED BY

Grace Toney Edwards

JoAnn Aust Asbury

Ricky L. Cox

The University of Tennessee Press / Knoxville

Copyright © 2006 by The University of Tennessee Press / Knoxville.
All Rights Reserved. Manufactured in the United States of America.
First printing, 2006; second printing, 2007.

Frontispiece: Subregions in Appalachia, as defined by the Appalachian Regional
Commission. Courtesy of Appalachian Regional Commission.

This book is printed on acid-free paper.

Library of Congress Cataloging-in-Publication Data
A handbook to Appalachia : an introduction to the region / edited by Grace Toney
Edwards, JoAnn Aust Asbury, Ricky L. Cox.—1st ed.
     p. cm.
Includes index.
ISBN 10: 1-57233-459-2
ISBN 13: 978-1-57233-459-5
  1. Appalachian Region.
  2. Appalachian Region—Handbooks, manuals, etc.
  I. Edwards, Grace Toney.
  II. Asbury, JoAnn Aust.
III. Cox, Ricky L.
F106.H23 2006
974—dc22   2005019799

CONTENTS

ILLUSTRATIONS

ACKNOWLEDGMENTS

The editors of this volume extend heartfelt thanks to the many contributors of manuscripts, photographs, and ideas. All have been amazingly patient and generous over the long process of bringing this book to print. We are especially indebted to Sandy Ballard, who played a major role in launching the project and supporting it through all the years. The Appalachian Studies Association's program committees offered a forum for discussion groups during multiple annual conferences. Radford University's Stevan Jackson and his students in APST 200, Introducing Appalachia, provided valuable feedback on the content and format of the manuscript. Southwest Virginia high school teachers Debbie Wilkerson and Selena Hillenberg have "adopted" the book in the Appalachian Studies classes even before its publication. The Appalachian Teachers' Network, based at Radford University, has provided a venue to showcase the content and authors of selected articles at the annual ATN conference over the past three years. The editorial staff at the University of Tennessee Press have encouraged and supported our efforts and have eased our way whenever they could. The Appalachian Regional Studies Center at Radford University has been our anchor during the entire process. For all the confidence and support, we are grateful. Finally, to our collective families, we offer our deepest appreciation for their understanding and love.

INTRODUCTION

People who teach, write, or speak about the Appalachian Mountains, about the land itself or the people who live there, are often asked to recommend a single book, *the* book, that explains in one volume every aspect of the history and culture of Appalachia. At least a dozen worthwhile titles could be listed for each of at least a dozen academic disciplines, with little overlap. No single full-time scholar, let alone student or professional working in the region, could read all the books, hear all the recordings, or view all the images necessary for a complete knowledge of the events and conditions, both human and natural, that shaped, and continue to shape, this place and the people who live in it. Nor could a single writer adequately condense this knowledge into a form compact and accessible enough for use as a handbook for professionals or as an introductory, interdisciplinary text for a secondary- or college-level course in Appalachian Studies. And finally, no single writer could anticipate the needs or inclinations of disparate thoughtful readers in perceiving that any single event or series of events, such as the Civil War, the unionization of coal mines, or out-migration from central Appalachia, has significant and lasting implications for the entire region.

The solution offered by *A Handbook to Appalachia* is a collection of concise, introductory overviews of the region as seen from thirteen different academic perspectives, all directed at a general audience yet necessarily flavored by the methods of inquiry and prose style characteristic of each discipline. While each essay stands alone and may profitably be read in isolation from the others, there is by design and by necessity much overlap. Perhaps the greatest revelation in editing the essays is that each is unique and yet all are interconnected.

Without doubt, the common goals of the contributors in writing their respective essays have led to this result. From the outset, authors and editors alike have aimed toward the following objectives: that the book reflect the thinking and input of as many Appalachian scholars as possible; that it be written in a prose style and layout appropriate for, and appealing to, a diverse audience, most of whom are not academics; that it include sources and resources for those who wish to know and do more; and that it be affordable to institutions and individuals. We believe the product reaches those goals.

In a beginning study of Appalachia, invariably the questions arise: Where is Appalachia? Who lives there? The simple answer to the first question is that it is the region upon and alongside the Appalachian mountain range, which extends from Quebec to the southernmost foothills in Alabama and Mississippi. However, the area called Appalachia does not include the entire Appalachian range. In the mid-1960s, as part of the War on Poverty effort, the federal Appalachian Regional Commission (ARC) was formed and charged with delineating the boundaries of Appalachia. Commonly accepted today as the political definition of Appalachia, then, if not the geographical and cultural, the region encompasses all or part of thirteen states. These include portions of New York, Pennsylvania, Ohio, and Maryland in the North, and in central and southern Appalachia, all of West Virginia (the only state entirely within Appalachia) and portions of Virginia, Kentucky, Tennessee, North Carolina, South Carolina, Georgia, Alabama, and Mississippi.

In the 410 counties that make up official Appalachia, some twenty-three million people live. A common misperception is that the inhabitants are largely homogeneous, but that is far from the truth, as several essays in the *Handbook* show. The people are a mix of racial and ethnic backgrounds, just as in America at large. They have, however, generally displayed characteristics and values that apply to a large segment of the population, with, as is always the case, some notable exceptions. These character traits, along with the rich cultural heritage, the natural resources, and the economic conditions of the region, make Appalachia a fertile and fascinating ground for study.

The topics of the essays in the *Handbook* have been chosen to encompass general areas of interest to students, scholars, and other readers. The essays are placed in an order designed to show roughly a chronological development of the Appalachian region and to show content relationships between essays. The authors reveal writing styles distinctive to their respective disciplines and voices unique to each individual writer. In most essays, the approach is relatively objective, as in "Appalachian History" or "Natural Resources and Environment of Appalachia," but in some, the writers' advocacy of a cause is evident, as in "The Politics of Change in Appalachia."

Richard Straw in "Appalachian History" provides an overview of the development of the region from the days of habitation solely by Native Americans to the industrialized society of the new millennium. He traces Appalachia through its agrarian beginnings into the harvesting of resources and subsequent industrialization. He focuses a considerable amount of attention on the coalfields but does not neglect such activities as tourism and second-home development in non-coal-producing areas. Stevan R. Jackson in "Peoples of Appalachia" complements "History" by adding detail about the various groups who inhabited the region in the earliest recorded history and those who continue to live in it. This essay dispels the myth of a homogeneous Appalachia through its enumeration of the variety of ethnic and racial groups populating the area. In "Natural Resources and Environment of Appalachia," David L. Rouse and L. Sue Greer-Pitt outline the conditions of waters, forests, wildlife, and minerals. Their essay links to both "History" and "Peoples" through its revelation of how resources have been used and, in many cases, abused.

Thomas R. Shannon in "The Economy of Appalachia" takes the foregoing information to the next step by analyzing how the resources and people have been utilized and exploited to create the economic picture in place today. "The Politics of Change in Appalachia," by Stephen L. Fisher, Patti Page Church, Christine Weiss Daugherty, Bennett M. Judkins, and Shaunna L. Scott, relates well to "Economy" as it details ways in which contemporary Appalachians have taken matters into their own hands to shape their communities and their means of livelihood, in contrast to years of exploitation largely by industrialists from outside the region. If Shannon's essay leaves a note of despair in the reader's mind, Fisher and company show another view of those who are fighting back to reclaim their own.

"Health Care in Appalachia" by Anne B. Blakeney depicts a region lacking essential medical facilities in many largely rural areas. The good news is that several regional and state universities have made improved health care a central mission and are currently implementing counteractive strategies. In "Education in Appalachia," Sharon Teets gives an overview of the regional history of education, moving from home schooling in the early days to one-room schools to a plethora of higher educational institutions today. Melinda Bollar Wagner in "Religion in Appalachia" outlines the history of religious movements and provides surprising numbers for the large variety of denominations currently in the region. Her essay draws on the values and characteristics of Appalachian people to explain the inherent propensities of various religious sects.

Since religion and folk belief are often closely intertwined, Deborah Thompson and Irene Moser's essay on "Appalachian Folklife" complements "Religion" in several ways. In addition to examining beliefs, superstitions, and other customs, the authors explore storytelling, music, dance, handcrafts, and more. Their essay is followed by Ted Olson and Ajay Kalra's contribution on "Appalachian Music." Olson and Kalra offer a history of musical development, taking the reader far beyond the expected traditional ballads, instrumentals, gospel, and bluegrass. Danny Miller, Sandra Ballard, Roberta Herrin, Stephen D. Mooney, Susan Underwood, and Jack Wright in "Appalachian Literature" provide a broad look at multiple genres with numerous authors and titles as examples. This essay offers a starting point for reading opportunities in virtually any category of creative literature, including fiction, poetry, drama, and children's literature. In "Visual Arts in Appalachia," M. Anna Fariello surveys art history to dispel yet another stereotype about the dearth of artistic productivity in the region. She details examples from fine art on display in museums nationwide to handcrafts produced for sale today.

Finally, the last essay in the collection is "Appalachians Outside the Region" by Phillip J. Obermiller, Michael E. Maloney, and Pauletta Hansel. They trace those who have migrated to urban areas, usually out of economic necessity. They give historical accounts of early out-migrants and current data from the 2000 census to show a picture of contemporary Appalachian out-migrants and their descendants. By necessity the last essay draws from many of those coming before since it combines a variety of topics to explain the present situation. It offers a fitting close to the *Handbook*.

Each essay is followed by suggested readings, provided in most cases by the authors and occasionally supplemented by the editors. All of the contributors to this book, including the editors, consider the essays to be starting points for the study of Appalachia; thus each essay concludes with suggested readings for greater in-depth exploration of any given topic.

The text of each essay is complemented by photographs that illustrate as much as possible the span of time and subject matter covered in the essay. In many instances, the photographs themselves tell a story that viewers/readers will want to know more about.

As indicated earlier, the editors believe this *Handbook* fills a void in the study of Appalachia. While it cannot possibly cover every topic of interest, it offers a wealth of information from authors whose careers are devoted to examination and analysis of the region. We extend to every reader a welcome to these pages and a wish that their reading experience will be rich and fulfilling.

Grace Toney Edwards
JoAnn Aust Asbury
Ricky L. Cox
Radford, Virginia
November 5, 2005

APPALACHIAN HISTORY

RICHARD STRAW

Appalachia is a place, a people, an idea, a culture, and it exists as much in the mind and imagination as on the map. While it can be defined in any number of ways depending upon the person defining it, its story is rich in everything that makes human history exciting and compelling. What ties mountain people together across the region is their shared geography, cultural traits, and common historical experience.

Native Americans

Long before adventurous Europeans set out to discover what lay in the backcountry of their coastal colonies, a diverse population of Native Americans had been living in the Appalachian Mountains for about three thousand years. The Iroquois, the dominant group in the region, entered from the West about 1300 B.C. and split into the northern Iroquois and the southern Cherokees. Like most eastern woodland Indians, the Cherokees were farmers and hunters who lived in small, separated, independent villages.

While Indians in the Appalachians had sporadic contacts with Europeans as early as 1540, it was not until the period from 1700 to 1761 that contact and conflict between the two cultures accelerated. The Europeans looked into the backcountry for room to expand their settlements and for sources of skins for trading, and the Indians opposed them in a desperate and ultimately futile attempt to save their homes and hunting grounds. The final defeat of the Cherokees by the British came in 1761, and after this date the number of whites on the Appalachian frontier grew rapidly.

Although there were some broad similarities between the European and Native American cultures, the main theme of their historical interaction was conflict. Perhaps the greatest difference between the two cultures was their contrary perception of the place people should occupy in relation to nature. For the Cherokees, language, names, and religious beliefs were based upon a special relationship between people and their environment. In a view characteristic of Native Americans in general, the Cherokees believed that humans were not superior to the natural world but were simply another part of it. They did not believe that people were superior to nature and the animals, but that man was a part of nature and its caretaker. Unlike Europeans, who believed that they were urged by God to conquer nature and be its master, the Indians acted on the belief that they were as dependent on nature for their well-being as any of the animals.

This belief system had special importance for one issue of near constant conflict between Indians and Europeans in America. The Indians' ideas about land, their relation to it, and how the land should be used caused explosive cultural conflict up and down the Appalachian frontier and beyond. While Indians reserved certain areas for specific tribal uses and fought with one another over tribal land claims, they did not believe as the Europeans did that the land itself could actually be owned, bought, and sold. This difference posed a chasm between these cultures that would never be bridged.

Despite Cherokee prosperity and their attempts to adopt the economic, political, and educational systems of the dominant white population, Congress passed the Indian Removal Act in 1831 and pursued an aggressive policy of forced Indian emigration. The Cherokees and many other Native American people were given little compensation for their confiscated land, and at least one-quarter of them died on the tragic 1838 trek westward, known as the Trail of Tears. Some one thousand managed to escape removal and fled into the mountains of North Carolina, where eventually they were allowed to settle in what became known as the Qualla Boundary.

European Settlement

The European resettlement of the southern Appalachians did not begin in earnest until the first half of the eighteenth century, and even then it was restricted largely to the Great Valley of Virginia. The push westward and southward was influenced by several factors. As life in the colonies became more settled and secure, immigrant populations began to grow, which put pressure on eastern towns and farmlands. The conquest of the Indian lands encouraged settlement, and land speculation on the Appalachian frontier ran rampant. Large tracts of land were also given out by English royalty as favors to their friends and relations. Many colonial leaders urged westward expansion as a vital key to a prosperous future. As a result of this early speculative land development, the Blue Ridge Mountains and the Great Valley of Virginia became the Appalachian and the American frontier in the several decades prior to the American Revolution.

The areas from which the earliest European settlers in Appalachia came and the routes they took into the backcountry were important elements in the formation of Appalachian culture. There were three major reservoirs of population from which people flowed into the Appalachian region in the eighteenth century: the central valley of Pennsylvania, the Piedmont of North Carolina, and western Pennsylvania.

The earliest European immigrants to the Appalachian frontier came out of eastern Pennsylvania, where, beginning around 1720, a steady buildup of the German and Scotch-Irish populations around Philadelphia began to move, many of them first into central Pennsylvania and then southward into the Shenandoah Valley. Over time they and their descendants pushed toward the New River, but instead of crossing the mountains into Indian country, most turned southeastward and settled in the Carolina Piedmont.

By the middle of the eighteenth century, this area began to fill with people, creating a second reservoir of population that would feed migrants into the mountains. The area became the significant source of early settlers into far southwestern Virginia, western North Carolina, and upper East Tennessee after 1761. By 1760, a significant number of Germans and Scotch-Irish were also coming into Appalachia from western Pennsylvania. These people drifted down the Ohio River and then followed tributaries into the mountains.

Appalachia and the New Nation

By 1763, settlers began to migrate into the western reaches of North Carolina, the river valleys of the Tennessee-Virginia border country, and even, just a few years later, into central Kentucky. The most important settlements were the Watauga settlements in East Tennessee founded by James Robertson and John Sevier, the Holston settlements of far southwestern Virginia and western North Carolina, and the Boonesborough and Harrodsburg settlements laid out by Daniel Boone in 1775. While many of these people did not own the land they lived on, it is nonetheless significant that on the eve of the American Revolution there were scattered settlements in the deep American frontier.

In addition, a smattering of British men and women, many from Wales, drifted into Appalachia directly from the east coast of Virginia in the mid-eighteenth century; some brought slaves. The British population in Appalachia was not large until after the American Revolution, and the African American population remained at around 10 percent throughout the entire period prior to the Civil War, though the percentage was higher in some parts of Appalachia.

The population of the southern mountains grew steadily from the 1760s until the 1820s, largely through immigration. Much of this sustained growth can be attributed to the impact of the American Revolution. Mountaineers were worried about protection from Indian attacks and wanted the removal of the Indians to make room for further settlement. They were also concerned about clear title to land they claimed and protecting their homesteads from wealthy land speculators and absentee owners. Political and economic issues began to emerge as tensions between mountain residents who grew corn on small farms and flatlanders who owned plantations escalated.

A longstanding hostility to political elites among farmers in the backcountry contributed significantly to their alienated and somewhat ambivalent feelings concerning the American Revolution in its earliest stages. Most settlers in the mountains eventually supported the war against England either out of an interest in religious freedom, which was the case for most Germans in Appalachia, or as a result of long-lived hatred of the British royalty among those of Scotch-Irish heritage.

Following the war, attitudes in the region over the adoption of the Constitution were mixed, and many of those who initially opposed the new Constitution were from the mountainous portions of the Appalachian states. They feared that a strong central government might limit local freedom and liberty. Significant support for the federal government came from Appalachia only after the election of Thomas Jefferson as president in 1800. Jefferson's political ideas, which emphasized small government, local power, widespread land ownership, an enlarged electorate, and self-determination, were immensely popular in the mountains. With the election in 1828 of Andrew Jackson as president, and the subsequent forced removal of the Cherokees, support of the federal government in Appalachia became even stronger.

As sectionalism began to emerge in the South between 1830 and 1861, the mountain counties, where the percentage of white slaveholders was typically only around 10 percent, and in the westernmost areas of the region as little as 5 percent, came into increasing conflict with their state governments. As a result, many mountaineers would carry strong feelings of support for the federal government into the coming disaster.

The decades prior to the Civil War set the stage on which the great drama of industrialization would be played out in Appalachia. It is important to know what the lives of the people in the southern mountains were like before industrialization, because their communities, their work patterns, their families, and even their images of and ideas about themselves would be altered dramatically by the coming of the railroads and various industries from about 1870 to the 1920s.

Preindustrial Society

The society that emerged in the mountains in the 1820s and 1830s was not unlike other rural American farm societies that were close to their frontier origins and dominated by the connections between land, family, and work. Until the era of industrialization, Appalachia was a region of small, open-country communities, or scattered settlements, concentrated in valleys and up into mountain coves and hollows. The separate settlements were integrated by transportation and communication systems, but only loosely. Each community of farmsteads was relatively self-sufficient socially and economically, and people tended to avoid routinely crossing mountains to reach another community.

What held these scattered farms together and molded the dispersed settlements into some semblance of community was a shared sense of identity, common ideals and values, and shared work and church. People exchanged food and shelter, worshiped in small, independent congregations, engaged in cooperative community service, had a sense of belonging to a larger family of friends and neighbors, and were united in their love of the land and the place they lived.

It has been widely asserted that the development of a strong sense of community in Appalachia was the result of longstanding cultural and geographic isolation. But in fact, for the first two-thirds of the nineteenth century, the Appalachian Mountains were not much more isolated than other rural, open country areas of the nation. Roads were as good, or as bad, and it was only with the marked increase in commerce in the rest of the nation that the mountain communities of Appalachia would appear to be more remote. Before railroads, a fairly constant stream of traffic eastward and westward kept the mountains in close touch with the low country. Marriage records, trade routes, and market reports make it clear that mountain people, especially men, had access to and contact with areas outside the mountains. Family histories also point to the fact that many people moved around a great deal within Appalachia.

The mountain economy was also similar in many ways to other preindustrial, traditional economies in rural America. There was a preponderance of noncommercial, self-sufficient farms, although there is reason to believe that in some areas of Appalachia, farming for an external market was more common than previously believed. Some small industries such as salt works, iron foundries, copper mines, and tanneries emerged in the mountains before the Civil War, but they had only a marginal effect on the total economy.

On the eve of industrialization in Appalachia, farm size averaged around two hundred acres each, with most of the acreage in woods and only a small amount of cultivated crop land. In some of the broad river valleys of Virginia and Tennessee there were much larger farms, and some used slaves to cultivate crops and raise livestock for sale at regional markets. Most Appalachian farmers relied on family labor to build homesteads along streams, cultivate orchards and small livestock pastures, grow large kitchen gardens, graze hogs in the woods, and sometimes raise flocks of turkeys and geese for market sale. The most commonly grown crop for both personal and commercial use was corn, which was milled locally and often sold for feed or made into liquor.

While most mountain communities were not divided rigidly between rich and poor, and while there were few hard and fast barriers to modestly improving one's economic position in society, mountain elites did exist. Usually they were the descendants of the earliest settlers in a particular region. They tended to have more frequent contacts outside the mountains.

In Appalachia, the family was at the center of preindustrial life, as it is in most traditional societies. The nuclear family was the basic social and economic unit around which nearly everything else revolved. Families were large—eight to fifteen children were common—and they provided the primary labor source in this agricultural world. The family was a working and consuming unit that functioned smoothly through the cooperation and interdependence of all its members.

Families also provided the framework within which education took place and social order and control were maintained. Politics and government also generally revolved around supporting and looking after the needs of the kin group. Gender and age roles were clearly defined and distinct in this society, and influence and respect grew with age for both men and women. While this was clearly a patriarchal society, women maintained strong and influential positions within the most important social unit in the mountain community.

Social activities for mountain residents involved either church, which tended to last all day, or community work, such as house and barn construction, clearing new ground, harvesting crops, preserving food, hog butchering, or husking corn. Road building and maintenance provided an opportunity for men to get together to work on the county's roads. Court and election days in the county seats were popular and festive events.

Civil War and Reconstruction

While slavery did not emerge in Appalachia as the dominant controversy of the Civil War era, this great conflict did have an impact there. In this land of relatively small and mostly self-sufficient farms, probably fewer than one in ten whites owned slaves, compared with about one in four in the South as a whole. The relative absence of slavery in the mountains was the result of its geographic and economic conditions. Because of the mountainous terrain, it was simply not profitable to develop commercial agriculture based upon a slave work force; slavery that did exist in Appalachia was concentrated in the larger valleys of Virginia and Tennessee. Most mountain families could not afford to maintain slaves on their small farms; as in the rest of the South, though, it is likely that had they possessed the financial resources to do so, most would have bought slaves. There was considerable industrial slavery in Appalachia in the tanning works, salt mines, and iron foundries of Virginia and in the brick mills of Tennessee and Kentucky.

While slavery was only marginally important in Appalachia, abolitionism was surprisingly not significant. A small minority of mountain whites, notably Quakers and Germans, opposed slavery on moral, ethical, and religious grounds, but others who openly objected to the peculiar institution did so for political and economic reasons. These grew out of longstanding feelings of distrust among mountaineers for the political power held by slaveholders in state government. Most mountain people were indifferent to the issue of slavery and abolitionism, but like most whites at the time, they disliked the presence of blacks in the region and favored colonization as a solution. If they spoke out against slavery at all, it was because of their belief that the power of the slaveholders posed a potential threat to their personal liberty as freeholding farmers and workers.

The Civil War was a watershed event in Appalachia, but not, as in the rest of the nation, because of slavery. The central issue in Appalachia was unionism: whether to maintain strong ties to the federal government or side with the Confederacy. Civil War divisions in this region of the South generally reflected old conflicts between low country areas and the mountains. These included political fights over building roads and other public improvements such as schools and canals; the dominance of slaveholders in state politics; and the debate over the economics, not the morality, of slavery versus free labor.

It was the unionist debate that divided Appalachia from the rest of the South and split counties and even families within the mountains. The whole fabric of mountain society was ripped apart during the Civil War as community was pitted against community, county against county, family against family, and even brother against brother. Though most Appalachian unionists disliked African Americans, most also were unwilling to destroy the federal union of states in order to preserve the institution of slavery.

The strongest areas of unionist sentiment in Appalachia were the western counties of Virginia, East Tennessee, western North Carolina, and eastern Kentucky. Even within these regions, however, there were mixed feelings. The best estimates place about one-third of Appalachia's residents in the Union camp and one-third in the Confederate camp. The other third were neutral. The strongest unionist sentiment in Appalachia was felt in the northwestern reaches of Virginia, where in 1861 twenty-seven counties met and declared the secession of their state illegal. It is important to note that these counties were not admitted to the United States as West Virginia until 1863 because the first two constitutions submitted by the new state did not include provisions for the abolition of slavery.

Pro-Confederate strength in Appalachia was certainly as important as unionist support. Allegiances to the seceded southern state governments and to the Confederacy itself were strongest in the valleys of Appalachia and in those mountain counties closest to the flat lands in the Blue Ridge region of Virginia and western North Carolina. Some historians believe that most who supported the Confederacy in Appalachia were from the economic and political elite, people like the larger valley farmers, the county-seat middle class, and small farmers and tenants who were dependent economically on the wealthier mountain residents. It is also noteworthy that slavery was more prevalent among these groups and that they had the strongest financial ties to the nonmountain areas of the southern states.

By the end of the Civil War the situation in the mountains, as in many areas of the South, was desperate. The Union and Confederate armies, both active in various parts of Appalachia throughout the war, followed a policy of living off the land. Crops and livestock were destroyed, homes robbed and burned, and civilians killed. Those who survived were confronted with shortages of food so severe that hunger was commonplace. All of this produced wounds so serious and deep that it would take generations for them to heal.

Abraham Lincoln promised loyal mountaineers in seceded states that he would do something to aid them after the war ended, but he was assassinated before he could extend a helping hand. During the era known as Radical Reconstruction, Republicans came to power in their states, and they were responsible for achieving some progressive reforms that helped the mountain counties. For example, state governments were reformed to provide for more equal representation between areas within the states, state taxation systems were improved, some efforts to create social welfare programs were initiated, and free public schools with compulsory attendance laws were established in some places.

These reforms were short lived, however, because of Republicans' ouster from power by the so-called Redemption Democrats during the 1870s. The new Democratic-controlled state legislatures ushered in an era of severe underfunding of public schools, transportation, and public services in general. Redemption meant the return of mountain counties to an era of neglect in social services and public needs. Lowland Democrats, once back in power, saw many mountaineers as traitors to the Lost Cause of the Confederacy; as a result, Appalachia entered a new era of gross neglect at the state level.

Ironically, while the mountain regions were being forgotten by their state governments, others, notably northern and foreign investors, were beginning to turn a covetous eye toward the natural resources of the area. Neglect, on the one hand, seemed to have opened the door to intense exploitation on the other, and by the 1880s Appalachia was on the verge of rediscovery and redefinition.

As the result of their Civil War experiences, a great many northerners came into contact with the southern mountains, and many were pleasantly surprised by what they found. Great mineral and timber wealth was coupled there with a romantic beauty and simplicity in the people just at a time when untamed urban growth, foreign immigration, and technological developments were beginning to unalterably change northern urban society. Capitalists responded to the call of profits, but writers, missionary workers, and teachers accompanied the industrialists into the mountains, and their work there was in some ways as substantial and the effects as long lasting as those of their entrepreneurial counterparts.

Early Industrialization and a Manufactured Image

The dominant stereotype of Appalachia which was formed during this era of industrial development and vast change was ironically an image of a society which had not changed and which still held within it much of its late-eighteenth-century frontier heritage. Mountain people were described as noble and savage, independent, proud, rugged, and violent, but also as dirty and uneducated yet crafty and practical. They drank too much and were lazy but managed to scare up the energy to produce excessively large families.

The people who were mostly responsible for this new image of Appalachia were writers collectively taking part in what is now called the Local Color movement. They described in influential and widely read journals, short stories, novels, and travel literature a land of pioneers, contemporary ancestors who were more Elizabethan than American. Violence, feuding, "moonshining," and a traditional culture existed, they wrote, in an Appalachia that had been untouched by the forces of modernization. Appalachia began to be seen and thought of as a region in stark contrast to the progressive, urban culture of the rest of America.

Gradually, through the writing of such popular authors as John Fox Jr., Appalachia came to represent the life of the past, and the rest of America represented the life of the modern present. Appalachia was depicted as the area of the United States least affected by progress, a place where time stood still and yesterday's people lived. Thus it seemed to many to be inherently picturesque and romantic, but to others it was appalling because of its perceived backwardness.

One of the most important results of this new definition of Appalachia was the urge felt by many people outside the region to improve conditions in the mountains and uplift the culture. These efforts were undertaken mostly by middle-class women who came into Appalachia from the Northeast with the goal of educating mountain people into the mainstream of American life and promoting cultural change. They typically perceived the regional culture as deficient in many ways, and they worked diligently to bring schools and modern middle-class values to the mountain people.

Ironically, a second feature of the response to this new image of Appalachia was a limited type of cultural preservation. What was thought by certain cultural workers to represent the best of mountain culture was preserved and kept from being contaminated by the evils of modernization. This preservation work was carried out by traveling folklorists such as Englishman Cecil Sharp and at folk schools like the one founded by Olive Dame Campbell in North Carolina to preserve mountain ballads, folk crafts, and dances. What they chose to preserve did not always reflect the reality and variety of Appalachian culture so much as an image of this culture, which was created and perpetuated by the cultural workers themselves. Between 1890 and 1930, nearly 250 church and settlement schools were founded in the southern mountains in response to the demands of this new image of Appalachian life and culture.

A third response to the backward image of Appalachia was to use economic development and industrialization as a way of promoting progress, since the local population was believed to be incapable of developing the mountains' human and natural resources on its own. Promoters of this idea asserted that uplift through economic development would provide needed discipline and order in the mountains, and that through participation in industrialization Appalachian people could contribute to the progress of the nation.

While many missionary workers and industrialists in the mountains, whether teachers, nurses, social workers, or entrepreneurs, did some real good, the overall result was that Appalachian people became objects to be used and explained. In a real sense they and their culture became as much a commodity as their coal and timber.

From 1865 to 1920, the United States progressed from being the world's fourth largest industrial nation to being its first. This growth was fueled by technological innovations and extraordinarily rapid urban growth, and both phenomena created demands for labor, minerals, and timber, all of which were abundant in Appalachia.

Coal was the primary resource driving the industrial revolution in Appalachia, but there were other, less significant resources. Land, mica, copper, timber, water, and human labor were natural resources, access to which depended first upon the building of an adequate transportation system into and out of, as well as within, the mountain regions of the South.

The great era of railroad building in Appalachia was between 1870 and 1910, although railroads were built in eastern Tennessee and southwestern Virginia before the Civil War. By the end of this period, the rail network was so vast that nearly every county in Appalachia could be reached by either a main or branch line. The impact of the railroads on practically every facet of life in Appalachia is hard to overestimate, but its most immediate and important effect was to unleash the full potential of the region's natural resources.

Coal was the most valuable natural resource in Appalachia. While its existence in Appalachia had been known for most of the time whites lived there, it was of little value until after the Civil War, when technological innovations in iron and steel making created a demand for Appalachian coal. Beginning about 1870, coal began to be mined in Appalachia and shipped out of the region to provide fuel for the nation's expanding industry.

The opening of the southern Appalachian coalfields was linked closely to the building of the rail network. The major fields in Appalachia were located in central and southern West Virginia, southwestern Virginia, eastern Tennessee, northern Alabama, and eastern Kentucky. Coal mining in these areas was not begun simultaneously but gradually, though by 1910 all the coal-mining regions of Appalachia were fully productive.

The men who opened and operated these mines were ambitious and college educated, from middle- or upper-middle-class backgrounds, possessed close ties to the railroads, and were largely from outside the Appalachian mountains. They believed they were a type of pioneer who, by bringing industry to the mountains, converted a wilderness into civilization. They established the company town system in Appalachia and wielded great, controlling political and economic power in the coalfields. In many locales, the coal operators not only

controlled the sources of income for the people and determined where workers would live in the coal districts but also influenced and manipulated the local
and state political system to their own and their industry's benefit, sometimes
to the long-term detriment of the local economy.

Like most other industrialists in the United States at this time, the coal
barons believed that power and authority should be in the hands of those who
demonstrated their ability by the accumulation of great material wealth. They
also valued harmony, order, and stability in the workplace, which meant that
they were bitterly anti-union. They were above all else committed to achieving
the highest profits for their companies, and when coal mining was no longer
profitable, most left, with little or no concern about the future economic well-
being of the region and its residents.

The men who worked in the mines and moved their families into company
towns were a varied lot. Three groups would eventually make up the coal-
mining work force in Appalachia: native Appalachians, African Americans, and
immigrants from southern and eastern Europe.

Historians disagree about the initial reaction of native Appalachians to the
prospect of work in the coal mines. Some think Appalachian farmers were re-
luctant to enter the mines because of the challenge industrial work presented
to their culture, especially to their ideas about working for a set period of time
for a fixed wage. Other historians find evidence that because of declining farm
size, the pressures of a steadily increasing population, and the few opportunities which existed to make a living outside farming, many Appalachian men
and women were anxious to move to the company towns and take up a job in
the mines because of the steady income it promised and the possibility of secur-
ing a better future for one's family. Whichever explanation is more accurate, the
fact remains that during the late nineteenth and early twentieth centuries,
thousands of Appalachian men and women moved their families into the hundreds of small and large company towns that dotted the region and willingly
took up picks, shovels, and axes for a coal company.

Impact of Industrialization

As the demand for coal increased in the United States, Appalachian coal operators sought out additional sources of labor. Recruiters were sent into the South
to entice African Americans to come to the coalfields, and many who were
already there because of previous work building the railroads also entered the
mine labor force. The numbers of African American coal miners were not evenly
distributed throughout the region and were more concentrated in southern
West Virginia and eastern Tennessee. African Americans, like white miners,
lived primarily in company towns and were, as in the country at large, rigidly

segregated in these industrial communities, although within the mines during working hours this was not the case.

The other major labor source for the coal mines was foreign immigrants. These workers, who came largely from areas of eastern and southern Europe (Italians, Poles, and Slavs predominated), were often preferred by the coal operators to either of the other two groups of miners. Many immigrants were single men who came to America hoping to make money quickly and then return to their homelands. Operators welcomed them because of their ambition, their work ethic, and the low likelihood that they would join a union. Company agents frequently met immigrant ships at Ellis Island, New York, and offered men transportation to the coalfields, the promise of a job, and a place to live. By 1900, this group had largely replaced the earlier work force of mostly native Appalachian farmers.

Work in the coal mines was extremely difficult and dangerous. Wages were low, the conditions in the mines were generally unsafe, and accidents were common. In 1900, wages in Appalachian mines averaged about two dollars per day based on a piece rate of thirty-eight cents per ton for coal mined. These wages were between twenty and ninety cents less than those paid to coal miners in the unionized fields of Pennsylvania, Ohio, and Indiana. At the turn of the century, coal mining was the most hazardous occupation in the United States. Explosions, poor ventilation, the presence of coal dust in the air, and rock and roof falls were constant dangers.

Since industrialization in Appalachia occurred in a completely rural area, it was necessary for the owners of the coal mines to build towns for the workers and their families. These towns, owned and controlled by the company, loom large in the history and folklore of Appalachia. The company towns were important institutions simply because so many thousands lived in them, but also because these company-owned villages were the primary means through which industrialization and modernization were brought to Appalachia.

From 1880 to 1930, there were over six hundred company towns built in the region, and they outnumbered independent towns by a margin of five to one. While there were also timber towns, textile mill towns, railroad towns, chemical towns, and paper mill towns scattered over the Appalachian landscape, the coal towns were the most widespread, influential, and infamous. At the height of the coal boom in the early years of the twentieth century, 78 percent of all coal miners and their families in Appalachia lived in a company-owned community.

Life in these communities, as described by historians and those who remember living in them, varied according to several factors. The quality of housing, the degree of overcrowding, the quality of sanitation and recreational facilities, the policies of the company store, and the degree to which the company sought to control people's activities in the town all determined whether the town was a decent or intolerable place in which to live.

While coal mining was certainly the most important industrial development in Appalachia, it was not the only one. From 1880 to 1930, industrialization also showed up in forestry and timber exploitation, textile mills, railroading, non-coal mineral mining, and chemicals production.

At the turn of the nineteenth century, one of the finest hardwood forests in the world stood on the hillsides of the Appalachian Mountains. While mountain farmers cut timber and floated it down rivers to markets in the mid-nineteenth century, it was not until the 1880s that an increased demand for timber was felt because of urban development in the Northeast. By this time, cutting logs was a major economic activity for some mountain farmers who lived along the region's larger streams and rivers. During the great timber boom between 1890 and 1910, the region's trees became a source of industrial activity when outside buyers came into the hills to purchase hundreds of thousands of acres of forest resources.

Many of the timber companies built camps to house their workers. These were short-lived versions of coal-mining company towns, but many thousands of mountain farmers found temporary employment there. Some cut timber from land which they had only recently sold to a lumber company. The height of the timber boom in Appalachia was reached in 1910. In that year, over 50 percent of the standing timber production in the United States came from the South, and most of that was from the mountains. Huge areas of Appalachia had been cut over by then, and production declined significantly thereafter.

The impact of industrialization in Appalachia has been, like the results of many things there, tinged with both good and bad features. Many people certainly believed that their lives, which had been lived harshly on the land, improved because of the steadier incomes and better housing offered them in the new towns that accompanied all forms of Appalachian industrial development. Many found a sense of community, belonging, and security in these places, but others surely pined for the beauty, cleanliness, quiet, and independence of their lost farms. Both hopefulness and helplessness were experienced and expressed by many thousands of mountain residents as they traveled the hard road of industrialism.

At the end of this era, fully two-thirds of Appalachian people made their living from nonfarm work, dependent upon a paycheck and not their ability to work the land. The economy had moved, by World War I, from a local or regional orientation to a national and international one. While most mountain people no longer earned their primary income from the land, an attachment to the land remained an important regional value. People still lived on and attempted to farm the land on a part-time basis, growing large gardens and raising a few head of livestock. Older values like strong family ties and conservative religious ideas remained central to regional culture despite the wrenching economic and social changes of the late nineteenth and early twentieth centuries.

One of the most important results of industrialization in Appalachia was its negative impact on the long-term economic health of the region. None of the industries in Appalachia encouraged rival or spin-off economic development during their boom years. The effect was sporadic economic growth without real economic development. Benefits throughout the region were not realized from the spectacular profits earned by largely absentee-owned corporations; when the boom periods ended or when technological changes occurred, Appalachia was largely left wanting for jobs and future economic prospects.

The Great Depression and the New Deal

The Great Depression of the 1930s actually began in Appalachia about a decade earlier, when the industrial system that had lured thousands off the farms of the region and thousands of others to the mountains collapsed under the weight of overproduction and increasing competition. Living in company towns, dependent upon a wage income, and fully integrated into a new social structure, people knew as the Depression deepened that they could not return to the old agricultural ways, yet there were no new economic opportunities opening up in the region.

By 1929, most mountain people were already suffering as the structure of industrialization built on coal mining, railroading, and timbering collapsed around them. The years of the Great Depression in Appalachia, from around the mid-1920s to the early 1940s, were marked by the most severe hardships—hunger, homelessness, and starvation. By the end of the 1930s, fully 75 percent of the mountain population would be on the receiving end of some type of government assistance.

Solutions to the tragedy were extremely limited as well. People by the thousands attempted to leave the coal camps and move back to their families' farms, but there were too many people and the actual size of most Appalachian farms had decreased because of industrialization. The result was more and more people living on smaller and smaller farms, but even with everyone working, not enough food could be grown to feed this growing rural population.

Many people in Appalachia did not even have this option and were forced either to move north into the industrial centers or stay in the coal camps after the companies shut down the mines. Some companies tried to sell the houses to their former employees, but with the industries either closed down or out of business entirely, few could afford to buy. Private charities were common in the region, but as in many other parts of the nation, the need for assistance among the poor was just too burdensome for the private resources that were available.

In areas of Appalachia that had remained rural and agricultural, where industry had not come to dominate life, there is considerable evidence to suggest that people weathered the economic storm of the 1930s without much change in their daily lives. Many continued their subsistence farming ways, raising a few head of livestock, hunting, fishing, and gathering wild foods, and growing big gardens and preserving their food in time-honored ways. In this manner, some in the mountains were able to live a life generally out of the mainstream of the industrial nightmare that haunted the rest of America.

In 1933, under the leadership of President Franklin Roosevelt, the federal government initiated a New Deal in order to lift the country out of the despair of economic depression. While the New Deal did not challenge or fix the structural problems which plagued the mountain economy, and while its programs generally only shifted the dependence of many mountain people from the coal companies to the federal government, its work and assistance programs did stave off starvation and gave thousands of men and women hope for a better future.

The Works Progress Administration, the Civilian Conservation Corps, and many other programs provided major employment opportunities in mountain counties. The Social Security Act, as well as programs to support dependent children, was also crucial in maintaining at least a subsistence level of survival in mountain communities during these hard times.

In 1935, Congress passed the Wagner Act, a bill of monumental importance in the Appalachian coalfields. This legislation legalized union organizations in the country and established federal guidelines to ensure that if workers wanted to join unions, that right would be protected. Labor relations within the Appalachian coalfields had witnessed some intense periods of union organization in the past and some spectacular episodes of violence, notably in southern West Virginia from 1912 to 1921, but the United Mine Workers of America (UMWA) had generally been unsuccessful in organizing southern Appalachia.

In the late 1930s, because of the Wagner Act, the pace of union organizing stepped up. Efforts were greatest in the coalfields of eastern Kentucky. The area received extraordinary media scrutiny and became known to the rest of the country as "Bloody Harlan," a term which referred to the often violent attempts to unionize coal miners in eastern Kentucky's Harlan County. Federal protection for the union movement eventually prevailed, and the UMWA became a

---

potent force in the lives of hundreds of thousands of people living in the coalfields of Appalachia.

In addition to the Wagner Act, another New Deal program affecting the lives of millions of people in Appalachia was the Tennessee Valley Authority (TVA). The purpose of the TVA was to develop the Tennessee River Valley by building a series of dams to generate electricity for rural areas and to use the energy to recruit industry to the region. In addition, TVA would help to regulate the river's flooding, restore eroded land, produce fertilizers to improve the soil, and generally benefit farmers who lived in the surrounding areas.

While some of the earliest planning in the TVA included provisions for broad-based community development schemes, eventually its major efforts focused on the production of electricity. Within a very short time it was obvious that the increased demands for electricity spawned by the TVA could not be met with hydroelectric dams alone, and as a result, in 1949 the TVA built nine coal-powered electrical generating plants along the Tennessee River. This move would have far-reaching effects on Appalachia. Because of the need for cheap electricity, the TVA was forced to go into the coal markets to find an inexpensive yet generous source of fuel. As a result of this demand, pressure increased in the Appalachian coalfields to shift from underground mining to the less expensive method of surface or strip mining. Ironically, as one Appalachian scholar has pointed out, the agency designed to restore and improve the land in the 1930s was by the 1950s and 1960s most responsible for the destruction of the Appalachian landscape through strip mining.

Appalachia at Midcentury and Beyond

World War II and the years immediately following it were turning points in the history of Appalachia, just as they were for the rest of America. During the war, men and women in Appalachia were uprooted and exposed to the world away from home in record numbers. Military service had an eye-opening impact on many thousands who were transported to military camps around the country and the world. In addition, work for women in war industries, both inside and outside the region, was transforming. For some men and women, this exposure expanded horizons, aspirations, and attitudes; for others, the exposure brought a greater sense of difference that created some feelings of inferiority. Once they returned home from their wartime experiences in factories or the armed forces, many young men and women focused on the lack of economic opportunities in Appalachia and began to look forward to moving out of the region in search of better jobs. This attitude provided the impetus for the great out-migration from Appalachia to the North and Midwest throughout the 1950s and 1960s.

RICHARD STRAW

After World War II, significant and far-reaching changes took place in Appalachia. During the war, coal companies began to mechanize their mining production, and this process continued and increased after the war. Demand for coal was up and production levels soared, but because of technological changes in deep mining and the widespread adoption of strip mining, more coal was mined with fewer men. In 1940, for example, there were 476,000 coal miners, but by 1960 there were fewer than 200,000.

Coal mining in Appalachia had not been accompanied by development of secondary or supportive industries, and as unemployment in the coal industry increased, migration out of the region was the only hope for thousands. Between 1945 and 1965, nearly 3.5 million people from Appalachia left their homes in search of a brighter economic future. They left for places such as Cincinnati, Columbus, Chicago, Cleveland, Detroit, Indianapolis, and Baltimore, and sizable subcultures of Appalachian migrants built up in these cities.

The 1950s was also a critical time in the history of Appalachia because this was when the southern mountains were again "discovered" by the rest of the nation. The late 1940s and the 1950s was a time of extreme poverty in some parts of America, including Appalachia, and as this fact became the subject of media reports, more and more attention centered on the mountains.

This renewed national attention to Appalachia was accelerated by the campaign for the Democratic presidential nomination in 1960, a battle which brought John F. Kennedy, Hubert Humphrey, and Lyndon Johnson into the mountains. Winning the West Virginia primary became central to Kennedy's campaign because he wanted to prove that a Catholic could win in the South. During his tour of that state, Kennedy visited some old coal camps and was visibly moved by the wretched living conditions and crushing poverty he discovered there. Because of his sympathetic reaction to the plight of Appalachia's poor and because of the media coverage of his visits, Kennedy won the primary, shot ahead in the national polls, and won the November election against Republican Richard Nixon.

The election heralded the beginning of an intensive media scrutiny of Appalachia, its economic problems, and its people. Immediately after the election, all the major television networks descended upon Appalachia, and several programs aired over the next few years focusing on the poverty and backwardness of the region and its people. While these programs and countless newspaper articles drew national attention to the region, they did so in a way that presented Appalachia in a uniformly negative light. The image that emerged, while accurate in an aggregate economic context, was resented by thousands of residents who did not like the way the media portrayed them as isolated, backward, ignorant, and pathetically impoverished. Appalachia was again represented to the country as a place that was indeed in America but not a part of modern American life.

Once in office, President Kennedy did not forget his commitment to Appalachia, although early efforts in the region of federally funded and directed economic development programs were meager and largely ineffective. In 1963, following Kennedy's death, President Lyndon Johnson pledged to fulfill Kennedy's programs. After a well-publicized trip to Inez, Kentucky, Johnson pushed the Appalachian Regional Development Act through Congress. The bill called for federal funding for secondary and vocational education programs, highway construction, timber management programs, and widespread promotion of tourism.

The bill also set up the Appalachian Regional Commission (ARC) and ushered in the War on Poverty. The commission worked in four areas: highway construction, resource development, flood control and water tower projects, and improvements in human services. When the act passed, it included in its definition of Appalachia 393 counties in thirteen states, stretching along the spine of the Appalachian Mountain chain from New York to Mississippi.

The Johnson administration's War on Poverty included many other provisions besides the ARC which had an impact on Appalachia. Among the most influential programs were the Office of Economic Opportunity (OEO), Volunteers in Service to America (VISTA), the Job Corps, and Head Start. The cornerstone of the government's antipoverty efforts was the OEO, a program that showed great promise initially but was, by 1968, diluted and made nearly ineffective. The original concept for the OEO provided for a direct relationship between federal, state, and local governments, and poor citizens, who would be organized directly into Community Action Programs. As the program evolved, the direct participation of the poor became weaker and weaker until the Community Action Programs withered as a force for real change in Appalachia.

VISTA attracted young, idealistic, new college graduates to the mountains, where they lived and worked within communities to organize poor people and improve the quality of their lives. Because of their values and ideals, VISTA workers frequently clashed with the sources of local economic and political influence. Head Start was one of the most famous and most successful of the antipoverty programs. It provided child care and preschool education for poor children, and while it is clear from many studies that this program brought positive results, it was chronically underfunded by the federal government.

While overall success of the War on Poverty was limited, there were some unexpected results in the mountains. In many communities there emerged the belief that change and improvement would come only through organizing at the grass-roots level. Hundreds of small and some large groups formed to address political, economic, educational, vocational, health, and environmental concerns that were not being adequately dealt with by the local political structure.

Much, although by no means all, of this grass-roots protest and organization was either influenced by or related in some way to issues surrounding the coal-mining industry. Protests against strip mining led to environmental and legal reforms, efforts to secure health benefits for victims of black lung disease led to greater scrutiny of occupational hazards in general, and it was a largely grass-roots effort that brought about a turbulent uprising within the United Mine Workers of America union in 1969.

By the mid-1970s, many of these groups had passed by the wayside, yet their efforts were remembered and enlarged upon by others in the region. For example, environmental protest became commonplace, and many communities in Appalachia were much more prone to organize in support of or against development projects, especially if these plans were formulated by outside agencies.

Another important result of the War on Poverty years in Appalachia was the emergence by the late 1970s of a strong sense of regional identity and the recognition of the need to express a positive image of Appalachia when writing or talking about its people, history, and culture. This was another form of grass-roots empowerment, as even the word "Appalachia" became more accepted than it had ever been. To many within the region, the culmination of the organizing and turbulence of the 1960s was an Appalachian renaissance filled with a strong dose of regional pride, which was associated for the first time in American history with being from the mountains.

Most historians who have studied the War on Poverty think that while it had some successes, generally it failed in Appalachia. The legacy in the mountains of the billions of dollars spent on highways and industries has been continued poverty amid pockets of prosperity. Economic development in the 1970s consisted of the coal boom of 1974–78, the tourism-generated land boom in East Tennessee and western North Carolina, a growth in textile production, some small-scale component part manufacturing, and the growth of the large-scale chain stores and fast food establishments located within the more prosperous areas.

Outside the few growing towns and cities, there are areas where poverty is still the norm. Here there are few opportunities for men, and the work force is made up largely of low-wage and minimum-wage jobs for women and young people. Dickenson County, Virginia, for example, deep in coal country, consistently achieves the highest unemployment rate in Virginia, with a figure that hovers around 25 percent.

And so Appalachia remains a contradiction in America: a region rich in natural resources yet a land of great poverty. From our earliest history as a nation, and even before, the mountains of the Appalachian frontier attracted visitors, those who were just passing through and permanent settlers. Such is still the case. The region is attractive today to both outsiders who are drawn to its natural beauty and economic potential and natives who take enormous pride in their heritage of independence, craftsmanship, hard work, family, and self-sufficiency. For some, the future may look bleak, while for others it holds great promise, but whatever path is taken in Appalachia, we can be certain that the region will play an important and vital role in America's future, just as it has in its past.

Hand-shocked corn on an Appalachian farm, c.1970. By Jack Jeffers.

RICHARD STRAW

The steam locomotive, an essential tool in the industrialization of Appalachia.
By Jack Jeffers.

Pouring metal at Bertha Iron Works, Pulaski, Virginia, c. 1910. Courtesy of the Raymond Ratcliffe Memorial Museum, Pulaski, Virginia.

Coal miners in Parrott, Virginia, at the end of a shift, c. 1935. From the collection of Ricky Cox.

Farmers in Floyd County, Virginia, display the benefits of chemical fertilizers, c. 1935.
Courtesy of Versie Hollandsworth Phillips.

Contemporary urban Appalachia: Roanoke, Virginia. By JoAnn Asbury.

Note

I would like to express my gratitude to Professor Ronald Eller of the University of Kentucky for sharing his ideas about Appalachian history with me. The list of Suggested Readings is adapted from a bibliography compiled by Gordon McKinney.

Suggested Readings

Berry, Chad. *Southern Migrants, Northern Exiles.* Urbana: Univ. of Illinois Press, 2000.

Blethen, H. Tyler, and Curtis Wood Jr. *Ulster and North America: Transatlantic Perspectives on the Scotch-Irish.* Tuscaloosa: Univ. of Alabama Press, 1997.

Corbin, David Alan. *Life, Work and Rebellion in the Coal Fields: The Southern West Virginia Miners, 1880–1920.* Urbana: Univ. of Illinois Press, 1981.

Davis, Donald Edward. *Where There Are Mountains: An Environmental History of the Southern Appalachians.* Athens: Univ. of Georgia Press, 2000.

Drake, Richard B. *A History of Appalachia.* Lexington: Univ. Press of Kentucky, 2001.

Dunn, Durwood. *Cades Cove: The Life and Death of a Southern Appalachian Community, 1818–1937.* Knoxville: Univ. of Tennessee Press, 1988.

Eller, Ronald D. *Miners, Millhands, and Mountaineers: Industrialization of the Appalachian South, 1880–1930.* Knoxville: Univ. of Tennessee Press, 1982.

Finger, John R. *Cherokee Americans: The Eastern Band of Cherokees in the Twentieth Century.* Lincoln: Univ. of Nebraska Press, 1991.

———. *The Eastern Band of Cherokees, 1819–1900.* Knoxville: Univ. of Tennessee Press, 1984.

Fischer, David Hackett. *Albion's Seed: Four British Folkways in America.* New York: Oxford Univ. Press, 1989.

Gaventa, John. *Power and Powerlessness: Quiescence and Rebellion in an Appalachian Valley.* Urbana: Univ. of Illinois Press, 1980.

Glen, John M. *Highlander: No Ordinary School, 1932–1962.* 2d ed. Knoxville: Univ. of Tennessee Press, 1996.

Inscoe, John C. *Mountain Masters: Slavery and the Sectional Crisis in Western North Carolina.* Knoxville: Univ. of Tennessee Press, 1989.

Inscoe, John C., and Gordon B. McKinney. *The Heart of Confederate Appalachia: Western North Carolina in the Civil War.* Chapel Hill: Univ. of North Carolina Press, 2000.

Koons, Kenneth E., and Warren R. Hofstra, eds. *After the Backcountry: Rural Life in the Great Valley of Virginia, 1800–1900.* Knoxville: Univ. of Tennessee Press, 2000.

Lewis, Ronald L. *Transforming the Appalachian Countryside: Railroads, Deforestation, and Social Change in West Virginia, 1880–1920.* Chapel Hill: Univ. of North Carolina Press, 1998.

McDonald, Michael J., and John Muldowny. *TVA and the Dispossessed: The Resettlement of Population in the Norris Dam Area.* Knoxville: Univ. of Tennessee Press, 1982.

McKinney, Gordon B. *Southern Mountain Republicans, 1865–1900: Politics and the Appalachian Community.* Chapel Hill: Univ. of North Carolina Press, 1978.

Noe, Kenneth W., and Shannon H. Wilson, eds. *The Civil War in Appalachia: Collected Essays.* Knoxville: Univ. of Tennessee Press, 1997.

Perdue, Theda. *Cherokee Women: Gender and Cultural Change, 1700–1835.* Lincoln: Univ. of Nebraska Press, 1998.

Salstrom, Paul. *Appalachia's Path to Dependency: Rethinking a Region's Economic History, 1730–1940.* Lexington: Univ. Press of Kentucky, 1994.

Schoenbaum, Thomas J. *The New River Controversy.* Winston-Salem, N.C.: John F. Blair, 1979.

Shapiro, Henry D. *Appalachia on Our Mind: The Southern Mountains and Mountaineers in the American Consciousness, 1870–1920.* Chapel Hill: Univ. of North Carolina Press, 1978.

Shifflett, Crandall A. *Coal Towns: Work and Culture in Company Towns of Southern Appalachia, 1880–1960.* Knoxville: Univ. of Tennessee Press, 1991.

Smith, Barbara Ellen. *Digging Our Own Graves: Coal Miners and the Struggle over Black Lung Disease.* Philadelphia: Temple Univ. Press, 1987.

Straw, Richard A., and H. Tyler Blethen, eds. *High Mountains Rising: Appalachia in Time and Place.* Urbana: Univ. of Illinois Press, 2004.

Waller, Altina L. *Feud: Hatfields, McCoys, and Social Change in Appalachia, 1860–1900.* Chapel Hill: Univ. of North Carolina Press, 1988.

Whisnant, David E. *All that Is Native and Fine: The Politics of Culture in an American Region.* Chapel Hill: Univ. of North Carolina Press, 1983.

———. *Modernizing the Mountaineer: Power and Planning in Appalachia.* Boone, N.C.: Appalachian Consortium Press, 1981.

Williams, John A. *Appalachia: A History.* Chapel Hill: Univ. of North Carolina Press, 2002.

PEOPLES OF APPALACHIA: CULTURAL DIVERSITY WITHIN THE MOUNTAIN REGION

STEVAN R. JACKSON

Of all the stereotypes that haunt Appalachia, perhaps the most deceptive is that Appalachians are a homogenous people with a single cultural heritage. Contrary to popular thought, Appalachia was not settled only by wild Celts from Scotland and Ireland or outlaws exiled to the mountains of Appalachia by England. Actually, Appalachia in the 1700s and beyond was settled not only by people of Ulster Scot descent but also by people from a host of other cultural backgrounds as well. And of course the Native American had been in Appalachia for centuries before white settlers of any heritage began moving into the region. Entire books can and have been written about each of these groups, but this work views them within one context—the heterogeneity of Appalachian heritage.

In addition to cultures that would shape the future of Appalachia, there were some that experienced the region without establishing extensive settlements. The first of such groups to visit the region were the Spanish, nearly five centuries ago. Though more famous for his travels through Central America and Peru, explorer and conquistador Hernando de Soto made an excursion into the Appalachian region as early as 1540, fully 130 years before any other Europeans.[1] De Soto and his men, who got lost in the southern Blue Ridge Mountains, may have given the region its name after encountering the Apalachee Indians, who contested the Spaniards' passage through northern Florida.[2]

Thus was born the European name for the Appalachian chain and the region around it, although the Native Americans already had names for the region. According to Dykeman, de Soto, ". . . having honed his appetite and aptitude for conquest in the subjugation of Peru, led his retinue of cavalry and footmen, Spanish aristocrats and royal representatives and Indian burden bearers, into the interior of eastern North America, seeking gold. . . ."[3]

The exact route taken by de Soto and his retinue is not known, but it is widely accepted that the Spaniards came as far north as the Appalachian portion of Tennessee along the Hiwassee and Tennessee Rivers before turning west and ending up at the Mississippi River near present-day Memphis. The Spaniards' reputations for kidnapping and enslaving native populations raced ahead of them, causing Cherokee women to flee into the wilderness.[4]

But with the possible exception of scattered progeny left in their wake, the Spaniards passed quickly out of the region. The first inhabitants of Appalachia, the Native Americans, would not be seriously disturbed again by Europeans until the Ulster Scots arrived, nearly two hundred years later. Beginning in the early 1700s, this mass migration carried with it tremendous cultural resources that would eventually supplant a Native American population and culture that had been in Appalachia for thousands of years.

And even though there was a tremendous amount of cultural baggage dropped off in Appalachia by the Ulster Scots, many other ethnic groups also have come to the mountains over the past three hundred years and brought their cultures with them. Among the many reasons for migrations by diverse groups into any region, the most compelling is the promise of good land and/or work. The latter part of the 1800s saw tremendous growth in an Appalachian coal industry that desperately needed bodies to go deep into the earth to bring the black diamond to the surface, and those bodies often came from a culturally diverse group of people. In fact, "[d]uring the 1870s and 1880s, campaigns were launched in every southern Appalachian state aimed at attracting foreign immigration and commercial investment."[5]

There was such an explosion in the coal industry that there were not enough local Appalachian residents to fill the shafts of the mines, nor could calls put out to the outlying regions of Appalachia provide enough laborers. When recruitment of workers from the Deep South also failed to satisfy the growing demand for labor, the Appalachian coal operators and absentee owners based in big eastern cities turned to Europe. They, along with shipping lines that desired to boost their industry as well, began to recruit millions of workers to send to America: "From Italy, Hungary, Poland, Rumania, Albania, and

Greece came shipments of immigrants, few of whom could either speak or comprehend a word of English."[6] Many of these culturally rich but economically poor individuals ended up in Appalachia, primarily working the coal mines and the railroads that brought workers in and took the coal out. Typically brought to the coal camps of Appalachia by rail, these newly arrived immigrants would often travel from a New York disembarkation center to the coal camps of Appalachia without leaving their train cars. At the end of this nightmarish trip, "[u]tterly mystified and astounded, smelling of garlic and carrying immense bundles of Old world shawls, dresses, petticoats, hats and accordions, they arrived in the middle of a brand-new [Appalachian] town."[7] In most cases, these immigrants found themselves in places even more foreign to them than other parts of America would have been. But neatly packed with their other bundles were the millions of memories and hundreds of old world customs they would share with their new country.

The growth of the coal-mining industry and the coming of roads to Appalachia brought cultural change to what were by now considered the "native" inhabitants of the region. By the late 1800s, the native population of Appalachia was indeed white, not the Native American aborigine of the past century. These primarily white families already living in the region ". . . were joined by immigrants from southern and eastern Europe, especially Italy, Poland, Hungary, and Slavic nations. Large numbers of African Americans also sought to escape the southern backlash against Reconstruction by moving to the coalfields."[8] The Europeans may have been the same skin color, but they spoke a different language and held different customs. Prejudices and stereotypes about these groups became commonplace.

The history of Appalachian coal mining is also the history of labor struggles. Immigrants played a big part in both the development of the industry and the ensuing labor struggles. Right off the boat from Europe, immigrants provided cheap labor for the coal bosses, often displacing local Appalachian workers, which of course did not put them in good stead with the local population. "These penniless 'transportation men,'" according to Caudill, "stepped from their cars at Jenkins, McRoberts, Benham, Lynch, Middlesboro, Wayland, Wheelwright [Kentucky] and numerous other wild coal towns, to jeers and hoots from crowds of mountaineers to whom they were more often than not simply 'dam furrin' sons of bitches.'"[9] These immigrants had made a journey across a goodly portion of two continents and an ocean in between, and they had personal commitments to do the best they could to be good Americans in hope of finding the freedom and prosperity promised them by the recruiters. Because they did not fit in, many of the new immigrants found themselves suffering not only the hardship of working in the coal mines but also the hardship of being despised, and sometimes cruelly beaten or even slain, by the native Appalachians. "In these early years of the mining industry, 'Wops,' 'Hunkies' and 'Pollocks' were regarded by the mountaineers, and by most of the camp overlords, as 'only one notch better than the niggers'—and this notch was a narrow one."[10] But even in these harsh contexts, the immigrants added cultural diversity to the Appalachian region.

The industrialization period from the 1870s to the 1920s, basically from the Reconstruction era through World War I, saw the metropolitan areas of America send workers of all ethnic types into Appalachia. Even though the influence of the Ulster Scots during the early migration period is undeniable and pervasive in some regions of Appalachia, this period brought new cultural influences to the mountains of Appalachia with migration from the rural South as well as from eastern and southern Europe. However, despite the growing cultural diversity within the region and the nation, and perhaps as a reaction to it, there was an attempt at this time to keep America and Appalachia homogeneous. During this period, working men throughout the region and in other parts of the country struggled for better living conditions and economic opportunities. Labor-management conflicts in the Pennsylvania Appalachian coalfields were sensationalized by the terrorist activities of the Irish immigrant workers called the Molly Maguires, adding to growing national resentment and distrust of newly arrived immigrants. Historian Darlene Wilson observes:

> Out of these crises of identity and purpose, whites fashioned legislative remedies, such as anti-immigration laws and the institutionalization of "Jim Crow." . . . Whites conducted "100% Americanization" campaigns in the schools and neighborhoods of European immigrants, African Americans, and southern mountaineers. Together these corrective measures acted to purge Americanism of any taint of otherness. Homogeneity topped the agenda; some white-enough men (including several so-called "race leaders" of mixed African American ancestry) were allowed into the inner circle, but women, as well as dark(er)-skinned Americans, Asian immigrants, and Hispanics, remained categorized as "others." Many were also contained in "domestic spheres," ghettos, shantytowns, and barrios that remained outside the boundaries of polite male-class(ed) America. By 1920, Appalachia, at least superficially, had come to better resemble the national norm of a society with two classes—men and not-men—and two castes—people of color and the uncolored.[11]

In spite of this national trend toward whiteness, Appalachia was becoming a rainbow of cultural colors and heritages. The sounds of blacks combined with the sounds of Irish, Slavs, Italians, Hungarians, and other peoples and cultures to create a symphonic cultural score that belies the aforementioned stereotype of homogeneity. And with each new non-native Appalachian, the cultural and ethnic diversity expanded, fueled by the tremendous increase in the number of immigrant miners in the region between the late nineteenth and early twentieth centuries, especially in northern Appalachia. There are no precise figures existing for the entire region, but it is estimated that the number of immigrants in northern Appalachia alone was at least one-quarter, and in some areas more, of the entire mine work force.

In West Virginia, for example, around 1870, near the beginning of this migration pattern, there were fewer than a thousand miners of foreign extraction in the overall labor force. This increased to nearly sixteen thousand by 1907, and by 1915, in the middle of World War I, foreign coal miners in West Virginia totaled nearly 32,000. This latter figure reflects the number remaining in West Virginia after the surge of immigrants had stopped, primarily because of the Great War. The feeling of ethnicity had remained so strong that many Europeans went back to fight for their native homelands. During this period, immigrants representing nearly all of the nations of Europe, each with its own unique cultural idiosyncrasies, came into Ellis Island and made their way eventually to Appalachia. "Many followed the typical chain migration pattern whereby family and friends established a 'beachhead' for others from the region who joined them later."[12] More often than not, once established, these ethnic groups remained to themselves, building churches, enjoying social clubs, and having their children marry through endogamous customs into their own ethnic group. And according to Couto, because these ethnic groups were characterized by large, stable, extended families, there are strong European ethnic identities that have held over into the later twentieth and early twenty-first centuries.[13]

The *1909 West Virginia Department of Mines, Report of the Chief Inspector* lists from four different counties (Fayette, Raleigh, Mercer, and McDowell) eighteen different types of racial or ethnic origins for their miners.[14] These were, in order of descending total population within these four counties, Native (white), Black, Italian, Hungarian, Slavish, Polish, Russian, Greek, English, German, Romanian, Scottish, Austrian, Lithuanian, Litvich, Swedish, Irish, and Syrian. The third largest number was reported as "Unknown/Other." The total miner population was 33,202, with 22,292 of them being from the diverse group of immigrants.[15] Similar numbers were reflected throughout the coalfields of Appalachia, only with differing emphasis on one immigrant population or another.

While deep within the earth digging coal, these immigrants looked essentially the same, but differences were very much accentuated above ground. Most lived in the infamous company towns, but these towns were very much segregated into Colored Town, Hunky Hollow, or Little Italy.[16] However, in an area that was fraught with economic ups and downs, the segregation of company towns often became blurred due to common economic interests. Cultural diversity had come to Appalachia by rail, and all the cultural baggage brought along began to intertwine through the commonality of hardships. And even though there was segregation, discrimination, and racism against blacks and immigrants by the native white population, Obermiller suggests "there is no evidence that Appalachians are more or less racist than any other group" of Americans.[17]

Appalachia, therefore, has historically been an extremely heterogeneous area of the country, although it has not been recognized as such. The stereotype of homogeneity has been particularly difficult to counter since it often has been perpetuated by academics. In referring to the contention by David Hackett Fischer that Appalachia's feuding tradition was brought to Appalachia by primarily Scotch-Irish immigrants, Blee and Billings suggest, "Not only is this carry-over [feuding] unlikely . . . but also the ethnic composition of Appalachia's early population remains in doubt, consisting of some unknown composition of English, German, French, Dutch, Welsh, and Scotch-Irish settlers."[18]

Native Americans

The first inhabitants of Appalachia were the Native Americans who occupied most of the Appalachian region at the coming of the first European white settlers in the early 1600s. There were at that time some fifteen to seventeen major Native American tribes living in the region, most of them sedentary agriculturalists and fishermen who supplemented their diets by hunting and gathering, and they belonged to two major linguistic groups.[19] It has been suggested that those Native Americans most associated with Appalachia, the Cherokee, or at least much of their traditional culture, originally came from Central or South America. Citing archaeological, historical, linguistic and ethnographic evidence, Evans suggests that the Cherokees may have been an amalgamation of several cultures that had become one by the time the Europeans arrived.[20]

Native Americans sometimes helped and sometimes hindered the European migration pattern that began in the early 1700s. White settlers in Appalachia learned, perhaps from the Cherokees, how to build cabins and how to use the slash-and-burn method of farming necessary in that region of the country but nonexistent in many of their previous habitations, particularly the north of Ireland. This migration, primarily of Ulster Scots and Germans, went peacefully unabated for the first half of the century. With the coming of more and more white settlers, there were more and more conflicts as the Native Americans began to be displaced by the newcomers. The French and Indian War, beginning in 1754, created a turbulent period for the white settlers. "The next ten years were marked by bloodshed, bitterness, constant anxiety, cruelty, and death to men, women, and children. Immigration from Ulster, as from Germany, almost ceased."[21] This midcentury crisis created by the war, especially battles taking place in Pennsylvania, made traveling south to Appalachia difficult and extremely dangerous, but the settlers persisted in their quest for new places and new lives. At this time, the two major tribes of the North Carolina Piedmont were the Cherokees and the Catawbas, who were usually friendly to the new white intruders. It was to the good fortune of the whites that the Catawbas fought against ". . . the Tuscaroras in the east and served as a barrier against tribes of the west" and that they ". . . were the hereditary enemies of the Cherokee."[22]

The western portion of North Carolina and that portion of the state that would become Tennessee held the Cherokees, who contributed greatly to the cultural history of the Appalachian region. The Cherokee named Sequoyah created an alphabet from the sounds of his language and thus "turned his people into a literate nation."[23] Assimilation into white society was feared by other Cherokees, such as Dragging Canoe, who led warriors against the whites to preserve the sanctity of Native American land. The Chickamauga Indians, around present-day Chattanooga, also fought the whites "to contest every acre of their shrinking land."[24]

But acculturation and assimilation took place within the Cherokee people perhaps more so than other Native American tribes. Many Ulster Scots and Cherokees intermarried and had children of mixed blood. ". . . Many of the great leaders of the nineteenth century were of Scottish ancestry (most notably John Ross, with a Scottish father and grandfather, and Major Ridge, with a Scottish grandfather)."[25] But there was a down side to intermarriage with the Cherokee culture. Those who intermarried, particularly Cherokee leaders, were more prone to accepting and adopting the white man's culture. In spite of this acculturation into white society, the Cherokee were still Native Americans and therefore culturally different from the whites around them. New laws passed by the white man allowed their lands to be taken, and eventually most of the

Cherokee were removed from Appalachia via the Trail of Tears, a forced march to Oklahoma that took place in 1838. According to the 1990 federal census, "Native Americans make up less than 1 percent of the population of the region and are concentrated primarily in western North Carolina."[26]

Melungeons

Adding to the cultural diversity of Appalachia are the Melungeons, a group whose origins are illusive and whose mysterious reputation has been enhanced by their relative isolation in northeast Tennessee, southwest Virginia, and northwest North Carolina, as well as by their Mediterranean complexions, blue eyes, high cheek bones, and straight, black hair. As early as 1690, they identified themselves as "Portyghee" to French settlers moving into the mountains of western North Carolina. The Ulster Scots found them in the 1750s in secluded areas of southwestern Virginian and northeast Tennessee.[27]

According to Lewis, "[T]he racially mixed Melungeons had resided in southern Appalachia since the earliest settlement days."[28] Today they are often identified by a relatively small number of surnames, and many still live in relatively isolated places, although their occupational profiles are similar to those of other Appalachians and include farmers owning their own land, farmers working for others, and laborers working in urban industrial plants or coal mines. Even in the twenty-first century, none of several theories concerning the origins of this obviously racially mixed group has been conclusively proven. Raitz and Ulack posit that the Melungeons may be a "mixture of Indian, black, and white."[29] They cite Edward Price, who determined through examining census schedules that Melungeons ". . . appeared to have migrated westward into the mountains from a few Piedmont counties on the North Carolina and Virginia border, where a large mixed-blood population is thought to have existed about 1790."[30]

A competing theory of the origin of the Melungeons is that they are the progeny of a group of shipwrecked Portuguese who wandered from the North Carolina coast to eastern Tennessee, married native Cherokees, and lived relatively undisturbed until the white man came in. An early but now less credible theory held that Melungeons were descendants of Sir Walter Raleigh's "Lost Colony," a group who disappeared from Roanoke Island, North Carolina, about twenty years before the first permanent English settlement at Jamestown, Virginia, in 1607. Based upon this theory, the Tennessee government, in 1887, actually recognized the Melungeons' legal existence, calling them "Croatan Indians."[31] Other suppositions about their origins include the possibility that they are descendants of ancient Phoenicians who migrated from Carthage to

Morocco, crossed the Strait of Gibraltar, and settled in northern Portugal. From there they were supposed to have come to North Carolina before the American War of Independence.[32] Though the Appalachian neighbors of the Melungeons and the surrounding world have been curious about the group's origins, they have not always been kind to them. "In central Appalachia, to call someone a Melungeon was an insult; no wonder it was a term the Melungeons themselves avoided like the plague."[33] The term was also used to scare children in Appalachia in the sense that, instead of the "boogie man" getting them, the Melungeons were the threat.

One prominent Melungeon historian, Brent Kennedy, asserts that

> the Anglo version of America's earliest settlements at Jamestown and Plymouth is reductive, obscuring the original melting-pot nature of the American people, dating back 1,200 years to the Muslim conquest of the Iberian Peninsula. The Melungeons of central Appalachia . . . are the prototypic "melange," or mixture, possessing Spanish, Portuguese, North African, Turkish, Semitic, Native-American, African-American, and, yes, northern European blood.[34]

Ulster Scots

Indeed, the cultural diversity of Appalachia is extensive. Yet through nothing but historical accident, the Ulster Scots delivered most of the settlers into the Appalachian region early in its settlement development and thus influenced that development heavily. Coming from Ulster, these Protestant, English-speaking Irish were the grandchildren and great-grandchildren of Presbyterian Scottish lowlanders who had migrated to and settled in nine counties in the north of Ireland during the Plantation Project period of England's Queen Elizabeth I and King James I.[35]

For a host of reasons, such as oppressive laws, taxes, unusually harsh winters, potato crop failures, epidemics among the livestock, and economic repression, these Protestant Ulster Scots joined their English, French, and Catholic Irish neighbors in following the watery road to the western shores of America. "If their forbears had subscribed to the belief that 'the best roads in Scotland were those leading out of it,' they extended that opinion to the roads of northern Ireland."[36] Most of these immigrants came to America via Philadelphia and took up residence in the Pennsylvania region before moving down the Shenandoah Valley into the Appalachian regions of Virginia and East Tennessee. Others went through the Piedmont region of North Carolina into the western portion of the state and on into Tennessee and Kentucky. But even these early migrants provided only part of the cultural diversity that would become an unheralded hallmark of Appalachia: "There were many English, some Germans—mainly from the Palatinate—and Welsh and Irish, a few [French] Huguenot; but the dominant character of Tennesseans came to be identified with that of the Scotch-Irish."[37] Following the War of Independence, in which they played a major role, these Ulster Scots continued to settle the Appalachian region. In the process, they spread the distinctive attitudes, beliefs, and customs, in short, the culture, that would come to be widely accepted as the only culture, rather than the dominant culture, of the entire region. "After 1782 . . . it seemed as if a considerable part of America was determined to go west; and in the vanguard of the pioneers were the restless Scotch-Irish."[38] Caudill suggests that in the Kentucky region of Appalachia, the family names that are heard today ". . . bespeak a peasant and yeoman ancestry who, for the most part, came from England itself and from Scotland and Ireland."[39] But in spite of the influx of Ulster Scots early in the history of Appalachia, there is a diversity that has been lost in the stereotyping of the culture. "Taking no note of the vast body of research by Appalachian scholars that has discredited the scholarship on which he relies, [David Hackett] Fischer describes the region as if it were little more than the New World survival of archaic Scotch-Irish culture."[40] But Appalachia is much more than the "survival of archaic Scotch-Irish culture."

English

The English, as major explorers of the globe, were also major contributors to the cultural diversity of Appalachia. As "owners" of the colonies, they were responsible for much of the cultural baggage brought to the New World and to Appalachia. As early as 1673, a little over a century before any struggle for independence by the American colonists, Englishmen James Needham and Gabriel Arthur were traversing the Great Valley of Tennessee during their explorations of the Alleghenies. They set the tone for white-red relations before the Ulster Scots made it into the region. Funded by fellow Englishman Abraham Wood, owner of a Virginia trading post, Needham and Arthur ". . . found, during their two journeys into the back country, a paradoxical range of experience—from murder to friendship—that would characterize generations of English-Cherokee relations."[41]

As most cultures were assimilating into the new American fabric, one enterprising group of Englishmen experimented with bringing English culture to Appalachia. In the Cumberland Mountains of Tennessee close to the Kentucky border, they founded the small town of Rugby with the intention of creating an

English village in the Appalachian Mountains. Begun in 1880, this little village experiment was funded by the royalties from *Tom Brown's School Days,* a successful novel authored by founder Thomas Hughes. His dream was to provide a place for the younger sons of English gentry to grow up. These young men were not allowed to inherit family estates or titles. Although they had been raised in an aristocratic atmosphere, they were legally denied any means with which to maintain their aristocracy.[42] Hence, Hughes began his proper English village in the middle of Appalachia as one solution to this problem. Literally in the middle of nowhere, Hughes created a library of some seven thousand volumes, established an Episcopal church, and imported a rosewood organ from England to provide music. He operated a well-financed school, held literary and dramatic presentations, ran an inn for visitors, and maintained swimming areas and tennis courts in the woods for recreation.[43] Although this is not typical of all English participation in the cultural diversity of Appalachia, it was not uncommon for many cultures to try to maintain their own cultural boundaries, which also had the effect of bringing diversity to Appalachia through non-assimilation.

African Americans

To trace the history of the African American culture in Appalachia, one would have to start with the institution of slavery, which began even before the country itself. However, the first people of African descent in America were probably the blacks who explored the regions with the Spaniards and the French in the 1500s: "The contact between the Black Africans and the native Americans of the Apalachee and Cherokee nations began . . . as early as 1526—including the cohabitation of the Cherokee Lady of Cofitachequi and the Spaniard's black slave."[44] The first black Appalachians did not live under the slavery of the plantation owners, therefore, but lived within the culture of the Cherokee Indians.[45] Later, black slaves ". . . accompanied the Spanish expeditions of Fernando de Soto in 1540 and Juan Pardo in 1566."[46]

There were not as many slaveholders in the Appalachian region as on the big plantations of the Deep South, but they did exist in the region. And black slaves, although brought to this country unwillingly, brought with them their cultural baggage as well. They were separated physically from their homeland, but they brought their memories, their heritage, language, songs, and certain customs, and they shared these elements of their culture with everyone who met them along the way, including the people of Appalachia.

Appalachia is also noted for disdaining the horrific institution of slavery, even before much of the rest of the country. In 1819, forty-two years before the beginning of the American Civil War, Tennessee's oldest town, Jonesborough, saw publication of the *Manumission Intelligencer* by the abolitionist Elihu Embree. He changed the newspaper in 1820 to a monthly and called it *The Emancipator,* making these the first antislavery journals in the United States.[47] On the eve of the American Civil War, Tennessee's total population included approximately 25 percent slaves. However, the Appalachian portion of the state in eastern Tennessee had only 8 percent slaves.[48]

After the Civil War, when the coal industry burst on the scene in Appalachia, it was only natural for blacks, both those living in Appalachia and those released from the plantations of the Deep South, to look for work in the mines. According to Lewis, "The preindustrial African American population of central Appalachia was relatively small, totaling only 14,360 in 1870, but by 1890 that figure had more than doubled to 30,226 and quadrupled to 64,251 by 1910."[49] The coal operators saw a new way to employ cheap labor in their mines and quickly took advantage of the many black railroad workers who laid the rails into Appalachia and needed work when that job was finished. Many stayed in Appalachia and became a part of the mining culture. "A separate section of each camp, usually known as 'Nigger Town,' was set aside for these Negroes," notes Caudill. "As reports from their new homes filtered south, scores and hundreds of other Negro families entered into the coalfields."[50]

These blacks become an integral part of the growing cultural diversity in Appalachia, finding their way into every aspect of Appalachian culture. As an example, blacks even participated in the extremely rare practice of serpent handling. In fact, Bishop W. L. Dickerson, the very first pastor of the Jolo church in West Virginia, was African American. He handled serpents in church, as did a few other African Americans who attended these types of services. Burton states that "Kenneth Ambrose found among the serpent-handling churches he studied that there was a strong belief, supported by their actions as well as their sermons, in people of all races being accepted in their congregations."[51]

Appalachian populations of blacks remained small; and in spite of being accepted in some religious circles, blacks, like the immigrants from other parts of the world, were discriminated against in Appalachia just as they were in the rest of the country. One African American said, "I was born in Charleston, West Virginia. . . . There was little interaction in the school between the middle-class whites from the suburbs, inner-city blacks, and the 'hillbillies' or 'creekers' from the surrounding hollows."[52]

Germans

The German culture moved into Appalachia very early in the region's history. Germans had settled in Pennsylvania and Maryland in the early 1700s, and it was only a matter of time before they would make the trek down the Shenandoah Valley into Virginia with their Ulster Scot friends. It was after 1727 that new German immigrants began to find the good ". . . Pennsylvania lands already taken, or too costly; and a new land policy was instituted by the governor of Virginia, William Gooch—the granting of great tracts of Valley land to individual enterprisers."[53] It looked as if the Germans would be the most prolific culture at that particular point in history to settle Appalachia.

It was not long before Germans made it into the heart of Appalachia. Christian Gottlieb Priber came into what would become Tennessee in 1736. Priber was not just any immigrant, but a very learned man who had mastered seven languages. He had left his family behind in Germany with the idea of starting a radically new system of government in the New World: "There, at Great Tellico, he exchanged his continental clothing for breechclout and moccasins and unpacked the tools of his trade, the weapons of his attack, his books."[54]

Like most of the cultures at this time in Appalachia, the Germans traded across cultural boundaries with all they met, particularly with the Ulster Scots, with whom they endured an extremely harsh land and an even harsher Indian war. German immigrants assimilated the Ulster Scot music into theirs and returned the cultural favor by providing the prototypes for the Appalachian dulcimer. The German and Ulster Scot folktale traditions, similar in structure, became amalgamated into a single tradition, stronger than in either motherland. The weaving together of the German and the Ulster Scot traditions provided a grounding on which other groups such as the English, Native Americans, and blacks could add their cultural touch.[55]

Italians

Italians came to Appalachia primarily because of the increased labor market that accompanied the aforementioned industrial boom of the mining era. Coal companies sent recruiting agents to Europe to attract miners to Appalachia with the promise of a better life. When many of these practices became illegal in the late nineteenth century due to immigration laws, the coal companies began to send their agents to Ellis Island, where most of the immigrants were coming into the country, and into the ethnic communities that had already formed in New York City and other northern towns. Work was scarce in the cities, and many immigrants, including a large number of Italians, were lured to the mountains by the agents' promises of a better life in the Appalachian mines.[56]

As with black miners, many of the new immigrants were not happy with their new Appalachian life. Many came not knowing what to expect, and many came unwillingly, clearly misled by their urban recruiters, or "padrones." The Italians were lied to about the location of the mines and about the kind of work they would be doing. They often lived under armed guards until they worked off the cost of their transportation, much like indentured servants of past centuries. There were even reports of forced labor in the Appalachian coal mines. In 1903, the New York Society for the Protection of Italian Immigrants sent an agent to Appalachia to investigate rumors of mistreatment. The labor practices and working conditions under which the Italian miners worked were condemned in his report. The complaints reached the Cabinet level of the federal government, and the governor of West Virginia, in 1907, actually admitted that foreign, as well as American, miners had been forced to work against their will by certain mine owners.[57]

There were many immigrants in the early part of the twentieth century who came to Appalachia for work, including Poles, Hungarians, and Slavs, but the largest ethnic group was the Italians. By 1910, there were seventy-six hundred Italian miners in West Virginia alone. Italians also worked on the railroads of Appalachia. Life for them in the mine and railroad company towns was generally the same as for the Appalachians already here. Many of them came from rural places not too different from Appalachia in makeup, save for the different languages and traditional cultures. Like many eastern Europeans, many Italians returned to their homeland at the outbreak of World War I to fight. Yet "[t]oday, one can find a sprinkling of Catholic churches and missions in the coal camps and mountaineers with Slavic and Italian sounding names—the last reminders of the thousands of immigrants who once played a major role in the region's history."[58]

Welsh, Hispanics, Asians, Jews, Amish, and Hungarians

Many other cultures left their mark on Appalachia. The Welsh, already used to coal mining in their own country, came to Appalachia in the late 1800s and early 1900s to join others with Welsh-sounding names who had been here since the days of the colonies. One can still find evidence of the Swiss culture in several parts of Appalachia, remnants of a past migration of Swiss countrymen.[59] In 1980, Asians in Appalachia numbered 84,092 (0.3 percent of the regional total), two-thirds of whom lived in urban areas.[60] There is a growing population of Hispanics, as well, some working as migrant farmers in the rural areas and some working in the urban areas.[61] And as early as 1748, an Englishman named Sir Alexander Cuming proposed to his government that he help create a new homeland for the Jewish people. He chose a place in the Cherokee part of Appalachia for this venture. He made some headway with Jewish leaders but never could get the three hundred thousand Jewish families to whom he made the request for resettlement to accept his offer.[62] There are also Amish in Appalachia, living primarily in the northern section of the region; they are "relatively dispersed but maintain connections through marketing, church, or school associations."[63]

As noted above, Appalachia provided an area for many social experiments. One such experiment involved a Hungarian immigrant who challenged not only the idea of the company town but also the economic system behind it. In 1917, Henrich Himler established a model cooperative mining town in Martin County, Kentucky, with a group of fellow Hungarians. Himler, a former coal miner, wanted a place for his countrymen to settle but also wanted to prove that labor and capital could work together, an extremely visionary idea in 1917, the year of the Bolshevik Revolution in Russia. According to Eller, "Most of the houses in Himlerville had five rooms, plastered walls, two fireplaces, gas and electricity, a miner's wash house, and a vegetable garden. Each room in the new houses had two windows, and all of the houses were equipped with a tub and shower."[64]

Most academics interested in Appalachia today accept the fact of diversity in the region. Besides David Hackett Fischer's, some of Harry Caudill's early ideas, often unsubstantiated, about the settlement of Appalachia have been repudiated by later academics. "Most historians agree," Donesky notes, "that the region was settled by a mixture of Scotch, Irish, English, Welsh, and Germans who came primarily from Virginia and the Carolinas with smaller migrations from Georgia and Pennsylvania."[65] But even William G. Frost, an early president of Berea College in Kentucky, often was ". . . uncomfortable with the cultural pluralism in America, and thus blind to the ethnic diversity within Appalachia."[66] It is through educational works such as this text, as well as the inevitable contact between cultures, that this blindness to diversity will be healed in all afflicted.

As was the case with the intertwining lives of immigrants and nationals throughout the history of Appalachia, the twenty-first century sees a burgeoning cultural diversity that destroys any stereotype of cultural homogeneity. With the exception of the Native American, the residents of Appalachia are all immigrants or the descendants of immigrants to the region. "All of these groups carried their own cultural traditions with them into the mountains and influenced others by their presence."[67]

Interior of a Cherokee council house in Oconaluftee Indian Village, a replica of a Cherokee village c. 1750, Cherokee, North Carolina. Courtesy of Oconaluftee Indian Village.

One man, one mule—typical in the settlement era and beyond. By Jack Jeffers.

Contemporary Scottish piper in full Highland dress. By Lora L. Gordon, Radford University.

Representative of an African American lodge of the Independent Order of the Oddfellows, c. 1915. Courtesy of Larry Clevinger II, Vintage Investments, Pulaski, Virginia.

The Emberti wedding party, Polish immigrants in Hazelton, Pennsylvania., c. 1918. Courtesy of Elaine Machelor.

Notes

1. Wilma Dykeman, *Tennessee: A History* (Newport, Tenn.: Wakestone Books, 1993), 22.
2. W. K. McNeil, ed. *Appalachian Images in Folk and Popular Culture* (Knoxville: Univ. of Tennessee Press, 1995), 1.
3. Dykeman, *Tennessee*, 22.
4. Ibid., 23.
5. Ronald D. Eller, *Miners, Millhands, and Mountaineers: Industrialization of the Appalachian South, 1880–1930* (Knoxville: Univ. of Tennessee Press, 1982), 46.
6. Harry M. Caudill, *Night Comes to the Cumberlands: A Biography of a Depressed Area* (Toronto: Little, Brown, 1962), 103.
7. Ibid., 104.
8. Denise Giardina, "Appalachian Images: A Personal History," in *Confronting Appalachian Stereotypes: Back Talk from an American Region,* ed. Dwight B. Billings, Gurney Norman, and Katherine Ledford (Lexington: Univ. Press of Kentucky, 1999), 172.
9. Caudill, *Night Comes to the Cumberlands,* 104.
10. Ibid.
11. Darlene Wilson, "A Judicious Combination of Incident and Psychology: John Fox, Jr. and the Southern Mountaineer Motif," in *Confronting Appalachian Stereotypes: Back Talk from an American Region,* ed. Dwight B. Billings, Gurney Norman, and Katherine Ledford (Lexington: Univ. Press of Kentucky, 1999), 100.
12. Ronald L. Lewis, "Beyond Isolation and Homogeneity: Diversity and the History of Appalachia," in *Confronting Appalachian Stereotypes: Back Talk from an American Region,* ed. Dwight B. Billings, Gurney Norman, and Katherine Ledford (Lexington: Univ. Press of Kentucky, 1999), 35–36.
13. Richard A. Couto, Nancy K. Simpson, and Gale Harris, eds., *Sowing Seeds in the Mountains: Community-Based Coalitions for Cancer Prevention and Control* (Rockville, Md.: Appalachia Leadership Initiative on Cancer, Cancer Control Sciences Program, Division of Cancer Prevention and Control, National Cancer Institute, 1994), 207.
14. West Virginia Department of Mines. *1909 West Virginia Department of Mines, Report of the Chief Inspector.* (Charleston: West Virginia Department of Mines, c. 1909).
15. Lewis, "Beyond Isolation," 37.
16. Ibid., 36.
17. Philip J. Obermiller, "Urban Organizations and the Image of Appalachians," in *Confronting Appalachian Stereotypes: Back Talk from an American Region,* ed. Dwight B. Billings, Gurney Norman, and Katherine Ledford (Lexington: Univ. Press of Kentucky, 1999), 259.
18. Kathleen Blee and Dwight B. Billings, "Where 'Bloodshed Is a Pastime,'" in *Confronting Appalachian Stereotypes: Back Talk from an American Region,* ed.

Dwight B. Billings, Gurney Norman, and Katherine Ledford (Lexington: Univ. Press of Kentucky, 1999), 128.

19. Karl B. Raitz and Richard Ulack, *Appalachia: A Regional Geography—Land, People and Development* (Boulder, Colo.: Westview Press, 1984), 87.

20. David K. Evans, "Pre-Columbian Cultural Contact Between Chibchan and Iroquoin Linguistic Groups," in *The Many Faces of Appalachia: Proceedings of the 7th Annual Appalachian Studies Conference,* ed. Sam Gray (Boone, N.C.: Appalachian Consortium Press, 1985), 57.

21. James G. Leyburn, *The Scotch-Irish: A Social History* (Chapel Hill: Univ. of North Carolina Press, 1962), 223.

22. Ibid., 217.

23. Dykeman, *Tennessee,* 19.

24. Ibid.

25. William L. Anderson, "The Impact of the Scots and Irish Among the Cherokees," in *Selected Readings: 1996 East Tennessee State University Appalachian-Scottish and Irish Studies,* ed. Stevan R. Jackson (Johnson City: East Tennessee State Univ., 1996), 33.

26. Couto, Simpson, and Harris, *Sowing Seeds,* 18.

27. Joan Vannorsdall Schroeder, "The Melungeons Revisited," *Blue Ridge Online,* 2000, http://www.blueridgecountry.com/melung/melung.html (n.d.).

28. Lewis, "Beyond Isolation," 38.

29. Raitz and Ulack, *Appalachia,* 183.

30. Ibid., 183–84.

31. Bonnie Ball, *The Melungeons: Notes on the Origin of a Race* (Johnson City, Tenn.: Overmountain Press, 1992), vi–vii.

32. Ibid., viii–ix.

33. Schroeder, "Melungeons Revisited."

34. Ibid.

35. Conor Cruise O'Brien and Maire O'Brien, *Ireland: A Concise History* (London: Thames and Hudson, 1997), 62–63.

36. Dykeman, *Tennessee,* 14–15.

37. Ibid.

38. Leyburn, *Scotch-Irish,* 232.

39. Caudill, *Night Comes to the Cumberlands,* 7.

40. Blee and Billings, "Where 'Bloodshed Is a Pastime,'" 120.

41. Dykeman, *Tennessee,* 24.

42. Ibid., 130–31.

43. Ibid., 131.

44. William H. Turner, "Introduction," in *Blacks in Appalachia,* ed. William H. Turner and Edward J. Cabbell (Lexington: Univ. Press of Kentucky, 1985), xviii.

45. Theda Perdue, "Red and Blacks in the Southern Appalachians," in *Blacks in Appalachia,* ed. William H. Turner and Edward J. Cabbell (Lexington: Univ. Press of Kentucky, 1985), 23.

46. Ibid., 23.
47. Dykeman, *Tennessee,* 19–20.
48. Ibid., 80.
49. Lewis, "Beyond Isolation," 35.
50. Caudill, *Night Comes to the Cumberlands,* 102–3.
51. Thomas G. Burton, *Serpent-Handling Believers* (Knoxville: Univ. of Tennessee Press, 1993), 166.
52. Stephen L. Fisher, "Appalachian Stepchild," in *Confronting Appalachian Stereotypes: Back Talk from an American Region,* ed. Dwight B. Billings, Gurney Norman, and Katherine Ledford (Lexington: Univ. Press of Kentucky, 1999), 187.
53. Leyburn, *Scotch-Irish,* 120.
54. Dykeman, *Tennessee,* 29–30.
55. McNeil, *Appalachian Images,* 309.
56. Eller, *Miners, Millhands, and Mountaineers,* 172.
57. Ibid., 172–75.
58. Ibid.
59. Leyburn, *Scotch-Irish,* 213.
60. Raitz and Ulack, *Appalachia,* 182.
61. Couto, Simpson, and Harris, *Sowing Seeds,* 207.
62. Dykeman, *Tennessee,* 128.
63. Couto, Simpson, and Harris, *Sowing Seeds,* 207–8.
64. Eller, *Miners, Millhands, and Mountaineers,* 191.
65. Finlay Donesky, "America Needs Hillbillies: The Case of the Kentucky Cycle," in *Confronting Appalachian Stereotypes: Back Talk from an American Region,* ed. Dwight B. Billings, Gurney Norman, and Katherine Ledford (Lexington: Univ. Press of Kentucky, 1999), 288.
66. Allen Batteau, "A Contribution to the Critique of Political Economy," in *The Many Faces of Appalachia: Proceedings of the 7th Annual Appalachian Studies Conference,* ed. Sam Gray (Boone, N.C.: Appalachian Consortium Press, 1985), 41–42.
67. Lewis, "Beyond Isolation," 38.

Suggested Readings

Anderson, William L. "The Impact of the Scots and Irish Among the Cherokees." In *Selected Readings: 1996 East Tennessee State University Appalachian-Scottish and Irish Studies,* edited by Stevan R. Jackson. Johnson City: East Tennessee State Univ., 1996.

Ball, Bonnie. *The Melungeons: Notes on the Origin of a Race.* Johnson City, Tenn.: Overmountain Press, 1992.

Batteau, Allen. "A Contribution to the Critique of Political Economy." In *The Many Faces of Appalachia: Proceedings of the 7th Annual Appalachian Studies Conference,* edited by Sam Gray. Boone, N.C.: Appalachian Consortium Press, 1985.

Blee, Kathleen M., and Dwight B. Billings. "Where 'Bloodshed Is a Pastime.'" In *Confronting Appalachian Stereotypes: Back Talk from an American Region*, edited by Dwight B. Billings, Gurney Norman, and Katherine Ledford. Lexington: Univ. Press of Kentucky, 1999.

Burton, Thomas G. *Serpent-Handling Believers*. Knoxville: Univ. of Tennessee Press, 1993.

Caudill, Harry M. *Night Comes to the Cumberlands: A Biography of a Depressed Area*. Boston: Little, Brown, 1962.

Couto, Richard A., Nancy K. Simpson, and Gale Harris, eds. *Sowing Seeds in the Mountains: Community-Based Coalitions for Cancer Prevention and Control*. Rockville, Md.: Appalachia Leadership Initiative on Cancer, Cancer Control Sciences Program, Division of Cancer Prevention and Control, National Cancer Institute, 1994.

Donesky, Finlay. "America Needs Hillbillies: The Case of the Kentucky Cycle." In *Confronting Appalachian Stereotypes: Back Talk from an American Region*, edited by Dwight B. Billings, Gurney Norman, and Katherine Ledford. Lexington: Univ. Press of Kentucky, 1999.

Dykeman, Wilma. *Tennessee: A History*. Newport, Tenn.: Wakestone Books, 1993.

Eller, Ronald D. *Miners, Millhands, and Mountaineers: Industrialization of the Appalachian South, 1880–1930*. Knoxville: Univ. of Tennessee Press, 1982.

Evans, David K. "Pre-Columbian Cultural Contact Between Chibchan and Iroquoin Linguistic Groups." In *The Many Faces of Appalachia: Proceedings of the 7th Annual Appalachian Studies Conference*, edited by Sam Gray. Boone, N.C.: Appalachian Consortium Press, 1985.

Giardina, Denise. "Appalachian Images: A Personal History." In *Confronting Appalachian Stereotypes: Back Talk from an American Region*, edited by Dwight B. Billings, Gurney Norman, and Katherine Ledford. Lexington: Univ. Press of Kentucky, 1999.

Fisher, Stephen L. "Appalachian Stepchild." In *Confronting Appalachian Stereotypes: Back Talk from an American Region*, edited by Dwight B. Billings, Gurney Norman, and Katherine Ledford. Lexington: Univ. Press of Kentucky, 1999.

Lewis, Ronald L. "Beyond Isolation and Homogeneity: Diversity and the History of Appalachia." In *Confronting Appalachian Stereotypes: Back Talk from an American Region*, edited by Dwight B. Billings, Gurney Norman, and Katherine Ledford. Lexington: Univ. Press of Kentucky, 1999.

Leyburn, James G. *The Scotch-Irish: A Social History*. Chapel Hill: Univ. of North Carolina Press, 1962.

McNeil, W. K., ed. *Appalachian Images in Folk and Popular Culture*. Knoxville: Univ. of Tennessee Press, 1995.

Obermiller, Phillip J. "Urban Organizations and the Image of Appalachians." In *Confronting Appalachian Stereotypes: Back Talk from an American Region*, edited by Dwight B. Billings, Gurney Norman, and Katherine Ledford. Lexington: Univ. Press of Kentucky, 1999.

O'Brien, Conor Cruise, and Marie O'Brien. *Ireland: A Concise History*. London: Thames and Hudson, 1997.

Perdue, Theda. "Red and Blacks in the Southern Appalachians." In *Blacks in Appalachia,* edited by William H. Turner and Edward J. Cabbell. Lexington: Univ. Press of Kentucky, 1985.

Raitz, Karl B., and Richard Ulack. *Appalachia: A Regional Geography—Land, People, and Development.* Boulder, Colo.: Westview Press, 1984.

Schroeder, Joan Vannorsdall. "The Melungeons Revisited." In *Blue Ridge Online,* 2000. Http://www.blueridgecountry.com/melung/melung.html (n.d.).

Turner, William H. "Introduction." In *Blacks in Appalachia,* edited by William H. Turner and Edward J. Cabbell. Lexington: Univ. Press of Kentucky, 1985.

NATURAL RESOURCES AND ENVIRONMENT OF APPALACHIA

DAVID L. ROUSE AND L. SUE GREER-PITT

Appalachian mountain topography can be divided into four principal areas. The Blue Ridge is the easternmost area, extending from northern Georgia through West Virginia and, according to some, Pennsylvania and Maryland. The Great Smoky Mountains are in western North Carolina and eastern Tennessee. The Black Mountains are in western North Carolina. Mount Mitchell, at 6,684 feet, is the highest point east of the Mississippi River. The Cumberland Mountains and Plateau extend along southeastern Kentucky, southwestern Virginia, eastern Tennessee, northern Georgia, and northeastern Alabama.

Rivers

Of the many resources of the central and southern Appalachian region, none is more important, or more undervalued, than its waters. Mountains are the natural collectors of rainwater, and the Appalachians serve this function for the eastern United States. Flowing eastward, eventually reaching the Atlantic Coast, are the Susquehanna, Potomac, James, Rappahannock, Roanoke (Staunton), Catawba, Yadkin (Pee Dee), Savannah, Ocmulgee, Oconee, and Altamaha. Feeding into the Ohio River are the Kentucky, Kanawha, Allegheny, Monongahela, and New River. Moving southward, we find the Cumberland and Tennessee River systems. The Holston, Clinch, French Broad, Hiwassee, and Duck feed the Tennessee. And this is to mention only a few of the important waterways flowing out of the mountains. Several of the rivers are actually older than the mountains. As the mountains were thrust up by plate tectonics, the rivers cut new courses, carving out spectacular gorges and bridges.

The rivers serve many functions. First and foremost, they are a source of drinking water for much of the eastern United States. They have been, and continue to be, transportation routes. They support rich resources of fish and game. They are major tourist attractions and provided the sites for white-water events in the Atlanta Olympic Games. The valleys formed by the rivers have been highly productive for agriculture, providing a livelihood first for Native American tribes and then for European settlers.

The impact of industrialization—logging, mining, paper and chemical manufacturing—on the rivers has been serious. The stripping of mountain slopes of trees has caused the buildup of silt on the river bottoms and been the cause of major flooding. The release of chemicals, including mercury and dioxins, has made fish unfit for consumption.

The glaciers of the last ice age did not affect the portion of the Appalachians from Pennsylvania southward. Consequently, there are few natural lakes. Large impoundments have been built along the rivers, principally by the Tennessee Valley Authority, to provide flood control and hydroelectric power. They also provide major recreational facilities.

Biodiversity

Missing the glaciers of the last ice age also means that Appalachia is one of the most diverse biological regions of North America. As the glaciers moved southward, northern species came to inhabit the southern areas, creating an unusually rich genetic pool. There are 690 vertebrate species and 2,245 higher plant species native to the region. The kinds of trees found today were here over fifty million years ago. Sixty of the vertebrate species and 83 of the plant species are threatened or endangered. The greatest negative impacts on the biodiversity of the region come from logging and mining, although air pollution is now affecting species at the higher elevations.

In addition to the commercially and ecologically valuable trees, there are plants appreciated for their sheer beauty. Spring brings the white flowering of dogwood, contrasting with the brightness of redbud. Later, the wild azaleas, laurel, and rhododendron, which thrive in the acid soils, add golds, purples, and reds to the mountain landscapes. Many tourists check with the Forest Service, Park Service, and local tourist centers in order to time their visits to the peak seasons for spring, early summer, and fall colors. Other plants such as ginseng and bloodroot are collected for their medicinal uses.

Native American and European settlers were attracted to the Appalachian Mountains not only by rich river valleys but also by the variety of game, much of which still abounds. One exception is the black bear, which is threatened by poaching. Their paws are sold as ornaments, and their gall bladders are used in oriental medicine. Nevertheless, they are still present in significant numbers and occasionally wander from the forests and parks into residential neighborhoods. Deer are also in abundance, and along with squirrel, rabbit, wild turkey, and ruffled grouse, they provide opportunities for the sport hunter. Fox and raccoon are also popular among hunters. In this case, however, the sport is rarely in the kill or providing meat for the table. Rather, it is in the training of the dogs for the chase.

There are ongoing programs to reintroduce species that have seriously declined or disappeared from the mountains. Successful reintroductions include beaver, wolves, elk, and the bald eagle. Gone, however, are mountain lion, golden eagle, and bison.

Streams, rivers, and man-made lakes provide ample opportunities for freshwater sports fishing. The native brook trout are found only in the remotest streams at higher elevations, having been replaced by the introduction of rainbow trout. Rainbow trout can now be caught in many of the streams and rivers, by fishing deep in the lakes, and below the dams. Perch, pickerel, muskellunge, catfish, crappie, and bass are in the rivers and lakes. Several streams are home to a rich variety of freshwater mussels, though these are increasingly threatened by pollution.

Forests

When Europeans settled the Appalachian region (between the 1720s and the 1830s), they found a region that was 80 to 90 percent forested. The original forest canopy was similar in species to present-day forests, with the exception of the now-extinct American chestnut. The chestnut dominated much of the forests until blight wiped it out. The fungus was first noticed in New York in 1904, and within twenty-five years, nearly all the trees in North Carolina and Tennessee were infected. Since the chestnut was a key element in the forest ecosystem, its death brought other major transformations. Loss of canopy caused major changes in the forest floor. Game that depended on the mast crop declined significantly. Farmers could no longer free range their hogs as they had since early settlement.

Remnants of old-growth forests can be seen in the few small coves of virgin timber preserved in national forests such as Sumter in South Carolina,

Chattahoochee in Georgia, Nantahala in North Carolina, Cherokee in Tennessee, and Robinson Forest, Lily Cornett Woods, and Blanton Forest in Kentucky.

At the upper elevations from Pennsylvania to Virginia, the dominant timber species was spruce and intermingled fir. At middle elevations, and from Tennessee and North Carolina to Georgia, hardwoods such as tulip poplar, red and white oak, ash, and maple were found. In the southern reaches of the Appalachian Mountains in Georgia and South Carolina were found varieties of pine. The cutting and milling of timber followed the settlers. Almost every mountain county had at least one sawmill. However, timber cutting was an adjunct activity to farming and it primarily supported building and commercial activity within the region. By 1900, fully 75 percent of the region was still wooded.

Commercial timbering for sale outside the region began as early as 1870. During the first decade of commercial timbering, cutting was done selectively of large, prime, hardwood trees. Timber companies purchased specific trees from private landholders, contracting the landholder to cut and deliver the timber to a distant sawmill.

Water was the primary means by which the cut timber was delivered to its destination. Farmers would construct temporary impoundments behind which they would place logs. When spring rains caused the rivers to rise, these "splash dams" would be opened, allowing the logs to float downriver to the mills. Lumbering continued to be a part-year activity for farming families. During this period, however, large commercial land and timber companies, financed and headquartered in northeastern cities such as Philadelphia and New York, began buying up great tracts of Appalachian timberland. More northern timber sources were already being exhausted. The social and technological changes of the 1890s would transform the timber industry in the Appalachian region. These changes included increased demand for hardwood and investment in building railroads deep into the mountain region. An important technological change was the development of huge bandsaws. The result was a timber boom after 1890. With access to rail transportation, large timber corporations from outside the region set up full-time operations, housing their workers in dormitories around huge band mills. Selective cutting was replaced by clear-cutting.

The timber boom transformed the region both socially and physically. Many residents found their first nonagricultural employment in the timber camps. The timbering practices of the period left millions of acres of denuded hillsides, resulting in extensive loss of watershed, soil erosion, and a greater potential for fire. The steam engine was the direct cause of most fires that swept across the region. Cinders escaping through the chimney or dumped with the ashes from the firebox ignited dry branches and leaves left exposed when the trees were cut. Millions of acres of timber were lost to fire. And as the fires smoldered, humus was depleted and the productive capacity of the soil was lost.

The physical devastation intensified after 1910, when the timber cutting and removal process was mechanized. The opening of paper pulp mills in the region, such as the Champion Mill in North Carolina, further accelerated the cutting, as the mills could utilize even the smallest trees. The devastation of the landscape drew concern both within and outside the region. Discussions of the reservation of forested land for aesthetic, recreational, and health purposes, in the form of a national park, began in the 1880s. By 1900, concern was also growing in professional forestry circles about the need to conserve the forest resource for future economic use. Conservation of forest lands for future use had extensive political support from Theodore Roosevelt and recently appointed chief forester Gifford Pinchot. However, Congress repeatedly refused to authorize the purchase of private lands, arguing that the Constitution provided no authority for such action. This changed in the decade following 1900, as watershed problems and serious flooding within the Appalachian region increased. It was effectively argued that the protection of the watershed of navigable streams and rivers was within the constitutional purview of the federal government.

The result was the 1911 Weeks Law, which authorized the purchase of private "forested, cut-over, or denuded lands within the watersheds of navigable streams." Within months, the U.S. Forest Service had purchased land within North Carolina that became the foundation for the Nantahala and Pisgah National Forests. Over the next decade, the Forest Service purchased lands throughout the Appalachian highlands. In most cases, the lands were purchased from the large land and timber companies that had come into the region in the late 1800s. They were generally pleased to be relieved of the tax burden of cut-over and less economically viable timberlands. In 1924, Congress passed the Clark-McNary Act, which authorized more funds for land acquisition and broadened the justification for purchase to also include fire protection. During the 1920s and 1930s, the Forest Service expanded its purchase program to include smaller parcels of land, taking advantage of economic hard times to consolidate acreage.

By the end of the 1930s, all of the currently existing national forests of the region had been organized: in Georgia, Chattahoochee; in South Carolina, Sumter; in North Carolina, Nantahala and Pisgah; in Tennessee, Cherokee; in Virginia, Jefferson and Washington; in Kentucky, Daniel Boone; in West Virginia, Monongahela; and in Pennsylvania, Allegheny. During the same general period, a significantly smaller proportion of Appalachian timberlands (both forested and cut-over) were preserved from future timbering in two national parks: the

Great Smoky Mountains on the border of Tennessee and North Carolina, and Shenandoah National Park in Virginia.

The Forest Service, with the assistance of the Civilian Conservation Corps, in the 1930s engaged in some reforestation on national forest lands. Primarily, however, the agency husbanded the natural reforestation process through fire and disease protection. By the time of the Forest Service's second Roadless Area Review and Evaluation (RARE II) in 1978, 95 percent of the national forest lands in the Appalachian region were considered to be commercial forests. At the time of RARE II, about two-thirds of the national forest acreage supported stands of timber of sawing size.

Forest Service land acquisition, which slowed to a dribble during the 1940s and 1950s, resumed again after Congress passed the 1964 Land and Water Conservation Act, which authorized funds for recreational land acquisition. More than four hundred thousand additional acres have been added to the Appalachian region national forests just since the early 1980s, for a total of nearly six and a half million acres. In comparison, fewer than one million acres are protected in the two national parks.

Yet the national forest lands account for less than 10 percent of the commercial forest land in the Appalachian region. Another 10 to 20 percent (depending on state and type of forest) is owned by timber corporations. In the 1980s, the Appalachian Landownership Task Force found that just six timber or wood products companies accounted for nearly seven hundred thousand acres of forest land in the Appalachian region. The majority of the timber stock of the Appalachian region is in a patchwork of private ownership. Some of it is in the hands of individual families; some is owned by coal, oil, and other mineral corporations. As the age and size of Appalachian forests increase, and as employment in coal mining wanes, the timber industry is becoming a more important economic force in the Appalachian region.

Two trends threaten the sustainability of the timber industry of Appalachia. First, as western forest reserves are depleted by overharvesting, the giant timber companies are moving back to the east. Second, numerous chip mills are being constructed throughout the Appalachian region. Chip mills reduce logs of any size to chips that can be used to manufacture a variety of products from wafer board to paper. The demand for wood chips is worldwide and so there is a strong export market. Since species, quality, and size are all irrelevant to the production of wood chips, the presence of the mills encourages clear-cutting.

Insects and disease remain serious threats to the forests. An insect only one-twenty-fifth of an inch long, the balsam woolly adelgid, imported from Europe to Maine, has devastated native stands of Fraser fir. The butternut has

been infected by a fungus that attacks not just the tree but also the nuts, keeping the tree from reproducing. The beech bark scale insect spreads a fungus that is fatal to the trees. Wild stands of dogwood are infected with anthracnose.

Another threat to the forests is air pollution. Tourists coming to the national parks to enjoy the spectacular views may find that visibility is low. The pollution that restricts their view is also causing increased acidity in the soils and streams through acid rain and acid clouds. That, in turn, is causing stress if not death in the forests. The primary sources for this pollution are the coal-fired power plants to the west of the forests. Automobiles also make a contribution, though a much smaller one.

Minerals

A variety of minerals is found in Appalachia. Copper was mined at the North Carolina, Tennessee, and Georgia border at the turn of this century. Aluminum, mica, and kaolin are also mined. Some gold is still found in South Carolina. No other mineral, however, has had the impact of coal.

Anthracite, a very hard coal with a high carbon content, is found in western Pennsylvania. Bituminous coal, softer and easier to ignite, is found southward through West Virginia, eastern Kentucky, southwestern Virginia, and eastern Tennessee into Alabama. The oft-cited portrayal of Appalachia as a rich land inhabited by poor people has more to do with the history of the bituminous coal industry than any other single factor.

The industrial expansion of the 1880s not only transformed the region by increasing the demand for timber but also brought increased demand for the region's coal. And like the demand for timber, the demand for coal brought speculative capital from the eastern United States and abroad, particularly England. Land ownership would be concentrated in the hands of a few corporations located outside the region; and farming, particularly in the coalfields, would fade into insignificance. The company town rather than the family farm would become the site of Appalachian life.

Boosters of the New South, through newspapers such as the *Richmond Whig,* the *Louisville Courier-Journal,* and the *Atlanta Constitution,* called for the rapid development of the South's "exhaustless treasures." State governments actively recruited not only foreign capital but also immigrant labor to mill the lumber and mine the coal. As the railroads extended into the region, they promoted further investment in timber and coal lands. Private speculators, many of whom first saw the region's natural wealth while serving as officers during the Civil War, envisioned "New Pittsburghs" being built to exploit the coal and iron, though the iron ore would prove to be of poor quality.

Many of the families determined to remain on the land as farmers were persuaded to sign what in eastern Kentucky was called a "broad form deed." It severed surface from mineral rights. Signed when minerals could only be obtained by deep mining with pick, shovel, and mule, these transactions would later be used by the coal companies to justify stripping the surface in order to obtain their minerals. During much of the twentieth century, the surface owner would have no legal recourse.

In other cases, mountain families found their deeds challenged. Companies would produce deeds based on land grants, recorded in Richmond or other state capitals, but not in local courthouses. The choice the mountaineer faced was to either undertake an expensive court battle that he might well lose or accept the offer that was given him by the company. Other land was obtained by having one of several heirs force a sale of property rather than divide it. By these and other means, many mountain families were forced off the land and into the labor camps of the industrial age.

Once the mountaineer became a miner, well-being depended upon the fluctuations of production and changes in mining technology. The following observations are based on the historical data compiled by the Mine Safety and Health Administration. They cover the years 1931 to 1992.

The peak years for employment in coal mining were 1941–45. Coal was needed to power the World War II effort. These were also the peak years for unionization. The National Labor Relations Act, passed as part of the New Deal, gave working people rights to organize that they had not had before—and have not had again since the Taft-Hartley amendment to that act. In 1944, miners worked 1.078 billion hours to produce 685 million tons of coal. In 1947, production was slightly higher, with slightly fewer hours worked.

It would be thirty-two years, 1979, before coal production would surpass the 1947 level. But the 741 million tons of coal produced in 1979 would require only 393 million hours of labor. In the 1970s, foreign oil-producing countries managed to put together a cartel that significantly raised oil prices. This led to a shift toward more coal-powered electricity production in the United States. Coal production has continued to increase since, but that increased production has required fewer and fewer mine workers. Coal producers continue to thrive, while unemployment in the coal-producing counties of Appalachia remains high.

Several factors have contributed to this poverty in the midst of wealth. One has been a shift from underground mining to surface mining. In 1931, there were sixty-seven miners working at underground operations for every miner working at a surface operation. By 1947, there were ten miners working at underground operations for every miner working at a surface operation. By 1983, there were 1.5 miners working at underground operations for every miner working at a surface operation. Not only has there been a change in how coal is mined within the Appalachian region, but an increasing amount of the nation's coal production takes place in western states. The top ten coal-producing states are, in descending order, Wyoming, Kentucky, West Virginia, Pennsylvania, Texas, Illinois, Virginia, Montana, North Dakota, and Indiana. With Appalachian reserves estimated at billions of tons, mining will continue to play a major role in the economy.

Underground mining itself has changed dramatically. In the early years, the miner went underground with a pick, shovel, and blasting powder. Each miner was assigned a "room" in the mine for which he and his helpers were responsible. He would make sure that timbers supported the roof. He would pick out the coal at the bottom of a seam, then he would drill holes at the top that he would fill with powder. He would then blast down the coal and load it into a car that a mule would pull out of the mine. The miner would be paid according to the amount of coal he produced. Family ties often conditioned the shares paid to his helpers.

The greater efficiencies in underground mining have come with mechanization. The first major change came with the mechanical loader. Arms in front of the machine pulled the coal onto a conveyer belt that then carried the coal out of the mine. Next came the continuous miner, capable of cutting the coal from the seam, eliminating the need for much of the underground drilling and blasting. The continuous miner also allowed higher levels of recovery. Continuous mining now accounts for 56 percent of underground production. The latest stage of mechanization has been the longwall miner. Resembling a large circular saw, the longwall miner moves back and forth across the seam, shearing the coal. Thirty-one percent of underground mining is now longwall.

Mechanization has reduced the number of underground workers and thus the overall number of people injured or killed in mining. But for those who continue mining and work the machines, risks to health and safety have increased. The pick and shovel mining of the past created relatively little dust. When the miner blasted his seam, he was well back from the worst of the dust. Today's miner, mounted on the machine he operates, is continually exposed to the dust, which is much greater in volume.

Health and safety laws require mine operators to monitor and reduce dust levels. Unfortunately, compliance has been spotty. The dust poses two threats to mine health and safety. First, exposure to coal dust results in "black lung," a progressive disease that causes the lungs to lose their elasticity. Second, the dust increases the risk of mine explosions. It can ignite with methane, a common gas in coal mines. While mine explosions make dramatic news events, however, most mine deaths are caused by roof falls. If mine roofs are not properly supported, the weight of the rock above can cause the roof to collapse. A miner caught in a roof fall can be killed or seriously injured.

Mining has taken its toll on both the people of the Appalachian coalfields and the land itself. The coal seams support the natural aquifers of the region. When the seams are mined, underground water is affected in several different ways. Individuals, or even entire communities, may lose their source of household water. When the low-grade iron ore that frequently accompanies coal is exposed to air, it oxidizes, releasing sulfuric acid that mixes with the water in the mine to cause acid mine drainage. When an underground mine is sealed, water can build up in the mine. Weak areas may "blow out," causing flash flooding.

Surface subsidence is another environmental problem caused by underground mining. Earlier mining techniques would leave pillars of coal in the mine to support the roof. When continuous miners are used, it is not uncommon to "pull" the pillars after the seam is finished and as the machinery is removed from the mine. Longwall mining might leave no support behind the mining machine. In both cases, the collapse of the mine roof can lead to the surface of the ground sinking.

Surface mining, particularly prior to the 1977 passage of the Surface Mine Control and Reclamation Act (SMCRA), has been even more devastating to the Appalachian environment. While deep mining follows the coal seam underground, surface mining removes whatever soil and rock cover the coal seam. This is done by cutting into the sides of mountains or digging pits into the ground, sometimes hundreds of feet deep. Prior to SMCRA, the coal operator would simply abandon a site after mining the coal. This left steep "high walls," on which no vegetation could grow, to erode into streams and sometimes collapse, as well as pits of poisonous acid water.

Even though SMCRA ended the worst of the environmental abuses of surface mining, land is rarely returned to the "higher and better use" the legislation called for. The enforcement mechanism is a five-year bond. Once the operator is released from the bond, he has no further responsibility. Thus the quickest and easiest route to bond release is most often followed. Postmine land use is designated to be "unmanaged pasture and forest." Fescue and lespedeza are hydro-seeded and a few white pines are planted where once grew forests of mixed species.

Levels of soil compaction are another problem following surface mining. The heavy machinery presses down on the rock and dirt that are placed back after mining. Plant roots cannot penetrate these compacted spoils, so revegetation is poor. The surface, however, does not get evenly compacted. As a result, it settles unevenly, and the settling damages construction on those surfaces.

Mountaintop removal is a form of surface mining that has become increasingly common and increasingly controversial. After the tops of mountains are blasted, draglines, which are mammoth shovels, remove the soil and rock, which are then dumped into the valleys. Coal is then loaded and hauled away. The method is used to reach successive seams of coal lying within the mountain. Mountaintop removal jobs are permitted under the "higher and better use" exception to SMCRA. In the process of filling the valleys, however, streams are covered with fill. Environmental groups in West Virginia and Kentucky have challenged valley fills in federal court as being in violation of the Clean Water Act. While they were successful in the Huntington District Court, the decision has been overturned in the Fourth Appellate Court. Legislation is currently before Congress which would make the practice illegal. The result of these efforts cannot be predicted at this time.

Coal refuse is another environmental problem of mining. Before shipping, coal is taken to a processing plant, where it is washed and sorted. The refuse is allowed to accumulate on the site. In dry piles, it can ignite and burn for years. Rainwater leaches acid out of the refuse, polluting both land and streams below. Refuse is also collected into sludge ponds. In October 2001, a Massey Coal Company pond in Martin County, Kentucky, failed, releasing 2.5 million gallons of coal sludge into tributaries of the Big Sandy River. The EPA called the event the worst environmental disaster ever in the southeastern United States.

The sandstones within which coal seams are found, as well as the seams themselves, often contain pockets of methane gas. Methane escaping into the mineshaft and building up to explosive levels is one of the constant dangers faced by the underground miner. The well-known "canary in the mines" was brought there to detect explosive levels of methane.

Today there is an increasing effort to tap coal-bed methane for commercial use. The gas is produced by drilling a well and then injecting chemicals to fracture the rock. Once the rock is fractured, gas can escape from the rock or coal into the well. Large quantities of briny water are also released in the process and must be pumped out prior to gas production. This water creates yet another environmental hazard for the coalfields. Industry preference is to inject these waste waters into previously drilled "dry" wells. Eventually these waters will reappear in the streams and drinking water.

Agriculture

While most of Appalachia is rural, it is not, in an economically significant sense, agricultural; that has not always been the case. Prior to timber and coal industrialization, agriculture dominated the region. The river valleys were first farmed by Native Americans, then by Europeans. Oak, walnut, hickory, and especially chestnut trees provided an abundant mast crop. European immigrants allowed hogs to "free range" in the woods, fattening on the mast. Hogs, and also turkeys, were driven to markets. Corn and whiskey could be shipped via the region's many waterways.

Farming did not completely disappear, and the culture of the family farm has lingered. In areas of East Tennessee, southwestern Virginia, and eastern Kentucky, particularly where limestone sweetens the soils, tobacco is still grown. Sorghum molasses is produced for local and regional markets. Livestock are grazed on gentler slopes and on some reclaimed strip mines. Christmas tree farms are found in many areas. Home gardens are found in every community, and the arts of canning and drying food are handed down through the generations.

There is a growing interest throughout the region in increasing agricultural production, particularly in sustainable crop production. In Dungannon, Virginia, environmental theologian Richard Cartwright Austin runs the Chestnut Ridge Farm and participates in regional marketing strategies for organic growers. On Austin's farm, raspberries are organically grown for fine restaurants, and over forty varieties of pepper are produced, also organically grown. Other small producers in the area have joined Austin, adding herbs, range-fed beef, and chickens to the list of organic farm products.

Horse logging is being revived as a way of producing timber through selective harvests without clear-cutting. Solar kiln drying of native hardwoods to be marketed to local craft and furniture producers is a way of adding value within the Appalachian economy instead of simply exporting a raw resource. In 1995, Austin and others involved in sustainable agriculture formed Appalachian Sustainable Development, a nonprofit organization with offices in Abingdon, Virginia.

The major obstacle to Appalachia returning to a diversified economy in which agriculture plays a significant role is the absentee, especially corporate, ownership of land. The scars of the industrial exploitation of natural resources are most visible on the mountainsides, but their concomitant legacies are also documented in the courthouse deed books.

Development

While many areas of Appalachia, particularly the coalfields, are suffering population loss, other areas are experiencing rapid growth. Increasing affluence across the nation means more people can afford vacation homes, and the scenic mountains of Appalachia are a favored place. Growing use of the Internet allows technology workers to live outside of crowded cities and suburbs, and many choose mountain communities. Consequently, an increasing number of these growing communities face the problem of controlling development so that the qualities that bring development to the mountains are not destroyed by that development. The university towns of Boone, North Carolina, and Blacksburg, Virginia, are two such areas that appeal to those who want the beauty of mountain life but also the conveniences of modern high-tech living. Once known for its steel industry, Pittsburgh has become a center of high tech, again boosted by its university communities.

Defense Department spending boosted growth in places like Oak Ridge and Kingsport, Tennessee, Huntsville, Alabama, and Radford, Virginia, but Radford, in particular, now suffers from the loss of defense dollars. The Appalachian Regional Commission, established by Congress in 1965 to promote economic development in the region, has focused mostly on highway construction. While improved roads have meant significant growth for some communities, such as Pikeville, Kentucky, others, like nearby Harlan, remain accessible only by narrow, two-lane roads damaged by heavy coal hauling.

For some communities that have previously considered themselves rural and isolated, keeping growth within the limits that can be accommodated by the existing infrastructure, such as roads, water and sewer systems, and protecting views from housing, business, and road construction, are new challenges. At the other end of the spectrum, communities like Ivanhoe, Virginia, and Sneedville, Tennessee, struggle to reverse declining revenues and population.

Little River, near its confluence with the New River in southwest Virginia. By Ricky Cox.

Typical hardwood forest in Appalachia. By Jack Jeffers.

A threatened species, the black bear. Courtesy of the U.S. Wildlife Service.

Mountaintop removal in the Black Mountains near Totz, Harlan County, Kentucky, spring 1999.
By Roy Silver.

Suggested Readings

Adams, Noah. *Far Appalachia: Following the New River North.* New York: Delacorte Press, 2001.

Appalachian Regional Commission. Http://www.arc.gov.

Appalachian Sustainable Development. Http://www.appsusdev.org.

Ayers, Harvard, Jenny Hager, and Charles E. Little, eds. *An Appalachian Tragedy: Air Pollution and Tree Death in the Eastern Forests of North America.* San Francisco: Sierra Club Books, 1998.

Brown, Margaret Lynn. *The Wild East: A Biography of the Great Smoky Mountains.* Gainesville: Univ. Press of Florida, 2000.

Davis, Donald Edward. *Where There Are Mountains: An Environmental History of the Southern Appalachians.* Athens: Univ. of Georgia Press, 2000.

Eller, Ronald D. *Miners, Millhands, and Mountaineers: Industrialization of the Appalachian South, 1880–1930.* Knoxville: Univ. of Tennessee Press, 1982.

Frome, Michael. *Strangers in High Places: The Story of the Great Smoky Mountains.* Knoxville: Univ. of Tennessee Press, 1994.

Jordan, Terry G., and Matti Kaups. *The American Backwoods Frontier: An Ethnic and Ecological Interpretation.* Baltimore: Johns Hopkins Univ. Press, 1989.

Kentucky Geological Survey. Coal. Http://www.uky.edu/KGS/coal/index.htm.

Lewis, Ronald L. *Transforming the Appalachian Countryside: Railroads, Deforestation, and Social Change in West Virginia, 1880–1920.* Chapel Hill: Univ. of North Carolina Press, 1998.

Pierce, Daniel S. *The Great Smokies: From Natural Habitat to National Park.* Knoxville: Univ. of Tennessee Press, 2000.

Ready for Harvest: Clearcutting in the Southern Appalachians. Produced and directed by Dee Davis. 29 min. Appalshop Film & Video, 1993. Videocassette.

Southern Appalachian Man and the Biosphere Cooperative. *The Southern Appalachian Assessment.* 5 vols. Atlanta: U.S. Dept. of Agriculture, Forest Service, Southern Region, 1996.

Sustainable Development Program. Appalachian State Univ. Http://www.acs.appstate.edu/dept/anthro/sd_index.html.

Swanson, Robert E. *A Field Guide to the Trees and Shrubs of the Southern Appalachians.* Baltimore: Johns Hopkins Univ. Press, 1994.

U.S. Department of Labor. Mine Safety and Health Administration. "Mining Industry Accident, Injuries, Employment, and Production Statistics." Http://www.msha.gov/ACCINJ/accinj.htm.

Weidensaul, Scott. *Mountains of the Heart: A Natural History of the Appalachians.* Golden, Colo.: Fulcrum, 1994.

THE ECONOMY OF APPALACHIA

THOMAS R. SHANNON

Much of the history, cultural development, and folklore, as well as the social problems, of Appalachia can be traced directly or indirectly to what has happened to its economy. Some of these economic developments were similar to those of other parts of the country. The decline of the small family farm, for example, is a story shared with the rest of rural America. Other economic activities, often linked to its particular geography, geology, and native flora, evolved in particular ways that set Appalachia apart from most of the country. The most obvious example is the soft-coal mining industry in the coal counties of West Virginia, Kentucky, Tennessee, and Virginia. The effects of that one industry have been pervasive and indelible in that part of the region.

The Agrarian Economy of the Mid-Nineteenth Century

By the middle part of the nineteenth century, most of Appalachia had developed a distinctive pattern of economic activity. The economy centered on the small farm household. The typical farm consisted of fewer than two hundred acres, which was usually divided between cleared bottom land planted in grain crops—especially corn, but also oats and wheat—open pasture land and hayfields, and often-rugged forest land. Settlement was generally sparse, and much of the land remained in open forest. Each farm had a large garden plot that provided vegetables, and many had orchards. Larger-scale commercial farms selling commodities to external markets were most common in the valleys, which had relatively large areas of level land and somewhat better transportation connections on main roads or rivers. The large landowners constituted an economic elite and were also likely to be engaged in non-agricultural commercial activities.

A large percentage of the diverse production of these farms was intended for direct use. Staple foods, vegetables, meat, wood products for household and farm use, most building materials, wild game, fruits, and herbs from the surrounding forest, some clothing, and numerous craft products from locally available materials were produced by each farm household. However, numerous necessities, from steel tools and guns to cloth, as well as various small luxuries, had to be purchased or bartered. Consequently, a major portion of farm production had to be devoted to things that could be sold or traded. The most important of these activities was livestock production. Hogs were allowed to forage free in the woods, and the cleared hillside land made excellent pasturage for cattle and sheep. By the middle of the nineteenth century, the southern Appalachian Mountains had become a major source of hogs for the eastern cities. Animals were sold or bartered to drovers, who assembled large herds of livestock which they then drove over the primitive roads to urban wholesale markets. Small-scale timber cutting was also a source of income. Logs were floated down streams to rivers during periods of high water and assembled into large rafts for the trip downriver to sawmills. Wild forest products, especially herbs such as ginseng, also provided something to sell or trade.

As a consequence of these production efforts, a successful farm household could provide for its basic necessities but was usually cash poor. The mostly home-based, handcrafted production involved time-consuming activity on the part of all family members. The available time and number of family members old enough to work set the limit on how much could be produced. A log cabin or small frame house, heated by fireplace or sometimes a wood cook stove, provided snug but cramped housing for an often large family. Most household goods were homemade, with a limited number of purchased utensils. Clothing was mostly home sewn and spun. With few exceptions, the family ate what it could produce, hunt, or gather. A few store-bought clothing items, guns, tools, and cherished household possessions rounded out the family's stock of material goods. By contemporary standards these households would be considered poor, although they generally had enough of the most basic necessities.

Nonfarm production was limited but not insignificant. Until the coming of the railroads, moving people or goods both within and outside of the region was difficult. Mostly, there were primitive, barely usable dirt roads and a few navigable rivers. Livestock could walk out and some timber could float out, but other production for external markets remained limited until after the Civil War. In some counties in Kentucky, salt was a valuable product that was fairly compact and suitable for transportation under difficult conditions. On the other hand, high transportation costs meant that some kinds of local production were often cheaper than goods produced outside the region. In the pre–

Civil War period, numerous water-driven mills produced lumber, flour, and even textiles. Small-scale manufacturing and iron production also developed to serve local markets.

Urban development was extremely limited in this period. For most rural residents, routine retail trade took place in a village that usually consisted of little more than a general store and a few other businesses, such as a blacksmith shop. Traders, making the rounds to these villages, also might provide opportunities for bartering farm and forest products, selling livestock, and purchasing special goods. Larger-scale commercial enterprises, law offices, small banks, and the like were to be found in widely scattered small towns, often along with courts and county offices at a county seat. In a few cases, towns also developed around a cluster of mills or small manufacturing enterprises.

This period of small-scale, independent farming frequently has been romanticized by both outside writers and Appalachians themselves. To be sure, these farm families enjoyed a degree of economic autonomy as the owners of their own small enterprises. They also developed impressive skills in utilizing locally available materials and lived in a beautiful and for the most part still-wild natural setting. However, at least in strictly economic terms, the people of the mountains also toiled long and hard for a relatively meager material return. Living conditions were arduous. The likelihood of children dying in the first year of life was high, and the cumulative effect of heavy labor, untreated injuries, the risks of childbirth for women, unbalanced diet, and so on made adults old and worn before their time. By the middle of the nineteenth century, division of farms through inheritance, increasing depletion of cultivated fields, increasing population, hunting out of wildlife, and the limited agricultural technology contributed to growing strain on this agricultural system. Well before the Civil War, many counties were increasingly divided between large landholders and small farmers, whose farms had shrunk from division as the result of inheritance to sizes that no longer were sufficient to meet the basic needs of their households. Hence, maintaining even the existing low level of consumption would not have been possible without major changes in technology and economic organization. Intervention by outside forces after this period, however, quickly overshadowed any indigenous efforts at economic change.

Extraction and Exploitation: 1870–1930

A series of technological changes and national economic trends after the Civil War set the stage for the economic transformation of much of Appalachia. Railroad technology finally improved to the extent that it was economical to tunnel, blast, and grade roadbeds through the mountains and along river valleys. More powerful steam engines made it possible to pull fairly long trains of bulk commodities such as coal even up long mountain grades. Rapid industrialization and urbanization of the East and Midwest created a huge market for coal for fuel and timber for construction. Mining technology improved to the point that large-scale, deep-shaft mining became possible. The evolution of ever larger private enterprises and the availability of large sums of capital for investment from domestic and British sources made it possible to attempt large-scale resource extraction projects involving long-term acquisition of huge tracts of land and major engineering efforts.

The result in Appalachia was a furious pace of railroad construction and land buying, or buying the timber and mineral rights on and under the land, by outside investors after 1880. Large-scale coal-mining operations and their accompanying coal towns sprang up in a belt of counties running from southern West Virginia through southwestern Virginia, eastern Tennessee, and eastern Kentucky. At about the same time, massive timber-cutting operations, with often temporary timber camps and mills, began clearing the forests of the region. By the end of the nineteenth century, outside industrialists also sought to take advantage of the availability of cheap labor to establish factories. Many of these manufacturing plants were located in separate company towns devoted to a single industry, for example, textiles, garment making, shoemaking, wool-based rayon fiber production, coal-based synthetic chemical production. Capital investment for the projects came almost exclusively from outside investors—wealthy entrepreneurs or corporations. At the same time, it should be noted that local business leaders, large landowners, and professionals played an active, very lucrative role in facilitating land acquisition and obtaining cooperation from local and state governments and courts.

By the beginning of the twentieth century, the economic and physical landscape of Appalachia had been transformed. The belt of coal counties was dotted by coal towns established by large coal companies. Control of vast stretches of land had passed to these corporations, either through outright purchase at low prices or even cheaper acquisition of mineral rights that allowed almost unlimited use and access to the land for mining purposes. In these counties, land ownership or effective control through ownership of mineral rights became, and remains today, heavily concentrated in the hands of large, usually corporate, landowners, and many small farm holdings were simply eliminated. Heavy recruitment of native workers for the mines was increasingly supplemented by European immigrants and African Americans from the rural South. By modern standards, labor in the mines was brutally hard, dangerous, and poorly paid. The mining industry was subject to extreme boom or bust cycles as demand for coal increased or decreased in the national economy.

Economic busts in the coal industry were made worse by the tendency toward overexpansion of capacity in boom periods. This made both employment and wage levels highly erratic in the industry. There were strong pressures to minimize costs by paying low wages. As time passed, mine owners also tried to cut costs through the introduction of laborsaving machinery. The coal companies, finding few existing communities near the coal deposits, literally created and owned the towns near the mines. As a result, the mine owners could control every aspect of community life. Most retail goods and services were only available through company-owned stores, hospitals, schools, and recreational facilities. County government was likewise under the sway of the companies through the cooperation of local business leaders and simple corruption of local officials. Coal and timber companies also exercised their influence in state government to assure favorable laws and court decisions for their operations.

It has been common for both contemporary observers and outside journalists to emphasize the relative poverty and lack of power of miners and their families in these towns. That characterization contains an element of truth. Small farmers were often cheated for their land, there was ruthless suppression of miners' unions, wages were low in comparison to the wages for many other industrial occupations, and hard times in the coalfields could create desperate poverty. On the other hand, conditions in the coal towns have to be compared to the increasingly impoverished condition of small Appalachian farmers whose holdings were growing ever smaller through the subdivision of land among heirs. Moreover, all mine owners were not the same. As Ronald Eller has pointed out, at least by the standards of the time, many owners tried to practice what they saw as a form of benign paternalism and create model communities that provided a wide range of services and even recreational opportunities.[1]

The timber industry created fewer permanent towns and more transitory camps and mill sites as it quickly depleted the timber supply in a given area. It too acquired vast tracts of land through conventional purchase or buying timber rights. By 1930, the bulk of the forest that had not been cleared for agriculture had been logged. Most of the forest land in Appalachia today is immature, second-growth forest that has grown up following the clear-cut removal of old-growth trees by the timber industry prior to 1930. The rapid destruction of the American chestnut from disease added to the destruction of the forest. The ecological damage caused by the wholesale destruction of the ancient forests was regionwide. Massive erosion, flash floods, destruction of wildlife habitat and native flora, and the displacement of agriculture followed in the wake of the timber industry. Substantial soil loss has left much of the region with badly damaged soil cover. Beginning at the turn of the century, federal land acquisition was designed to create large areas of national forest in which more scientific controlled logging could occur. Major portions of the regional forest are now incorporated into that federal forest system. However, huge tracts of second-growth forest are still concentrated in the hand of large private owners and are potentially available for cutting again in the next few decades.

Manufacturers, most in search of a low-wage labor force under conditions that protected them from unionization, completed the transformation of the Appalachian economy after the Civil War. Among the most prominent industries that moved factories to Appalachia were those dealing in textiles, garment making, shoe manufacturing, and furniture making. Many of these factories were built in new company towns along rail lines and rivers. Others located in existing towns, but the industry came to dominate the economic life of the community. Furniture factories concentrated in western North Carolina and spilled over into southwestern Virginia. Textile mills were most common on the eastern edge of the region in the Piedmont of North Carolina, South Carolina, Georgia, and Alabama but drew heavily upon labor recruited from the mountains. A minority of textile mills was actually located in the mountains proper. Like coal towns, mill towns were characterized by the almost total domination of a single employer. Housing, community services, and even retail stores were either provided by the company or tailored to the company's preferences and needs as a result of the company's overwhelming economic and political power in the community. In comparison to national standards at the time, wages were low and working conditions poor. For example, in 1897 southern textile mills paid 40 percent less than those in the North, and the working day was 24 percent longer.[2] At the turn of the century, a majority of the workers in textiles were women and children, favored for their docility, dexterity, and willingness to work for low wages.

While few counties escaped the ravages of the timber industry, only a minority of Appalachian counties actually participated directly in the other economic changes just discussed. The majority remained relatively isolated and predominantly agricultural. However, traditional agriculture could not survive unchanged in the new conditions. A long list of problems beset Appalachian agriculture: soil depletion; the ecological disruption of logging; continual subdivision of farms by inheritance; land acquisition by coal and timber companies, followed by the creation of the federal forest system; the competition for livestock and other markets from larger, commercial farms in the Midwest; the loss of open forest land on which to let livestock range; the unsuitability of small mountain farms for mechanization; and the loss of local markets to national distribution systems (e.g., use of canned goods). As a consequence, Appalachian farms became less economically viable as relatively self-sufficient enterprises capable of meeting the basic needs of a large household. Smaller and smaller farms provided a more marginal existence as the producer of limited amounts of row crops and small livestock herds. Under these increasingly difficult circumstances, the attraction of Appalachian workers to the mines and mill towns is understandable. By 1930, only about three-fifths of the labor force was still engaged in agriculture. More and more farmers also sought part-time or seasonal work to supplement their farm income. Increased numbers of farmers were tenants rather than owners. Predominantly agricultural counties began to lose population, and farm abandonment became more and more common.[3]

By 1930, the basic new pattern of the Appalachian economy had been established. Agriculture provided an impoverished existence for a steadily declining number of Appalachians. The timber industry had virtually completed its clear-cutting of the region, and large-scale timber cutting was disappearing. Dozens of counties concentrated in the northern part of the region had become the center of large-scale coal mining. Several hundred thousand miners labored underground in dangerous and arduous conditions for wages kept low by overproduction, intense competition in the coal industry, and the power of the coal companies. Numerous other workers concentrated in mill towns, producing labor-intensive, low-wage manufactured goods.

It is hard not to see this economic pattern as one in which outside interests exploited the region. There were some real benefits—employment opportunities outside of a declining agriculture; education, health, and other benefits available in the coal and mill towns; and a vastly improved transportation and communication infrastructure—yet such gains came at a high cost. A partial list of these costs includes environmental destruction; political and economic domination by outside corporate interests; concentration of mineral wealth in a few hands; harsh industrial discipline; low wages; destruction of a system of small, independent farms; and the less tangible, but no less real, disruption of a valued cultural tradition. Appalachia was integrated into the national economy primarily as a producer of cheap fuels, raw materials, and low-wage industrial goods. Indisputably, the bulk of the wealth created by the new enterprises left the region in the form of profits for outside owners.

Numerous observers have pointed out the rough similarity between this form of economic development and Third World colonialism or neocolonialism. As in much of the Third World, economic development primarily benefited outside investors and a small group of local elites, often business and political leaders. The more general benefits of industrialization went primarily to the urban populations outside of the region, who enjoyed major improvements in their standard of living while the people of Appalachia remained, at least in comparison, relatively deprived.

THOMAS R. SHANNON

Stagnation and Decline: 1930–1960

Even before the Great Depression of the 1930s, the Appalachian coal industry was in crisis. Overcapacity from the boom of World War I led to steadily falling prices in the 1920s. The industry cut wages and services in the coal towns severely. Many mines closed. By the end of the 1920s, unemployment, short hours, and low wages had brought destitution to the coalfields. Mill towns fared only slightly better, but the textile industry was also in trouble. Low agricultural prices likewise had a depressing effect on the regional farm economy.[4]

The national economic collapse of the 1930s made a bad situation in the region into an economic catastrophe. Cold, hunger, and disease stalked the mountains. Average income among coal miners, already at a poverty level, dropped two-thirds, and farm cash income almost vanished. Many families, unable to find work, returned to relatives or even abandoned farms in the mountains to eke out a subsistence living by farming.

Partial economic recovery provided some relief for the coal and textile industries in the last half of the decade. A resurgent United Mine Workers of America union, benefiting from changing labor laws and a more favorable national political climate, began to make real inroads in organizing the Appalachian coalfields. New Deal agricultural subsidy and general relief programs provided a critical measure of assistance to the destitute of the region. Yet the extent of continued poverty was reflected in the fact that about half the families of the region were receiving federal assistance in 1936. Other New Deal programs had fewer benefits for the people of Appalachia. Expansion of federal forest lands displaced farmers and withdrew land from the local tax rolls.[5]

The Tennessee Valley Authority (TVA) was billed as an economic development program for the region. Substantial flood control, improved river navigation, and the provision of cheap power did benefit those downriver and electrify many mountain communities. On other hand, the promised benefits to East Tennessee mountain agriculture and economic development proved to be marginal at best. By the end of the 1930s, the TVA was already narrowing its focus in the direction of electrical generation rather than regional economic development. It would continue to evolve in that direction in the 1940s and 1950s.

War production brought a brief boom to coal and the other industries of the region. However, the region did not participate in the general prosperity of the postwar period. Hardest hit were the coal counties. The United Mineworkers had entered the postwar period in firm control of the large, deep-shaft mining operations and were in the position to make significant improvements in wages and benefits. These gains were in exchange for allowing major technological changes in the mines that steadily reduced the numbers of mineworkers needed to produce the same amount of coal. At the same time, coal was replaced as a railroad fuel by diesel oil and as source of space heating by natural gas and heating oil. The Appalachian deep-shaft mines were also faced with competing strip mines, in the region and elsewhere, which used fewer, non-union workers. Coal-mining employment collapsed from a high of almost half a million in 1945 to around two hundred thousand in 1960. The coal-hauling railroads also experienced a 40 percent drop in employment from 1950 to 1960. Older textile mills faced fierce competition from overseas, and most other Appalachian plants were also in stagnant or declining industries. Appalachian agriculture continued its long-term decline as smaller, less viable farms ceased being capable of generating enough income to support a household. Farms were either abandoned or became part-time enterprises combined with low-wage industrial employment.

The most obvious effect of these economic difficulties was a period of tremendous out-migration. Almost three million economic refugees had left the region, mostly for metropolitan areas in the South and Midwest, by 1960. Both coal counties and primarily agricultural counties experienced major population declines. The region as a whole, thanks to a still-high birth rate, maintained its overall population of about ten million in a context of rapid national population growth, the baby boom. National average income rose substantially, and poverty rates fell. Yet Appalachia maintained its position as a low-wage, low-income region. In 1960, the number of households in the region with income below the poverty line exceeded one-third, compared to one-fifth of the households nationwide. Poor nutrition, low levels of educational achievement, low levels of human services (e.g., medical care), and poor housing completed the picture. Appalachia was officially labeled as an economically depressed region by the federal government.

The Mirage of Economic Development: 1960–1980

By the early 1960s, especially following the 1960 Kennedy presidential campaign, Appalachia had become a visible symbol of the continuing problem of rural poverty. There followed a period in which the federal government adopted a series of programs to deal with regional poverty. These programs were intended to either stimulate economic development in the region or address the problem of poverty nationally with programs that also were implemented regionally.

Although TVA still claimed some role in bettering the region's economy, by the 1950s, it had essentially become nothing more than a publicly owned electrical utility. In fact, many critics claimed that its policies contributed to the problems of East Tennessee. Its focus on cheap power had resulted in increasing reliance on coal-fired generators. The TVA sought the cheapest sources of coal from environmentally destructive strip mines and other low-wage, non-union sources, a policy that only further weakened the bargaining position and employment opportunities for unionized miners. Its plants contributed to the air-quality problems associated with coal-fired electrical generation. Continued dam construction created both local opposition and raised environmental concerns. Its switch to a nuclear power strategy not only raised safety concerns but also proved to be a fiscal disaster that forced it to raise rates.

The central strategy to deal with the problems of Appalachia in the 1960s and 1970s was based on the "modernization theory," a view that saw the region's problems as similar to those of poor, Third World countries. In this view, what Appalachia needed was economic development aid to modernize its economy. This aid would establish conditions under which private investment would be attracted to the region to create modern industrial and service jobs. The focus was on providing assistance to produce infrastructure such as highways, subsidies to attract private investment, and a regional economic planning system. Some aid was also to be used to invest in human capital to raise the educational and health conditions of workers to make them more attractive to industry.

A preliminary effort to assist all depressed areas, including Appalachia, came in 1961 with the creation of the Area Redevelopment Administration (ARA). The ARA was intended to provide low-interest loans to private investors who were willing to invest in an economic activity that was part of a locally planned community development program. It also was designed to assist in training workers and providing financial assistance in creating necessary public infrastructure. In practice, ARA only provided limited funding to Appalachian projects, and its long-term impact was virtually nil.

Dissatisfaction with the ARA led to the creation of the Appalachian Regional Commission (ARC) in 1965. Central to the ARC strategy was the creation of infrastructure, especially highways, to encourage private investment. The ARC staff envisioned urban growth centers or growth corridors along this highway network. Workers and population in the region would move to these areas to take advantage of new employment opportunities. The ARC was also committed to providing indirect subsidies, such as industrial site development and worker training programs, to investors who funded manufacturing and service activities consistent with the plan. To carry out the plan at the local level, a system of planning districts was created. As the ARC evolved, it eventually made some limited investments in public service provision (e.g., health care).

The most visible impact of the ARC was the significant upgrading of thousands of miles of primary highways and roads in the region. Its industrial development program had limited impact, mostly in attracting industries interested in low-wage workers. Some additional tourist attractions, offering mostly low-wage and/or seasonal employment, were developed or improved. Further, road building may have had some impact in certain areas in attracting large retirement enclaves (see below). ARC's service activities were too limited in scope to have any real overall effect on the region, however. Some urban growth centers, mostly in existing urban areas on the fringes of the region and/or along the interstate highway system, did indeed emerge, but it is not clear that ARC's role was crucial in this development. Overall, larger-scale economic trends and general national policies, rather than ARC, seem to have been most crucial to what has happened in the region since 1960.

The War on Poverty programs of the 1960s were also intended to help the region. As a depressed region with a higher than average level of poverty, a large percentage of the people of the region qualified for these programs. There was a flurry of initial activity and the creation of a number of antipoverty programs, including a controversial program to mobilize poor communities (Community Action Programs). After that, funding and goals for the programs were steadily reduced. By the early 1970s, the war was essentially over. Its effect on the overall level of poverty and/or opportunity for the poor was small, both nationally and regionally. However, it left in its wake several changes that increased the levels of government support for the poor. Generally speaking, states had increased the availability of general welfare (Aid to Families with Dependent Children, or AFDC), the Food Stamp Program created a significant supplement to the standard of living of the working and nonworking poor, some minimal health care (Medicaid) was made available for some, and a few specific programs survived that benefited some groups among the poor (e.g., Head Start and Women's and Infants Nutrition, or WIN). At the same time, the federal government embarked on a major effort to reduce poverty among the elderly. Social Security benefits were increased, and the Medicare system was created in the early 1970s. Extreme poverty among the elderly was consequently substantially reduced. The elderly now have the lowest rate of poverty of any age group in the country. Young women with children have the highest.

The government support programs were particularly important in the economy of Appalachia after 1970. In the poorest coal counties and declining agricultural counties, high unemployment and the out-migration of younger workers left a population heavily dependent on either welfare benefits or Social Security. In these counties, welfare and Social Security became major props for a weak local economy. They made the difference between people being just poor and not having their basic survival needs met. For the rest of the region, generally higher than national average levels of poverty continued to make them more sensitive to levels of government support for the poor. The Food Stamp Program became an important income supplement for many of the very low wage workers in the region.

Despite these disappointing and limited government initiatives, the regional economy of the late 1960s and most of the 1970s saw some signs of growth. This growth reflected national economic, demographic, and social trends. The energy supply concerns of the 1970s and rising use of coal for electrical generation contributed to an increase in demand for Appalachian coal, temporarily reversing the downward slide of employment in the coalfields. Some coal counties actually experienced minor economic booms. Increasing international competition and slower economic growth led a growing number of employers to look for low-wage, low-tax, weak-regulation locations to locate their industrial facilities. Many industries chose Third World locations from the beginning, but the South, including Appalachia, benefited from this search. Reliance on trucks for transportation meant that the most likely industrial locations were along the now almost complete interstate highway system.

Appalachia's traditional manufacturing enjoyed mixed results during the 1960–80 period. For example, textiles and apparel enjoyed a competitive advantage with older centers of the industry, primarily because of continued wage and other cost advantages. About 10 percent of the entire labor force remained employed in these industries in 1980. On the other hand, despite tariff protections, they faced increasing Third World competition, especially after 1970. The furniture industry held its own. The chemical industry, heavily dependent on the textile, steel, and paper industries for sales, also remained stable, providing about one hundred thousand jobs in the region.

Agriculture, as a result of the trends discussed above, continued its long-term decline. Fewer and fewer farms were commercially viable operations. The relatively low productivity of most Appalachian farmland meant that less farm consolidation occurred. Getting bigger, the economic strategy of farmers elsewhere, consequently did not make sense in Appalachia. Instead, the trend in Appalachia was toward either abandonment of farmland or the continuation of small-scale farming supplemented by outside employment.

Reflecting national trends, the largest source of economic and employment growth was the service sector, although the rate of growth was below the national average. In Appalachia, the largest proportion of service sector growth (two-thirds of the employment growth in services from 1970 to 1980) was in health services, retail trade, and education. The extreme concentration in these kinds of services reflected the fact that Appalachia was not a good location for metropolitan-based services such as finance, marketing, wholesale trade, and business services. It is worth noting that most of the services that expanded offered a high percentage of low-skill and relatively low-wage jobs.

Both reflecting and reinforcing these economic changes was a dramatic change in demographic trends in the 1970–80 period. More isolated, rural counties continued to lose population to out-migration. Yet overall net migration (movement in minus movement out) was positive and substantial. In other words, fewer young workers were leaving the region and more people from outside the region were moving in.

While retention of more young workers reflected the economic trends, attraction of new residents reflected a number of other factors. Some urban Appalachians in the North responded to the improving economic conditions back home or returned home to retire. In addition, a growing number of relatively affluent retirees, mostly from northern metropolitan regions, sought Appalachia's milder climate, lower living costs, and scenic rural settings. A number of counties of the southern mountains became the destination of these affluent retirees (e.g., around Boone, North Carolina). Major growth of regional colleges and universities also benefited a small number of counties. Nationwide, the 1970s witnessed an increased preference for country living that encouraged those who could to choose rural locations near small towns or, more commonly, "exurban" counties near metropolitan areas. A number of Appalachian counties within commuting distance of a major metropolitan region (e.g., Atlanta) or a regional state university benefited from the back-to-the-country trend.

Thus, the end of the 1970s was a period of modestly hopeful signs about the economic prospects for the region. There were lingering problems of higher-than-average poverty and unemployment and continued low-wage rates, but the period of steady economic decline and population loss seemed to be ending.

Disappointment and Continued Problems: 1980–2000

A severe national recession in the early 1980s was particularly deep in Appalachia because a number of traditional manufacturing industries and coal mining were especially hard hit by national economic stagnation. As a whole, the regional economy never regained its former momentum. Some counties near metropolitan areas continued to experience exurban growth. The retirement counties in the North Carolina mountains continued to attract retirees and retail businesses serving their growing, generally affluent populations. Tourism continued to grow. These areas were islands of relative prosperity in a sea of economic and demographic stagnation or decline.

The long-term prospects of traditional manufacturing industry and coal mining were almost uniformly dismal. Textiles, apparel, furniture, and chemicals all faced substantial foreign competition, and the expectation is that all will experience major employment declines into the next century as the result of lost markets and/or automation (especially in textiles). The labor-intensive nature of the apparel industry makes it especially vulnerable to the extremely low-wage producers in the Third World. Coal-mining employment resumed its long-term decline as a result of very rapid mine automation, intense competition for foreign markets, the long-term decline in steel industry demand for coal, and the switch to strip mining, both within the region and in newer coal producing areas in the West. The maturation of second-growth forests will probably increase logging operations and provide a modest amount of additional employment, but the increase raises serious ecological and other concerns. The brief attraction of Appalachia as a location for runaway plants from high-wage metropolitan areas also faded in the 1980s. The kind of industry that the region might attract (employing semiskilled, low-wage workers) increasingly chose Third World locations for their plants in the 1980s. Indeed, some plants that came to the region in the 1970s have subsequently relocated again, this time to the Third World. High-tech industry generally has a set of requirements that few areas in the region can match: a well-educated labor pool, excellent infrastructure, an established network of research centers and scientific personnel, and the urban amenities expected by the professional staffs of these firms.

Poverty continued at a level higher than the national level. Counties with high levels of poverty and welfare dependency faced another challenge as a result of the Welfare Reform Act of 1996. The new welfare system sets absolute time limits on how long a household can receive benefits. Consequently, numerous households exhausted their benefits as the decade closed.

The general conclusion seems to be that large-scale modernization of the regional economy by attracting large manufacturing facilities to growth centers has little chance of success. Even most of the traditional sources of manufacturing employment have an uncertain future. A few favorably situated areas will continue to attract certain industries where the mix of labor costs and geographical location are favorable. Retirement and tourism seem likely to continue to flourish in a few areas also. However, even the ARC has quietly abandoned its strategy of large-scale modernization. In its place are modest projects to encourage developments of particular areas. It seems likely that each community ". . . needs to begin to think in terms of how to tailor . . . [its] . . . resources to meet the particular problems . . . [it is] . . . likely to face. In doing so . . . [it] . . . will have to rethink what constitutes acceptable solutions to the problems and create new organizational structures to implement . . . new strategies."[6]

Number 11 Mine, New River and Pocahontas Consolidated Coal Company, Capels, McDowell County, West Virginia, c. 1935. Courtesy of Eastern Regional Coal Archives, Bluefield, West Virginia.

Loaded coal trucks in eastern Kentucky. By Ricky Cox.

Steam-driven sawmill, typical of small-scale lumber milling, c.1925. From the collection of Ricky Cox.

Vegetable gardens provide a means of preserving traditions and supplementing incomes throughout the region. From the collection of Grace Toney Edwards.

Pulaski, Virginia, iron foundry, c. 1900. Courtesy of the Raymond Ratcliffe Memorial Museum, Pulaski, Virginia.

A Wal-Mart store, representative of service-industry employment in Appalachia. By Ricky Cox.

Notes

I wish to acknowledge the help of Katrina Landon in preparing this chapter.

1. Ronald D Eller, *Miners, Millhands, and Mountaineers: Industrialization of the Appalachian South, 1880–1930* (Knoxville: Univ. of Tennessee Press, 1982).
2. Ibid., 125.
3. Ibid., 229–30.
4. Ibid., 238.
5. Ibid., 239–40.
6. Thomas R. Shannon, "Surviving the 1990's: Inter-Regional Variation in Economic Problems," in *The Many Faces of Appalachia: Proceedings of the 7th Annual Appalachian Studies Conference,* ed. Sam Gray. (Boone, N.C.: Appalachian Consortium Press, 1985), 35–136.

Suggested Readings

"Appalachian Outlook Through the 1980s." *Appalachia* 17, no. 2 (1983): 1–14.

Billings, Dwight B., and Kathleen M. Blee. *The Road to Poverty: The Making of Wealth and Hardship in Appalachia.* Cambridge: Cambridge Univ. Press, 2000.

Billings, Dwight B., and Ann Tickameyer. "Uneven Development in Appalachia." In *Forgotten Places: Uneven Development in Rural America,* edited by Thomas Lyson and William Falk. Lawrence: Univ. Press of Kansas, 1993.

Branscome, James. *The Federal Government in Appalachia.* New York: Field Foundation, 1977.

Couto, Richard A. *An American Challenge: A Report on Economic Trends and Social Issues in Appalachia.* Dubuque, Iowa: Kendall-Hunt, 1994.

Eller, Ronald D. *Miners, Millhands, and Mountaineers: Industrialization of the Appalachian South, 1880–1930.* Knoxville: Univ. of Tennessee Press, 1982.

Hansen, Niles. "The Appalachian Region." In *Appalachia: Its People, Heritage and Problems,* edited by Frank S. Riddel. Dubuque, Iowa: Kendall-Hunt, 1974.

Lewis, Helen M., Linda Johnson, and Donald Askins, eds. *Colonialism in Modern America: The Appalachian Case.* Boone, N.C.: Appalachian Consortium Press, 1978.

Packard, Jerome. "Appalachia's Decade of Change—A Decade of Immigration." *Appalachia* 15, no.1 (1981): 24–28.

Selznick, David. *TVA and the Grassroots.* Berkeley and Los Angeles: Univ. of California Press, 1949.

Shannon, Thomas. "Surviving the 1990's: Inter-Regional Variation in Economic Problems." In *The Many Faces of Appalachia: Proceedings of the 7th Annual Appalachian Studies Conference,* edited by Sam Gray. Boone, N.C.: Appalachian Consortium Press, 1985.

Whisnant, David E. *Modernizing the Mountaineer: People, Power, and Planning in Appalachia.* Boone, N.C.: Appalachian Consortium Press, 1980.

THE POLITICS OF CHANGE IN APPALACHIA

STEPHEN L. FISHER, PATTI PAGE CHURCH, CHRISTINE WEISS DAUGHERTY, BENNETT M. JUDKINS, AND SHAUNNA L. SCOTT

Contrary to popular images of Appalachians as passive victims of corporate greed, there exists throughout the Appalachian Mountains a tradition of individual and organized efforts to establish community services and jobs, win and maintain safe workplaces, and preserve one's homeplace and community values.

The Politics of Change Prior to 1960

The Appalachian region has never lacked a politics of change and alternative economic development. But what stands out in the literature describing life in Appalachia before 1960 is not the extent of change efforts but the obstacles to change, the conditions leading to quiescence. The industrialization of Appalachia was characterized by single-industry economies; the control of land and resources by large absentee companies; high levels of poverty and unemployment; the frequent use of Red baiting, intimidation, and physical force to squelch dissent; political corruption; and a highly stratified and oppressive class system. Collective struggles for change were further undermined by cultural traditions that stressed individualism, the strength of capitalist ideology, racism and sexism, the lack of strong local organizations, high illiteracy rates, and poor transportation and communication systems.

During this period, one could find throughout Appalachia examples of the starkest political and economic oppression in American society. Yet people there found ways to resist. The organized efforts of workers in the coal, textile, and steel industries to improve their working and living conditions are well documented. But in other parts of the Appalachian Mountains, responses to these conditions often assumed forms far less visible than picket lines and organized movements and included such individual acts of behavior as gossip, back talk, holding on to one's dialect, and refusal to cooperate with outside authority figures.

Increasingly, we are coming to recognize the existence and significance of such protest in Appalachia's history and to understand that it has most frequently occurred in struggles to preserve traditional values and ways of life against the forces of modernization. This point is demonstrated in several important studies. Helen Lewis, Sue Kobak, and Linda Johnson describe the various ways in which mountain families and churches became defensive and inward in order to protect their members from some of the harmful impacts of industrialization and the actions of outside change agents. Kathleen Blee and Dwight Billings reinterpret early ethnographic studies of the region to show that work attitudes and other practices previously viewed as traits of a culture of poverty could better be understood as forms of resistance to the capitalist separation of work and control. Altina Waller argues that the legendary Hatfield-McCoy feud can be seen as a battle between local defenders of community autonomy and outside industrial interests. These and similar studies broaden our understanding of the nature and extent of resistance by rural working-class and poor people in Appalachia prior to 1960.

Community Organizing since 1960

Many of the obstacles that made collective struggles so difficult throughout Appalachia's history are still present today, and individual protests continue on a number of fronts. But new conditions after 1960 provided impetus and support to organized resistance efforts throughout Appalachia. The civil rights movement helped legitimize the notion of dissent in general and the strategy of nonviolent civil disobedience in particular throughout the region and the nation. The environmental and women's movements offered resources for local groups in the mountains and provided the impetus for national legislation that created opportunities for local organizations fighting to save their land and communities from environmental destruction or working to create alternative economic opportunities for women. The antiwar and student movements called into question the notions of "progress," "modernization," and "national interest" that had been used for so long to justify the destruction of traditional ways of life in Appalachia.

Building on past resistance struggles, people in the region cast around for help wherever they could get it. The War on Poverty spawned the Appalachian Volunteers and community action agencies throughout the mountains. While these programs had many weaknesses, they did bring young organizers into the region and provided opportunities for local leadership development. Mainstream churches, reflecting a new social consciousness, sent to Appalachia clergy and other church workers who were committed to working for social and economic justice. The construction of more and better roads, the availability of video recording equipment, open meeting and record laws, and increased church and foundation funding of Appalachian citizen groups also contributed to local organizing efforts.

These changes and new opportunities, when combined with a variety of indigenous factors, strengthened ongoing efforts and led to an outburst of new grass-roots community organizing across Appalachia in the late 1960s and early 1970s. Local residents, depending upon their location in the region, fought to prevent the destruction of their land and homes by strip miners, dam and highway builders, the U.S. Forest Service, toxic-waste dumpers, and recreation and second-home developers. People organized to secure welfare benefits, enact tax reform, build rural community centers and health clinics, fight for better schools for their children, and establish programs in literacy and child care. Community groups pursued a wide variety of alternative economic development strategies that resulted in agricultural and craft cooperatives, worker-owned factories, and new job opportunities for women. Efforts to preserve and celebrate local culture flourished in the mountains, as people began to develop a consciousness of and pride in being Appalachian.

Today, people across Appalachia are still fighting back, often around similar issues. The battle over strip mining continues as local groups challenge the devastating effects of mountaintop removal and join with other groups to lobby Washington for better water protection laws. Communities throughout rural Appalachia struggle to prevent their landfills from becoming the dumping ground for the nation's trash, sludge, and toxic waste and to save their forests from clearcutting and chip mills. Kentucky Resources Council, Georgia Forestwatch, West Virginia Highlands Conservancy, Virginia Forest Watch, the Oak Ridge Environmental Peace Alliance in East Tennessee, the Dogwood Alliance in western North Carolina, the Buckeye Forest Council in Ohio, and the Mountain Watershed Association in western Pennsylvania are just a few of the groups

88

across the region fighting the poisoning and destruction of their land, air, forests, and water. The Ohio Valley Environmental Coalition organizes around mountaintop removal and industrial pollution where Ohio, Kentucky, and West Virginia meet. The Appalachian Women's Alliance and the Center for Economic Options in West Virginia work to improve the social and economic position of women in the region.

In sum, since the 1960s, hundreds of new citizen groups have been organized throughout Appalachia. Most arose in response to a particular issue. These single-issue groups have worked together from time to time, helped create local leadership, and won important victories. But because they have focused on a single issue, many of these groups have been short lived, disappearing once their issues have been resolved. Thus, one of the most exciting and hopeful developments in community organizing in Appalachia in recent years has been the establishment and success of thriving and influential multi-issue, membership-driven organizations such as Save Our Cumberland Mountains (SOCM), Kentuckians For The Commonwealth (KFTC), the Community Farm Alliance (CFA), and the Virginia Organizing Project (VOP).

Organized in 1972 to fight strip mining in a five-county area in the northern coalfields of Tennessee, SOCM changed from a single-issue, staff-run group to a multi-issue, grass-roots organization able to exercise influence at the state and national level. KFTC, started in mid-1981 by a small group of eastern Kentucky residents who wanted to address community problems that crossed county lines, has grown into a powerful statewide, multi-issue, social justice organization. The CFA was transformed from a handful of people who were replicating the mistakes of the national farm movement of the 1980s to a growing and successful membership-based organization with over a dozen chapters across Kentucky. And VOP, begun in 1995 with strong chapters in southwest Virginia, has grown into a statewide grass-roots organization committed to challenging injustice by empowering people in local communities to address issues that affect the quality of their lives.

These groups pursue an organizing approach that is flexible, pragmatic, and grounded in the past and present of members' lives. But unlike the narrow single-issue organizing of the past, these groups' primary concern is to empower their members for the long haul—to provide schooling in politics and personal empowerment. They do so by offering a self-conscious leadership training program designed to develop democratic skills and build a sense of ownership and community. These organizations provide the space where participants can begin to see the connection between their concerns and those of other exploited people, where members can come to confront issues of racism and sexism, and where people can start to envision new alternatives to the world in which they live. As Connie White, a past SOCM president puts it, "We don't care just about winning issues; we care more about helping people get stronger. In the long run, that is how you win issues and make real changes."

Alternative Economic Development since 1960

In the last forty years, two styles of economic development have emerged in the Appalachians. The first, practiced by state and local governments, is highly competitive, and success is measured solely by the number of jobs created. Businesses are recruited from other parts of the country, loans are subsidized, and taxes are forgiven. Because some of the counties that make up the Appalachian region are among the most impoverished in the nation, there are few standards for the jobs created, and economic development authorities often recruit and lend to businesses that exploit both their workers and the public.

In contrast, an alternative strategy, community-based economic development (CED), is also creating jobs in rural and urban areas of Appalachia. Community-based economic development is a citizen-initiated approach designed to revitalize the local economy and all its citizens, including the most disadvantaged. CED recognizes that increasing literacy, improving educational and health-care opportunities, providing access to affordable day care, and ensuring tax equity are essential components of an economic development process. While CED uses some of the traditional methods to create businesses (market studies, business plans, etc.), it does so with the avowed purpose of achieving social goals as well as economic ones. Thus, people are at the center of this development. CED strategies are small, achievable, and often labor intensive, using the particular talents and skills of people in the community.

One example of this strategy is Appalachian by Design (ABD) in southern West Virginia. A nonprofit organization, ABD has spent the last fourteen years developing the machine knitting industry in West Virginia and mid-Appalachia, and funders and policy makers now view it as a model of an innovative rural sectoral initiative. Finding that the sectoral initiative framework provides the most relevant context for its efforts, Appalachian by Design

• Targets a specific industry;
• Develops deep knowledge of the sector by becoming a "player" in the industry;
• Implements training and other strategies that benefit low-income individuals;
• Works toward systemic change.

ABD targets handloom knitting because it fits the lives of many rural Appalachian people. Working at home in rural areas where there are few jobs in the formal sector, women and men choose to become self-employed in the garment industry, producing hand-knitted clothing marketed by ABD. Located in Lewisburg, West Virginia, ABD has built a national wholesale marketing program and a retail business at a premier resort in West Virginia in order to become a true player in the industry. The technical training program works one-on-one with women (and some men), 80 percent of whom are low income by HUD standards. Efforts to raise the value of the trade and wages through accessing high-end market channels is creating systemic change both in individual lives and in the wider perception of cottage industry. In sum, since its inception in 1991, ABD has pioneered new ways of providing rural people with income and sustainable security.

Many other alternative economic development strategies have been pursued in Appalachia. In the 1980s and 1990s, the Ivanhoe Civic League and the Dungannon Development Commission in southwest Virginia received regional and national publicity for their innovative grass-roots community development plans. For over thirty years the Human/Economic Appalachian Development Corporation (HEAD) has struggled in the trenches to foster cooperatives, worker-controlled industry, and community-based development. In rural areas where hospitals are closing and consolidating, entrepreneurs are opening preventive-care centers, home health-care businesses, and birthing centers. Micro-enterprise loan funds and programs are nurturing small businesses in urban areas such as Knoxville and Asheville. All of these job creation efforts help to empower local people who want to stay and raise families in their own communities.

Labor Organizing since 1960

The story of central Appalachia is primarily of domination by one industry—coal—with an overwhelmingly male work force and a long history of militant trade unionism. For over one hundred years, members of the United Mine Workers of America (UMWA) have made great personal sacrifices in their commitment to bring about change in the coalfield communities in which they work and live. Throughout the first part of this century, they sought and won collective bargaining rights that led to fairer wages, safer jobs, accessible and affordable health care, and retirement with dignity. By the 1960s, many of these gains had been undermined by the mechanization of the mines, corporate greed, government indifference, and an unresponsive and corrupt union leadership. Union miners and pensioners and their wives and widows responded to these developments with one of the most militant rank-and-file mobilizations in the postwar labor movement.

This rebellion began with the black lung movement, which addressed the issue of coal workers' pneumoconiosis, a lung disease caused by the inhalation of coal dust. Despite years of rank-and-file pressure to link black lung disease to working conditions, top union officials ignored the problem. Company officials refused to acknowledge that black lung disease existed, and some company doctors even suggested that coal dust was "beneficial." But West Virginia doctors I. E. Buff, Donald Rasmussen, and Howley A. Wells founded Physicians for Miners' Health and Safety and traveled throughout the state informing miners of the deadly effects of coal dust. In 1968, these doctors, along with consumer-protection activist Ralph Nader and West Virginia congressman Ken Hechler, helped a group of miners form the Black Lung Association (BLA). The BLA lobbied, rallied, and won passage of the nation's first state black lung compensation bill. After seventy-eight coal miners were killed in a November 1968 mine explosion at Farmington, West Virginia, Congress passed the 1969 Coal Mine Health and Safety Act, which included federal black lung compensation.

Members of the BLA criticized the union leadership's lack of commitment to coal miners' health and safety issues and supported Joseph "Jock" Yablonski's effort to unseat UMWA president Tony Boyle in 1969. Boyle won reelection, but Yablonski filed complaints of election fraud with the Department of Labor (DOL). In December 1969, Yablonski, his wife, and daughter were murdered as they lay sleeping in their beds. Boyle was convicted in 1974 for his role in the conspiracy to murder Yablonski.

After the DOL overturned the 1969 election results, Yablonski's supporters formed Miners for Democracy (MFD) to continue their reform efforts. Arnold Miller, a BLA activist, was selected to head the MFD ticket, and in 1972 the MFD's slate defeated Boyle's bid for reelection. Coal miners' health and safety, however, has been a continuing struggle even with a more supportive UMWA leadership. Over the last thirty years, the coal industry has sought in a variety of ways to weaken the Coal Mine Health and Safety Act, especially the legislation dealing with compensation for black lung. For example, in 2001, the National Mining Association sued to overturn Clinton-era regulations that made it easier for coal miners and their survivors to receive black lung benefits. Strong resistance from coal miners and the UMWA forced the Bush administration to defend the regulations.

There was widespread and intense labor activity on other fronts in Appalachia during the 1960s and 1970s. Women's organizations arose to fight for women's employment rights in nontraditional areas such as highway jobs and the building trades. Especially important was the Coal Employment Project's effort to end gender discrimination in the coal mines. The Amalgamated Clothing and Textile Workers Union (ACTWU) conducted a successful nationwide boycott of J. P. Stevens, which was, at the time, the second largest textile company in the country. Textile workers organized the Carolina Brown Lung Association to clean up their workplaces and obtain compensation for those afflicted with byssinosis, a lung disease caused by the inhalation of cotton dust.

The period since the 1980s has been disastrous for organized labor in Appalachia and throughout the United States. In 2004, 12.4 percent of the American work force was unionized, compared to almost 36 percent half a century ago. Membership in the UMWA fell from 160,000 in 1978 to below 20,000 working members today. During the same period, the United Steelworkers of America (USWA) lost 58 percent of its members. Along with a decrease in membership has come a loss of labor rights in the workplace, deteriorating working conditions, a decline in bargaining power, and, for many workers, a drop in real wages.

But some workers in Appalachia have fought back. The employees of Weirton Steel Company in the small town of Weirton, West Virginia, responded to the threatened closure of their plant by organizing an employee-stock ownership plan that eventually enabled them to become the nation's largest, wholly employee-owned company. Steelworkers from western Pennsylvania, northern West Virginia, and eastern Ohio formed the Tri-State Conference on Steel to fight for job retention and renewal. In 1992, in a well-orchestrated campaign, the USWA was able to defeat an effort by billionaire commodities trader Marc Rich's global corporation to destroy the union at the Ravenswood Aluminum Corporation in West Virginia.

In 1989, temporary workers in Morristown, Tennessee, organized Citizens against Temporary Services to push for legislation that would limit temporary assignments and force employers to give long-term employees regular pay and benefits. Activists in Appalachian Ohio established the Appalachian Center for Economic Networks (ACEnet) to help worker-owned businesses get off the ground. There have also been successes in the service sector, with two of the largest chains of nursing homes and several major hospitals now organized in West Virginia and eastern Kentucky.

The ACTWU began to have success in organizing related industries, such as seat covers and tires. In a wave of elections at a dozen plants in 1993, over thirty-five hundred workers voted to join ACTWU, the most new members for the union in a decade. In July 1995, ACTWU joined with the International Ladies Garment Workers Union (ILGWU) to form the Union of Needletrades, Industrial & Textile Employees (UNITE), which has won a number of organizing drives throughout Appalachia and the South.

Retired and disabled Appalachian coal miners in the Black Lung Association, southern textile workers in the Brown Lung Association, and asbestos workers in the White Lung Association formed the Breath of Life Coalition to fight for a federal program that challenges many of the prevailing assumptions and practices regarding compensation and occupational health issues. Although their efforts were unsuccessful, the importance of coalition building between workers and their supporters from different industries was an important lesson for future struggles.

In 1989, after working more than eighteen months without a contract, the UMWA went on strike against Pittston Coal Company in an effort to retain adequate health care, pensions, and job security for its members. Most observers predicted a quick victory for Pittston, but they underestimated the preparedness, discipline, and unity of the UMWA. Union members, families, and supporters waged a massive civil disobedience campaign, using tactics reminiscent of the civil rights movement of the 1960s. The UMWA's takeover of Pittston's Moss 3 preparation plant sparked a visit by Secretary of Labor Elizabeth Dole, leading to appointment of a federal mediator and settlement of the ten-month strike.

Workers and union officials in Appalachia and across the nation are increasingly aware of the need to adopt new tactics and strategies to confront corporate owners in an international economy. In some of the struggles mentioned above, UNITE, USWA, and the UMWA effectively used corporate campaigns to win concessions. These campaigns are designed to take the battle away from the work site and disrupt a company's relationship with stockholders or lending institutions by publicizing the company's poor record in financial, labor, environmental, or other policy areas. Unions began pursuing a variety of electoral strategies, including running their own political candidates as Democrats or independents. The UMWA's Coal Miner's Political Action Committee (COMPAC) has been particularly successful in this regard, electing a number of UMWA members to serve as mayors, county commissioners, school board members, county judges, and state legislators. Some unions, especially UNITE and the UAW, are rethinking traditional labor-management relations and are considering ways to restructure work systems and production policies in order to increase employee involvement in decision making in the workplace and in corporate boardrooms. Union leaders are coming to recognize that the only effective response by workers to the increasing integration of the world economy is to coordinate their strategies both at home and abroad. Tens of thousands of workers from all over the country traveled to southwest Virginia to support union miners during the Pittston strike. UNITE has worked diligently to build solidarity between South African and North American clothing and textile workers. Australian miners and Japanese and Italian steelworkers took part in the organizing campaign against Pittston. The steelworkers at Ravenswood received crucial support from the Geneva-based International Metal-workers Federation and the Brussels-based International Federation of Chemical, Energy and General Workers' Union. These union solidarity efforts provide a framework through which workers and their families in Appalachia can begin to understand the impact of national and global events and institutions on their lives and communities.

Women and the Politics of Change

Appalachian women's and men's political activities and ideologies have changed through time, in response to interactions and developments within their families, communities, region, nation, and, increasingly, the global economic and political system. Gender plays important roles in structuring these political practices and ideologies, but its role is complicated by interacting factors, including class, race, ethnicity, religion, and education. For example, contemporary Appalachian women may be united across race, class, and ethnicity in a struggle against domestic violence while, simultaneously, they may disagree about abortion and reproductive choices.

Some of the most exciting work in recent Appalachian scholarship examines how class, race, and gender conflicts express themselves today in cultural and political formations in Appalachia. Those interested in such analyses should consult many of the works listed in the bibliography at the end of this essay.

Before coal mines and other industries were commercially developed, economic interdependence between women and men and a kinship-based economic and political system provided avenues of power and influence for women. But the development of the industrial economy led to the removal of men from the domestic realm, which, by increasing familial dependence upon male wage earning, changed the political dynamics between women and men. This development often resulted in the devaluation of women's economic activity and curtailment of their political influence in Appalachia.

There are important caveats to be made here, however. First, in other parts of Appalachia the labor market provided white women with as many or more wage-earning opportunities than men, although they were not generally as lucrative as men's coal-mining jobs. In North Carolina, for instance, white women were employed quite extensively in cotton mills and mica-processing plants. Second, coalfield women have been active in a variety of political movements, including the labor unionization movement, the anti–strip mining and environment protection movements, the welfare rights movement, educational reform efforts, and community and economic development projects. Finally, women did make some inroads into coal-mining jobs during the late 1970s.

Since 1980, economic restructuring and automation have eliminated thousands of jobs throughout Appalachia, resulting in high rates of poverty and unemployment. Many families have responded by migrating out of the region in search of work. Sometimes only men migrate or commute to alternative jobs while women and children remain behind to survive on the money they send home, on government transfer payments, and on informal economic activities. Increasingly, however, Appalachian women are taking advantage of new educational and economic opportunities that have emerged during the last thirty years. The female labor force participation rate has increased dramatically since 1960, doubling and even tripling in some counties. Women students predominate in college and community college classes. As women attain education and employment, they also gain power, both formally and informally, publicly and privately.

This economic and political transition has been marked by a variety of other social developments, not all of them positive. It is important to note that most female service jobs do not pay as much as male union mining jobs did. As is true throughout the United States and the world, Appalachian families with female wage earners make less than those with male wage earners, and Appalachian women do not receive the same economic return on their educational investment as men do. Economic restructuring has placed a stress on families and marriages; divorce rates have increased, and there is some evidence that domestic violence has increased.

On the positive side, Appalachian women are flexing their political muscles at home, in their community, and beyond. Many of the citizen groups discussed above, including KFTC, SOCM, the Ivanhoe Civic League, and the Dungannon Development Commission, draw their energy and leadership from a strong cadre of active, vocal, and talented women. In Whitesburg, Kentucky, women play key directing, producing, and leadership roles at Appalshop, an important regional arts, cultural, and media cooperative. Women have been leaders in educational and health reform efforts throughout the region. Women professionals predominate in social services fields. More and more women are serving on boards of education, city councils, and in other important local offices. Clearly, much has changed in the gender politics of Appalachia, though much remains to be done.

Efforts to Create an Appalachian Movement

Since the 1960s, activists have attempted to organize citizen and labor organizations in the Appalachian mountains into a regionwide grass-roots social movement. The most important attempts were by the Council of the Southern Mountains, the People's Appalachia Research Collective, the Congress for

Appalachian Development, the Highlander Research and Education Center, and the Appalachian Alliance. These attempts to build a unified movement failed for a variety of reasons, but primarily because, unlike class, race, and gender, region in the United States does not provide an adequate political and economic focus for social movements.

This failure to create a social movement in Appalachia similar to the civil rights or women's movement does not mean that change efforts in the region have occurred in isolation. While many of these struggles have been local and concerned with a single issue, they have often been assisted by and associated with other groups and individuals within a loose alliance or network of Appalachian organizations. At times the network has had a name; at other times, it has been little more than an informal chain of individuals and groups. Organizations and activists come and go, and financial support is rarely stable, but the network persists, and there are few like it in the United States. Key players in this network today include the Highlander Research and Education Center, an adult education center in eastern Tennessee that has served as a meeting place, training center, and catalyst for social action throughout Appalachia and the South; the Southern Empowerment Project, an organizer training program established and controlled by grass-roots community groups; and the Appalachian Community Fund, a community-controlled foundation that provides seed money and small grants to groups in the Appalachian region.

As Bill Horton points out, this loose, informal network "is the form that the Appalachian social movement has taken—slowly winning victories, working together, laying the groundwork, building or trying to build democratic organizations. Perhaps this is the way the movement will be built, piece by piece like a patchwork quilt until it comes together to rid the region of oppressive structures and practices, in turn becoming a piece of a much larger quilt that must be created to rid the nation of those same structures and practices."

Women pickets facing state police at Consolidated Coal's Owings mine, Shinnston, West Virginia, June 1925. Courtesy of West Virginia State Archives, West Virginia State Police Collection.

Protesting a proposed natural gas pipeline, Floyd County, Virginia, 2003. By Ricky Cox.

Teri Blanton, chairperson of Kentuckians for the Commonwealth, in Dayhoit, Kentucky, by a stream polluted by coal runoff. Courtesy of Roy Silver.

Denise Giardina, 2000 Mountain Party candidate for governor of West Virginia. Courtesy of the West Virginia Humanities Council.

Note

We would like to thank Mary Anglin, Sally Maggard, and Joe Szakos for their insightful critiques of this essay.

Suggested Readings

Anglin, Mary K. *Women, Power, and Dissent in the Hills of Carolina.* Urbana: Univ. of Illinois Press, 2002.

Blee, Kathleen, and Dwight B. Billings. "Reconstructing Daily Life in the Past: An Hermeneutical Approach to Ethnographic Data." *Sociological Quarterly* 27 (Winter 1986): 443–62.

Brisbin, Richard A., Jr. *A Strike Like No Other Strike: Law and Resistance During the Pittston Coal Strike of 1989–1990.* Baltimore: Johns Hopkins Univ. Press, 2002.

Clark, Paul F. *The Miners' Fight for Democracy: Arnold Miller and the Reform of the United Mine Workers.* Ithaca, N.Y.: Cornell Univ., 1981.

Couto, Richard A. *Making Democracy Work Better: Mediating Structures, Social Capital, and the Democratic Prospect.* Chapel Hill: Univ. of North Carolina Press, 1999.

Fisher, Stephen L. *Fighting Back in Appalachia: Traditions of Resistance and Change.* Philadelphia: Temple Univ. Press, 1993.

Fox, Maier B. *United We Stand: The United Mine Workers of America, 1890–1990.* Washington, D.C.: United Mine Workers of America, 1990.

Glen, John M. *Highlander: No Ordinary School, 1932–1962.* 2d ed. Knoxville: Univ. of Tennessee Press, 1996.

Hinsdale, Mary Ann, Helen M. Lewis, and S. Maxine Waller. *It Comes from the People: Community Development and Local Theology.* Philadelphia: Temple Univ. Press, 1995.

Horton, Bill. Review of *Highlander: No Ordinary School, 1932–1962,* by John Glen. *Appalachian Journal* 16 (Summer 1989): 370.

Judkins, Bennett M. *We Offer Ourselves as Evidence: Toward Workers' Control of Occupational Health.* New York: Greenwood Press, 1986.

Juravich, Tom, and Kate Bronfenbrenner. *Ravenswood: The Steelworkers' Victory and the Revival of American Labor.* Ithaca, N.Y.: ILR Press, 1999.

Lewis, Helen M., Sue E. Kobak, and Linda Johnson. "Family, Religion, and Colonialism in Central Appalachia or Bury My Rifle in Big Stone Gap." In *Colonialism in Modern America: The Appalachian Case,* edited by Helen M. Lewis, Linda Johnson, and Donald Askins. Boone, N.C.: Appalachian Consortium Press, 1978.

Loker, Suzanne, and Elizabeth Scannell. "The Unique Nature of Textile and Craft Home-Based Workers: A Comparison." *Journal of Family and Economic Issues* 13 (Fall 1992): 263–77.

Montrie, Chad. *To Save the Land and People: A History of Opposition to Surface Coal Mining in Appalachia.* Chapel Hill: Univ. of North Carolina Press, 2003.

Moore, Marat. *Women in the Mines: Stories of Life and Work.* New York: Twayne, 1996.

Scott, Shaunna L. *Two Sides to Everything: The Cultural Construction of Class Conscious-ness in Harlan County, Kentucky.* Albany: State Univ. of New York Press, 1995.

Seitz, Virginia R. *Women, Development, and Communities for Empowerment in Appalachia.* Albany: State Univ. of New York Press, 1995.

Smith, Barbara Ellen. *Digging Our Own Graves: Coal Miners and the Struggle over Black Lung Disease.* Philadelphia: Temple Univ. Press, 1987.

Waller, Altina L. *Feud: Hatfields, McCoys, and Social Change in Appalachia, 1860–1900.* Chapel Hill: Univ. of North Carolina Press, 1988.

Whisnant, David E. *Modernizing the Mountaineer: People, Power, and Planning in Appalachia.* Boone, N.C.: Appalachian Consortium Press, 1980.

HEALTH CARE IN APPALACHIA

ANNE B. BLAKENEY

In recent decades, health care has become a major concern for Americans. Across the nation, people are increasingly worried about the rising cost of health care. Whether they live in large cities or in rural areas, many Americans are concerned about "managed care" and what it will mean for them. The future of the American health-care system itself is the subject of political debates and sidewalk conversations. Those who live in Appalachia share these same concerns.

However, there are additional long-term health issues in Appalachia that predate these current national concerns. Three issues that have had a persistent effect upon health care in Appalachia are (1) the accessibility of health-care services to all citizens within the region, (2) the education of health professionals, and (3) the importance of providing culturally sensitive health-care services.

Social Capital and Accessibility to Health Care

Accessibility to health care has been a longstanding concern in Appalachia. Richard Couto argues that this problem, as well as other economic and social needs, is basically a factor of social capital, that is, the investment which is made to produce and reproduce human beings in communities.[1]

In American society, private capital serves as the means for producing and distributing goods and services. The goal of private capital is to generate profit for private business investors. Social capital is the investment made in such areas as education, housing, health care, culture, and the environment. In most cases, social capital follows upon the needs of private capital. In a capitalist society such as ours, the primary goal of investing in social capital is to ensure the production, reproduction and distribution of workers for a labor force. Thus, the vast majority of social capital is invested in American communities to maintain people as workers. Much smaller amounts are invested in people as citizens, parents, community members, or in other public roles.[2]

America's history reveals a longstanding emphasis on the private provision of social capital. For example, workers' wages are tapped as a primary source of many social capital investments; employers are expected to serve as a secondary source. American public policy requires that workers use their wages to obtain housing, transportation, and recreational opportunities. Health-care insurance is another aspect of social capital linked to the worker's wage. Thus, as a form of social capital, health insurance depends upon a person's place in the economy.[3]

Because health insurance is so closely tied to the workplace, increasing numbers of people remain in dangerous or unrewarding work situations in order to maintain their access to health insurance, even when their health-care benefits become limited. Others may be forced to work in jobs that do not provide them with health insurance. This is particularly true in rural areas of Appalachia, where people are likely to work in agricultural enterprises or in small businesses that do not or cannot provide employees with health insurance.[4]

During the early part of the twentieth century, private capital invested heavily in coal, steel, and textile businesses throughout Appalachia.[5] Initially, private capital invested in social capital in order to produce and reproduce an Appalachian work force. In many places, company towns were built, providing housing, education, health care, and recreation. Although not all companies provided the same degree of social capital investment, some were considered to have created model communities.[6] When the coal industry was thriving, social capital investments were made for miners through their union, the United Mine Workers of America (UMWA), for health-care services as well as for disability and retirement benefits.[7]

Richard Couto argues that when groups of people have subordinate roles in the economy, the social capital invested in them is modest. When people have no role in the economy, even less social capital is invested in them. Thus, when a community's economic conditions change, so will the social capital invested in it.[8]

When the American economy shifted in the latter part of the twentieth century and the need for a large labor force diminished in Appalachia, the social capital investment in the region dried up. Coal towns began to decline,[9] and many steel towns[10] and textile towns eventually followed.[11] As the coal industry became increasingly mechanized and the steel and textile industries began to move out of the country into the global market place, fewer and fewer workers were needed in many northern and central Appalachian communities. The result was that large numbers of workers were unable to find employment.[12] Millions of those who had the means to do so left Appalachia in search of work elsewhere, while others either could not or would not go, hoping that the economy would recover at home.

As the economy declined throughout the region, German automobile manufacturers moved into the foothills of Appalachia in northern South Carolina. These manufacturers generated increased social capital investment there, resulting in improved schools, health-care systems, and housing in a limited number of southern Appalachian counties.[13]

Throughout much of northern, central, and southern Appalachia, as the demand for a skilled labor force continues to decline into the twenty-first century, so does the incentive for social capital investment. Thus, the housing crisis, the educational crisis, and the health crisis in Appalachia are all interrelated. They represent a deficit in the social capital budget. This deficit has increased as public policy continues to entrust the distribution of necessary resources to private capital, even as businesses downsize or leave Appalachia altogether.[14]

The picture of health care that emerges in Appalachia today is complex and eludes simple generalizations. The family, the first means of social capital, is the primary source for the creation and sustenance of healthy people in our society. Yet the changes in work and income in Appalachia during the latter part of the twentieth century have meant that many families live in poverty and have access to increasingly fewer resources. This has had a severe impact on children in many parts of the region. Increasing numbers of Appalachia's children are growing up in poverty during a time of unprecedented economic prosperity in the rest of the nation.[15]

The poverty of central Appalachia remains the highest in the region, almost twice the national rate. Thus, despite the fact that improvements were made between 1970 and 1990 in the overall poverty rate in central Appalachia, one in four people continued to live in poverty in the early 1990s.[16] Central Appalachian families have the very lowest incomes in the region, especially those living in eastern Kentucky. Thus, the poverty of central Appalachia is chronic, as both private capital and public programs continue a steady decline. As an example, the welfare reform legislation passed by Congress in 1996 rests upon the assumption that those on welfare will be able to find jobs as they move from welfare to work. The jobs which once supported families in Appalachia have largely disappeared and been replaced by a limited number of jobs in the service sector that pay wages insufficient to support families. Thus, as more people are removed from the welfare rolls, if jobs are not created to provide work and adequate incomes for them, we can predict that even more Appalachian families will move deeper into poverty.

The federal government makes it possible for the most rural states in the nation to pursue additional Medicaid coverage for pregnant women and for all children under the age of eighteen who need health care. However, Kentucky and West Virginia have not exercised this option. By maintaining highly restrictive Medicaid eligibility requirements, these states, and several of the southern Appalachian states, have excluded many women and children from access to health-care services.[17]

In northern Appalachia, there is new poverty as a result of the decline of work and wages for the middle class. The urban areas of northern Appalachia have particularly declined, with inner-city incomes for many families coming closer to those of families living in economically distressed rural Appalachian communities.[18]

However, with the exception of West Virginia, the northern Appalachian states provide better access to health care than do the central and southern Appalachian states. This means that people in northern Appalachia are more likely to be medically insured or to have access to Medicaid and that they have more access to primary and prenatal care.[19] Among Appalachian states, New York ranks the highest in providing community health services, including per capita spending on health care, sanitation, sewage, and public-health workers. Pennsylvania and Mississippi rank the lowest in public-health spending in the region.

Appalachia has obtained some federal funding for community health centers to fill the gap created when private capital withdrew from the region, leaving health-care needs largely unmet. In 1992, 13 percent of all federal grant support for community health centers nationwide came to centers in Appalachia. These centers serve patients with low incomes or those who are eligible for Medicaid or Medicare benefits.[20] West Virginia reported community health centers in 77 percent of its medically underserved counties. These centers serve 25 percent of all the people throughout the entire Appalachian region who receive health care in community centers. No other Appalachian state demonstrates the same commitment to community health care. The Appalachian counties of Tennessee have almost as many community health centers, but far fewer people are served in them (111,558 West Virginians vs. 47,511 Tennesseans).[21]

Despite the gains made in numbers of community health centers in the region, many of the more rural economically distressed communities in Appalachia continue to struggle with achieving accessibility to health care. This means that too many Appalachian women do not receive needed prenatal care and too many babies born in Appalachia are classified as "low birth weight."[22] Often referred to as "the working poor," these women and their families fall through the cracks in the health-care system, frequently going without much-needed care.

Appalachia also lags behind the rest of the nation in numbers of health professionals. This continues to create problems for citizens seeking accessible health care. Progress has been made in increasing the numbers of health professionals in the region, with Pennsylvania and North Carolina demonstrating the most significant gains of health professionals in federally designated Health Professional Shortage Areas.[23] However, rural communities in other Appalachian states continue to struggle to recruit qualified health professionals.

Thus, even among rural Appalachians who have insurance or the financial means to pay for health care, access to needed services remains inadequate due to shortages of health-care professionals.[24] As an example, the termination of the National Health Service Corps scholarship program in 1981 dramatically reduced the total number of physicians available in rural areas throughout the country.[25] In many rural Appalachian communities, recruitment and retention of qualified health-care professionals continues to be a persistent and unresolved problem.[26]

In 1995, the Kentucky Appalachian Task Force described the following roadblocks that create critical problems for Appalachians as they seek health care:

> Health services are fragmented, driven by profit motives in many cases, and are reimbursed in a way to *devalue* rural health issues, primary care, prevention, and collaboration, while *fostering* procedurally-oriented illness care. Health professions learners are actively educated to *avoid* prevention, rural communities, and primary care. It is a highly perverse health care system which fails to address population health issues. The gulf between private illness and public health care systems exemplifies a basic flaw in the American health system. It is magnified in rural communities, and perpetuated by existing models of health professions education and training. There is great risk that rural problems will be exacerbated as legislative efforts at both state and federal levels, driven in part by large urban insurance and managed care organizations, seek to impose urban solutions on rural communities. Since rural health care problems are uniquely different from urban problems, unique rural solutions *must* be applied.[27]

The report of the Kentucky Appalachian Task Force focused upon specific issues within the Appalachian communities of eastern Kentucky. However, the current status of rural health care as described by the report may well define many of the major limitations in the health-care system throughout much of central and southern Appalachia.

Individuals or groups who attempt to promote access to health care within their local communities can be described as social capital entrepreneurs.[28] They seek to bring new investment in people. They also frequently address broader political, economic, and environmental issues that have an impact on the health status of their entire communities. Eula Hall's efforts to obtain clean drinking water for the people served by the Mud Creek Clinic in Floyd County, Kentucky, provide an example. A longtime advocate for health-care accessibility for all citizens in her community, Eula Hall has also been instrumental in obtaining access to clean drinking water and improving housing conditions along Mud Creek. In addition, she has continued to work tirelessly over the years to recruit and retain qualified health professionals to serve the citizens of Mud Creek.

Recruiting health-care professionals into rural Appalachian communities requires ongoing, persistent efforts by community organizers such as Eula Hall. That such recruitment efforts remain difficult is explained, in part, by the fact that the investment in social capital in Appalachia has not changed significantly during previous decades. Additionally, the content, the process, and the location of health professionals' education is directly linked to the ongoing problems of recruitment and retention in many rural Appalachian communities.[29]

Educating Health Professionals

More than twenty years ago, James Branscome of the Appalachian Regional Commission's youth leadership programs, discussed the absence of appropriate educational materials regarding Appalachia within many different disciplines.[30] Specifically regarding the training of students in the health professions, Branscome noted, "Medical students are taught to treat medulla tissue on the brain, but know next to nothing about how to practice in rural areas. Nursing students graduate with experience in urban and local hospitals, but few have real training in public health with field work in the region. . . . In fact, no institution of American society is more divorced from Appalachia than the higher educational system which resides within it."[31]

In 1988, Couto noted that little had changed since Branscome's earlier assessment of the deficiencies within medical education. If anything, the medical students of the late 1980s were prepared to practice medicine in a much more narrow sense than those who had preceded them into community health. Couto described these more recent young physicians as

> more concerned about salaries and finances. . . . They think like stock-brokers and expect a six-figure salary the first year out of training. This

attitude is not a personal and individual matter but a reflection of the inadequacy of medical school training. Medical schools emphasize acquiring credentials, board certification, and specializing in a narrow field of medicine, leaving medical students with substantial debts to pay off. All of these factors push ... the social commitment of medical students off to the edges of their personal agendas.[32]

The 1995 report of the Kentucky Appalachian Task Force indicates that the problems noted by both Branscome and Couto continue to persist well into the 1990s. To address these longstanding problems, the report suggests major re-structuring and reordering of health professionals' education, including (1) educating providers *within the Appalachian region,* (2) making greater efforts to recruit and educate people *locally* to become health-care providers, and (3) including *values and ethics* as a foundation within the curriculum of all health-care professions. Similar suggestions have been offered in the past and are well supported in the literature on recruitment and retention of health profession-als in rural areas.[33]

There are some notable efforts being made toward training health-care stu-dents within rural Appalachia. For example, the University of Kentucky Center for Rural Health, located in Hazard, Kentucky, is currently attempting to recruit and train health professionals within eastern Kentucky. Marshall University has demonstrated a long-term commitment within its medical school to train physi-cians in family medicine for practice in rural West Virginia. Radford University has a family practitioner nursing program for rural communities. In addition, the medical school at East Tennessee State University has attempted to incor-porate clinical rotations throughout rural East Tennessee in an effort to provide students with exposure to rural health practice. Were these models to be system-atically implemented at other universities throughout region, we could dramat-ically improve the educational process of many of the professionals who deliver health care in Appalachia.

Providing Culturally Sensitive Health Care

Recruiting Appalachian students into the health professions and educating them within the region are important strategies for increasing the accessibility to health-care services for many people living within rural mountain communi-ties. However, simply providing the standard medical education in a rural loca-tion is not enough to ensure that people gain real access to health care. Includ-ing content about Appalachian culture within the educational curriculum is absolutely critical for the success of any strategy designed to increase accessibil-ity to health care in Appalachia.[34] Without an informed cultural context within which to interpret actual clinical experiences, students cannot achieve the maximum benefits of their education as health professionals, whether they are natives of Appalachia or coming into the region for the first time.

It is not uncommon to encounter technically competent health-care professionals who make derogatory comments about Appalachian people. This is particularly true if patients are from rural communities or if they are perceived to be poor or working-class individuals. These Appalachian patients are often described as ignorant, uncooperative, difficult to manage, and unwilling to communicate with health professionals. In addition, their religious beliefs and family relationships are often poorly understood by non-Appalachian health-care providers.[35]

Patients are sometimes judged as failing to follow through on treatment goals established "in their best interest." At times, they are even discharged prematurely because some health professionals state that they simply do not want to bother with people who are not motivated to improve themselves.[36]

Even the accent of mountain people may be the object of ridicule among health professionals. And patterns of speech are often so poorly understood that miscommunication occurs. For instance, a physical therapist originally from New York who was working in central Appalachia related the following episode.[37] Every day this young therapist entered the hospital room of an elderly mountain woman. After introducing herself, the therapist then asked the patient if it would be all right to do the exercises which the doctor had ordered for her. The patient would respond, "Well, I don't care to." For several days, the therapist immediately left the room and officially recorded that the patient had "refused" therapy. Shortly thereafter, the patient was discharged from therapy as "non-compliant."

It was not until months later that this therapist overheard a local colleague using the same expression and discovered that she should have been interpreting "I don't care to" as "I don't mind" doing those exercises now. This young woman was technically a very competent physical therapist who was willing to work in rural Appalachia. However, she had little knowledge of local culture, especially as it influenced patterns of speech. Although she was physically accessible and willing to deliver health-care services, she was culturally inaccessible, and in some instances this resulted in the actual loss of health-care services.

It is not enough simply to take students into the region and then provide the experiences of a "typical" medical education for them once they are there. Nor is it enough to recruit students from within the region and then provide them with a medical education that often demeans their local experience and devalues their cultural knowledge. Too often Appalachian students are taught to feel ashamed of their culture during their academic experiences, and in response they may reject it.[38] Far too many of these students leave the region after becoming educated.

Drawing on Appalachian Scholarship in Health-Care Education

What can be done to change this situation? Infusing the curricula of the health professions with information on Appalachian culture is an important first step. Using the scholarship from within the region can provide students with insights into the context of the daily lives of their patients. Too often, students in the health-care fields are "trained" to develop highly technical health-care skills but are not "educated" to consider the broader issues they will encounter once they enter Appalachia and begin to work.

Students within the health-care professions are traditionally trained to look very carefully at the individual patient and his or her pathology, then to focus intervention strategies on a one-to-one basis with the person who is ill. They often do not understand anything about the local political economic systems, nor how these fit into broader national and international systems.[39] They do not see that health and illness are social phenomena, nor do they recognize that individuals usually have little control over the forces that cause them to be sick. At times, they may become very harsh in the judgments they make about their patients.

For example, health professionals may blame all of the unemployed for not working, rather than realizing that few jobs exist locally within the political economy of many mountain communities. Sometimes professionals also view the unemployed as undeserving of health-care services. Providers may also judge some of their patients as not trying hard enough to take care of themselves without fully realizing the very real constraints which poverty places upon the daily lives of those whom they are supposed to be serving.[40]

If health-care professionals are not educated regarding the social, political, and economic realities of the society in which they will eventually live and work, they cannot formulate intervention strategies that are grounded within the social and cultural context of their patients. As a result, they may blame the poor for being poor, blame the sick for "bad health habits," and blame the "culture" of their patients for any behaviors that they fail to understand.[41]

Because Appalachian culture is frequently presented within stereotypes in the society at large, many health professionals are unaware that any other notions about the culture exist. Their perspectives on Appalachia may be informed solely by stereotypical images. They may make judgments based upon stereotypes and fail to see how limited their reasoning is.[42]

ANNE B. BLAKENEY

For example, elderly patients who lack many years of formal education within the region's schools may be judged to be "uneducated" altogether rather than being seen as possessing knowledge and skills gained through years of lived experience in a rural environment. Therefore, the knowledge and skills that such patients bring into the health-care setting often go unrecognized. The opportunity for the health professional to tap into a patient's knowledge to strengthen a clinical intervention strategy is often lost as a result.[43]

Thus, a patient who might be willing to move a painful arthritic shoulder if encouraged to work in the garden daily may not be as willing to complete a set of isolated shoulder exercises which are painful as well as unrelated to his or her daily life tasks. The patient may eventually develop a frozen shoulder as a result of restricted movement in the shoulder joint and ultimately be labeled as "noncompliant" with treatment recommendations. In such instances, health professionals have applied their technical competence to a situation that demands social and cultural competence as well. Such scenarios are repeated all too often in Appalachian communities when health professionals have not been introduced to an informed cultural context as part of their educational process.[44] Introducing health professionals to Appalachian scholarship and/or encouraging their participation in the Appalachian Studies Association are two ways to begin to address this lack of knowledge.

Drawing on Creative Literature and the Arts

Introducing students to the creative literature and to the arts within Appalachia is another way of expanding the depth of their awareness of Appalachian culture. At Eastern Kentucky University, some occupational therapy students choose to complete a required community-based clinical education course in the mountains of southeastern Kentucky during a special four-week intersession experience. During this month-long health-care course, these students are exposed to an intensive combination of both clinical and cultural educational experiences. At the same time, they are delivering health-care services in underserved rural communities under the direction of faculty mentors.

In addition to the technical skills they are expected to master, the students are required to read either a novel or a collection of short stories by an Appalachian author. They may choose a book from a selection of titles provided by their instructors. While completing this additional reading, students are often able to make connections to the social and cultural context in which they are immersed.

For example, strip mines that are passed daily while traveling to and from clinical sites take on a different meaning when students are reading *Hell and*

Ohio by Chris Holbrook or *The Unquiet Earth* by Denise Giardina. The complexities of family conflicts are viewed from a different perspective when students are reading *The Doll Maker* by Harriette Arnow, *River of Earth* by James Still, or *The Devil's Dream, Saving Grace,* and *Family Linen* by Lee Smith. Sorting out the strong feelings often expressed by local people who are either pro- or anti-union is better understood as students read Denise Giardina's *Storming Heaven.* Recognizing cultural folklore and traditions within contemporary Appalachian life becomes easier for students who are reading *She Walks These Hills* or *The Hangman's Beautiful Daughter* by Sharyn McCrumb or *The Mountains Won't Remember Us* by Robert Morgan and *I Am One of You Forever* by Fred Chappell.

Rather than viewing Appalachian people and their culture as "odd" or "different," students who simultaneously explore the region and the literature are better able to make culturally informed decisions about the patients whom they encounter in health-care settings. These students are encouraged to use their novels or collections of short stories in posing questions that they have about their daily experiences during this course. They are also urged to begin to make their own connections between art and the lived experiences of their patients as they start to answer their own questions.

In addition to reading the creative literature from the region, the students in this clinical course are taken on field trips to such places as Appalshop, where they meet filmmakers and view some of the films that document the life and culture of Appalachia. They also explore the area through hikes in the mountains and visits to museums and community development centers.

When this month-long course was first moved into the mountains of southeastern Kentucky in 1990, there were no more than four occupational therapists working in rural mountain communities. Six years later, 38 therapists, or slightly more than a third of 112 students who completed the course, had gone into eastern Kentucky communities to live and work.[45]

In evaluating their course experiences, students generally state that while the novel or short story collection was initially resisted as "extra work," they would strongly recommend that it be continued as an assignment for future students. When students meet to discuss their books, they are able to reflect upon how they were helped to see the complexities of local issues as a result of having read works of fiction. They also see the value of the additional films and field trips in balancing the final perspective they gained about the entire region.

Appalachians share many of the same concerns as other Americans regarding the current upheaval in American health care. As for-profit corporations control

ANNE B. BLAKENEY

112

more and more of the health-care services which are delivered throughout the nation, many people in rural Appalachian communities wonder what kind of health care will ultimately be available to them.

In addition to these current concerns, there are health-care issues in Appalachia that have persisted for decades. These include the challenge of guaranteeing accessibility to health-care services for all citizens in the region in a period of declining investment in social capital, the failure of medical models of education to go beyond strictly technical competence, and the persistent need for culturally sensitive health-care services. While there are examples of medical and allied health education programs that do address the social and cultural aspects of health and illness, they continue to be in the minority throughout the region. In addition, recruitment and retention of qualified health professionals in the most rural communities continues to be a challenge.

If these problems are to be addressed in the future, we will have to pay more attention to the ways in which students are educated to become health professionals in Appalachia. We must also insist upon rural models of service delivery that emphasize local needs rather than settle for inadequate transplanted urban models of health-care delivery. Finally, we all will have to work toward more investment in the social capital of the region, as Richard Couto urges us to do, in order to improve the quality of life for all of Appalachia's citizens.[46]

Midwife Amanda Gardner Hollandsworth, Indian Valley, Virginia, c. 1940.
Courtesy of Versie Hollandsworth Phillips.

off

HEALTH CARE IN APPALACHIA

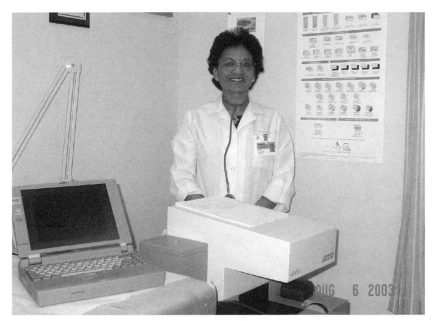

Dr. Sudesh Tayal, promoter of women's health through bone-density screening, at New River Valley Medical Center, Radford, Virginia. By Grace Toney Edwards.

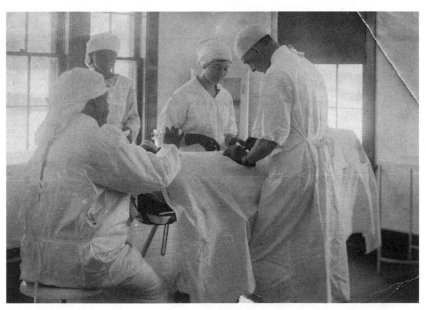

Christiansburg Institute's infirmary, early health care for African Americans, 1918. Courtesy of Ann S. Bailey.

New River Valley Medical Center, Radford, Virginia, a multipurpose regional facility.
By Grace Toney Edwards.

Mobile Health Unit, Waldron College of Health and Human Services, Radford University.
By Lora L. Gordon, Radford University.

Notes

1. Richard A. Couto, *An American Challenge: A Report on Economic Trends and Social Issues in Appalachia* (Dubuque, Iowa: Kendall/Hunt, 1994), 9–11.
2. Ibid., 10.
3. Ibid.
4. Dana Hughes and Sara Rosenbaum, "An Overview of Maternal and Infant Health Services in Rural America," *Journal of Rural Health* 5, no. 4 (1989): 299–319.
5. Couto, *American Challenge*, 10.
6. Ronald D Eller, *Miners, Millhands, and Mountaineers: Industrialization of the Appalachian South, 1880–1930* (Knoxville: Univ. of Tennessee Press, 1982), n.p.
7. Richard Mulcahy, "A New Deal for Coal Miners: The UMWA Welfare and Retirement Fund and the Reorganization of Health Care in Appalachia," *Journal of Appalachian Studies* 2, no. 1 (1996): 29–52.
8. Couto, *American Challenge*, n.p.
9. Crandall A. Shifflett, *Coaltowns: Life, Work, and Culture in Company Towns of Southern Appalachia, 1880–1960* (Knoxville: Univ. of Tennessee Press, 1991), n.p.
10. William Serrin, *Homestead: The Glory and Tragedy of an American Steel Town* (New York: Vintage Books, 1992), n.p.
11. Edward H. Beardsley, *A History of Neglect: Health Care for Blacks and Mill Workers in the Twentieth Century South* (Knoxville: Univ. of Tennessee Press, 1987), n.p.
12. John Gaventa, Barbara Ellen Smith, and Alex Willingham, eds., *Communities in Crisis: Appalachia and the South* (Philadelphia: Temple Univ. Press, 1990), n.p.
13. Couto, *American Challenge*, n.p.
14. Ibid.
15. Ibid.
16. Ibid., 160–66.
17. Ibid., n.p.
18. Ibid.
19. Ibid., 171–72.
20. Ibid.
21. Ibid.
22. Ibid, n.p.
23. Ibid., 173.
24. Kentucky Appalachian Task Force, "Health Issues Committee Report," in *Communities of Hope: Preparing for the Future in Appalachian Kentucky* (Lexington: Appalachian Center, Univ. of Kentucky, 1995), n.p.
25. Hughes and Rosenbaum, "Overview," n.p.
26. Lee Crandall, Jeffrey Dwyer, and R. Paul Duncan, "Recruitment and Retention of Rural Physicians: Issues for the 1990s," *Journal of Rural Health* 6 (1990): 1.
27. Kentucky Appalachian Task Force, "Health Issues Committee Report," 35.
28. Richard A. Couto, "The Political Economy of Appalachian Health," in *Health in Appalachia: Proceedings from the 1988 Conference on Appalachia* (Lexington: Appalachian Center, Univ. of Kentucky, 1988), 14.

29. Crandall, Dwyer, and Duncan, "Recruitment and Retention," n.p.

30. Bruce Ergood and Bruce E. Kuhre, eds., *Appalachia: Social Context Past and Present* (Dubuque, Iowa: Kendall/Hunt, 1976), 3.

31. James Branscome, cited in Ergood and Kuhre, *Appalachia,* 3.

32. Couto, "Political Economy," 11.

33. Crandall, Dwyer, and Duncan, "Recruitment and Retention," n.p.

34. Anne B. Blakeney, "Appalachian Values: Implications for Occupational Therapists," in *Sociocultural Implications in Treatment in Occupational Therapy,* ed. F. Cromwell (New York: Haworth Press, 1987), n.p.

35. Ibid.

36. Ibid.

37. Ibid.

38. Bill Best, "To See Ourselves," in *The Great Appalachian Sperm Bank and Other Writings* (Berea, Ky.: Kentucky Imprints, 1986), 41–58.

39. John Donahue and Meredith B. McGuire, "The Political Economy of Responsibility in Health and Illness," *Social Science and Medicine* 40, no. 1 (1995): 47–53.

40. Ruth Finerman and Linda A. Bennett, "Guilt, Blame and Shame: Responsibility in Health and Illness," in *Social Science and Medicine* 40, no. 1 (1995): 1–3.

41. Donahue and McGuire, "Political Economy of Responsibility," 47–53.

42. Susan E. Keefe, ed., *Appalachian Mental Health* (Lexington: Univ. Press of Kentucky, 1988), n.p.

43. Blakeney, "Appalachian Values," n.p.

44. Ibid.

45. This data was obtained from the Kentucky Occupational Therapy Board. The board is located in Frankfort, Kentucky, and may be reached through state government offices there.

46. Couto, "Political Economy," n.p.

Suggested Readings

Barney, Sandra L. *Authorized to Heal: Gender, Class, and the Transformation of Medicine in Central Appalachia, 1880–1930.* Chapel Hill: Univ. of North Carolina Press, 2000.

Beardsley, Edward H. A. *History of Neglect: Health Care for Blacks and Mill Workers in the Twentieth Century South.* Knoxville: Univ. of Tennessee Press, 1987.

Best, Bill. "To See Ourselves." In *The Great Appalachian Sperm Bank and Other Writings.* Berea, Ky.: Kentucky Imprints, 1986.

Blakeney, Anne B. "Appalachian Values: Implications for Occupational Therapists." In *Sociocultural Implications in Treatment Planning in Occupational Therapy,* edited by F. Cromwell. New York: Haworth Press, 1987.

Couto, Richard A. *An American Challenge: A Report on Economic Trends and Social Issues in Appalachia.* Dubuque, Iowa: Kendall/Hunt, 1994.

———. "The Political Economy of Appalachian Health." In *Health in Appalachia: Proceedings from the 1988 Conference on Appalachia.* Lexington: Appalachian Center, Univ. of Kentucky, 1988.

Couto, Richard A., Nancy K. Simpson, and Gale Harris, eds. *Sowing Seeds in the Mountains: Community-Based Coalitions for Cancer Prevention and Control.* Rockville, Md.: Appalachia Leadership Initiative on Cancer, Cancer Control Sciences Program, Division of Cancer Prevention and Control, National Cancer Institute, 1994.

Crandall, Lee, Jeffrey Dwyer, and R. Paul Duncan. "Recruitment and Retention of Rural Physicians: Issues for the 1990's." *Journal of Rural Health* 6, no. 1 (1990):19–38.

Davis, Carlton. "Domestic Food Programs, Hunger and Undernutrition in Rural America: How Secure Is the Safety Net?" *Review of Black Political Economy* 22, no. 4 (1994): 179–203.

Denham, Sharon A. "Family Health in a Rural Appalachian Ohio County." *Journal of Appalachian Studies* 2, no. 2 (1996): 299–310.

Donahue, John, and Meredith B. McGuire. "The Political Economy of Responsibility in Health and Illness." *Social Science and Medicine* 40, no. 1 (1995): 47–53.

Eller, Ronald D. *Miners, Millhands, and Mountaineers: Industrialization of the Appalachian South 1880–1930.* Knoxville: Univ. of Tennessee Press, 1982.

Ergood, Bruce, and Bruce E. Kuhre. *Appalachia: Social Context Past and Present.* Dubuque, Iowa: Kendall/Hunt, 1976.

Fiene, Judith Ivy. "The Stigma of Mental Illness: The Labeling of Low-Status Appalachian Women." In *Health in Appalachia: Proceedings from the 1988 Conference on Appalachia.* Lexington: Appalachian Center, Univ. of Kentucky, 1988.

Finerman, Ruth, and Linda A. Bennett. "Guilt, Blame and Shame: Responsibility in Health and Illness." *Social Science and Medicine* 40, no. 1 (1995): 1–3.

Gaventa, John, Barbara Ellen Smith, and Alex Willingham, eds. *Communities in Crisis: Appalachia and the South.* Philadelphia: Temple Univ. Press, 1990.

Hochstrasser, Donald, and Gerry Gairola. "Family Planning and Fertility in Southern Appalachia: A Community Study." *Human Organization* 50, no. 4 (1991): 393–405.

Hughes, Dana, and Sara Rosenbaum. "An Overview of Maternal and Infant Health Services in Rural America." *Journal of Rural Health* 5, no. 4 (1989): 299–319.

Judkins, Bennett M. "The People's Respirator: Coalition Building and the Black Lung Association." In *Fighting Back in Appalachia: Traditions of Resistance and Change,* edited by Stephen L. Fisher. Philadelphia: Temple Univ. Press, 1993.

Keefe, Susan E., ed. *Appalachian Mental Health.* Lexington: Univ. Press of Kentucky, 1988.

Kentucky Appalachian Task Force. "Health Issues Committee Report." In *Communities of Hope: Preparing for the Future in Appalachian Kentucky.* Lexington: Appalachian Center, Univ. of Kentucky, 1995.

Merrifield, Juliet. *Putting the Scientists in Their Place: Research in Environmental and Occupational Health.* New Market, Tenn.: Highlander Center, 1989.

Mulcahy, Richard. "Health Care in the Coal Fields: The Miners Memorial Hospital Association." *Historian* 55 (Summer 1993): 4.

———. "A New Deal for Coal Miners: The UMWA Welfare and Retirement Fund and the Reorganization of Health Care in Appalachia." *Journal of Appalachian Studies* 2 (1996): 29–52.

ANNE B. BLAKENEY

Pearles, Caesar, and Lauren Young, eds. *Women, Health and Poverty.* New York: Hawthorn Press, 1988.

Roberts, Allan, Laurence Davis, and James Well. "Where Physicians Practicing in Appalachia in 1978–1990 Were Trained and How They Were Distributed in Urban and Rural Appalachia." *Academic Medicine* 66 (1991): 682–86.

Serrin, William. *Homestead: The Glory and Tragedy of an American Steel Town.* New York: Vintage Books, 1992.

Shifflett, Crandall A. *Coaltowns: Life, Work, and Culture in Company Towns of Southern Appalachia, 1880–1960.* Knoxville: Univ. of Tennessee Press, 1991.

Shortland, Jeffrey, and Deanne Loonlin. *Off to a Poor Start: Infant Health in Rural America.* Washington, D.C.: Public Voice for Food and Health Policy, 1988.

Turner, John. "High Country Hunger: Adapting to Less Food Assistance." *Journal of the Appalachian Studies Association* 6 (1994): 48–58.

EDUCATION IN APPALACHIA

SHARON TEETS

In our culture, the word "education" is often misused. It is not uncommon to hear someone say, "It's important to get a good education" or "I want to get my education finished before I start my family." But "education" derives from the Latin *educare,* which literally means "drawing out," implying that education is a process by which the human potential within each individual is "drawn out" or maximized. Properly defined, then, education is the lifelong process by which an individual maximizes his or her own capacity for all aspects of development, and that definition acknowledges that education occurs in a variety of settings other than schools.[1] If education in Appalachia were examined from this perspective, volumes of personal accounts would have to be written; in fact, much of what we know about the diversity of educational experiences in Appalachia comes from individual accounts. Reviewing the contributions of the Highlander Center in East Tennessee, for example, has filled more than one book, and a brief mention in this chapter would not do it justice. In a broader sense, the U.S. Department of Agriculture Extension Service provided practical education for farmers and homemakers and leadership training for youth throughout the Appalachian region.[2] As the region was rediscovered in the 1960s, the role of the federal government through the funding of Head Start, the Appalachian Regional Commission, and the Appalachian Educational Laboratory would likewise fill chapters, if not books. In order to be practical, however, this chapter focuses on issues and developments related to the traditional educational institutions: schools, colleges, and universities.

Educational Patterns in Colonial America

The nature of Appalachian educational institutions may be understood better within the context of educational patterns that developed throughout the United States during the colonial period. In the early beginnings of the New England colonies, education was a focus of attention, a focus driven primarily by the belief that the Bible must be read for salvation. In order to be saved, everyone needed to be able to read. As early as the 1600s, legislative acts established a pattern of compulsory schooling for all children, although not necessarily providing for the funding that would support education for all children. The Old Deluder Satan Act of 1647 required that towns with more than fifty persons had to provide reading and writing instruction for their children, and provisions were made for families who were not able to pay for their children to attend. Although this functioned as a sort of compulsory school law, the first true compulsory school law was enacted in Massachusetts in 1852.[3]

The Puritan settlers of the New England colonies devised a curriculum that focused primarily on reading skills to facilitate religious instruction, and discipline took the form of corporal punishment, with a heavy reliance on the Old Testament mandate, "Spare the rod and spoil the child." Before any schools were established, any education that children received was in the form of home schooling by parents and/or older siblings. When towns became more populated, the early schools in New England built on the home-schooling idea by educating both young boys and girls at home in what were known as dame schools. This very basic instruction in reading, writing, and arithmetic was followed by instruction, primarily for males of elementary-school age, in a one-room schoolhouse led by a clergyman. Only a privileged few children went on to Latin grammar schools, which would be the equivalent of college preparatory schools, or colleges, the earliest of which was established in 1636.

Throughout the colonies, different patterns of education, which reflected the needs of each region's settlers, emerged. Settlers of the middle colonies came from more diverse backgrounds and were eager to make available a variety of religious instruction for their children; hence, private schools sponsored by given denominations were established as a pattern in the middle colonial region. In the southern region, a two-tiered system of education developed. Due in some part to the distance between families, wealthy landowners provided private tutors for their children (particularly males), while children of some poorer families were provided a minimal education by the Society for the Propagation of the Gospel in Foreign Parts. Because reading was not directly tied to salvation here, education was not as urgent a matter as it had been in New England. Although there continued to be somewhat of a religious influence on schooling from the Anglican settlers in the South, the belief was not so strong that children must be taught to read the Bible as the means to their salvation. In general, the quality of education for poorer children was inferior to that of their wealthier counterparts. In some areas, property taxes were used to fund schools, and as poor families owned little property, little money was available for the education of their children.[4]

Throughout the colonial period, then, patterns of education that varied from region to region emerged. Schools were held for different lengths of time, generally more often for males who were from relatively affluent families, and school facilities and materials varied greatly according to the amount of money available to fund the schools. By the time of the Revolutionary War, even though regional variations still occurred, the patterns of local control, education for all citizens, and some sort of tax support for schools had been established. When the Constitution was written, however, no specific provision was made for education. By default, the Tenth Amendment, which states that "powers not delegated to the United States by the Constitution, nor prohibited by it to the states, are reserved to the states respectively, or to the people," created a system of education that depends heavily upon individual states for direction and funding.

States generally attended to the issue of schooling in their earliest legislative documents, but predictably, levels of interest and support varied widely. Some states, such as Kentucky, initially expressed the belief that education should be a private matter. Others made provisions for public education but left it up to localities to determine the nature of the school, including the length of the school term. Some local communities developed a system of subscription schools, which were open to those who could pay for the cost of the schooling for themselves. Regardless of initial differences, one dominant pattern—one that continues to the present—quickly emerged: that of mandating public education activities without the guarantee of sufficient funding to implement the programs for the poorest of children.[5]

Reformers at the federal level were not long in attempting to shape decisions made by individual states or to act in their absence. For example, the Land Ordinance and Northwest Ordinance Acts of 1785 and 1787 provided for funding for schools. Landmark legal cases also set important precedents. The ruling in the Kalamazoo case of 1874 provided for state funding for high schools in the state of Michigan. This case set a precedent for other states to pass legislation to fund not only elementary school education but high school education as well.[6]

Education in Appalachia

During the first one hundred years of the settlement of the Appalachian region, the patterns of schooling most closely mirror those of New England, beginning with home schooling and followed, as communities developed, by the one-room school house for elementary-aged children, which operated for varying periods of time during the year. These patterns seemed to have persisted throughout the nineteenth century.[7] Due largely to the geography of the region and its impact on settlement patterns, Appalachia can be characterized well into the twentieth century as having had many small schools that were integral parts of the community. For example, in 1904, Wilkes County in North Carolina reported a total of seventy-four schools for white children and forty for Negro children. Public education in Appalachia departed from the New England model, however, in that compulsory attendance laws did not appear until after 1900, more than fifty years after the first such law was enacted in Massachusetts. In the first published accounts of public education in the Appalachian region, the level of education of its people, and the resources available to them, have been targets of concern, if not ridicule. For example, in one of the more widely read accounts published in the early 1900s, Semple had this to say about education:

> The Kentucky mountaineers are shut off from the inspiration to higher living that is found in the world of books. Isolation, poverty, sparsity of population, and impassability of roads make an education difficult, if not impossible; the effect of these conditions is to be seen in the large percentage of illiterates in this section. Of the women over twenty-five years old and men over forty, 80 percent can neither read nor write. It is quite the usual thing to meet men of clear, vigorous intellects and marked capacity in practical affairs who cannot sign their own names.[8]

If the people of the region were seen to be poorly educated, Semple and other writers were quick to point out the inadequacies of the schools that were designed to serve the region. In an article published by Hitch some decades after the Semple article, one school experience was described:

> Twenty-two years ago, six years ago, two years ago, the past summer and autumn—these are the only times when school terms were held in this community during the past half century. And none save the last term (of eight months) has exceeded three months in length. The teacher of one term was a fourteen-year-old fourth grade girl, who married and thereupon closed the school before the term was completed. At a meeting held one night in the little school house during the sixth, and supposedly final, month of the past term, the patrons signed a petition for

an additional two months of school. Of the fourteen present eleven signed with a cross, only three being able to write their names. This community, isolated and untutored is a part of the Old Dominion state, the first settled, and lies within seventy-five miles of the nation's capital.[9]

Since the publication of this and other early accounts of the region, writers have been fascinated with strategies to improve the quality of education in the region. Even though early patterns of education in southern Appalachia had mirrored the beginnings of formal education systems in other regions, by the time of the Civil War, larger discrepancies existed between the educational levels of individuals from affluent families and those from poorer backgrounds. The education of slaves was prohibited in some states. With the outcome of the Civil War, and with the requirement that all former slaves be included in schooling experiences, southern states provided two separate systems of education, one for whites and one for blacks. Because of the heavy reliance upon local funding, the schools for whites were almost certainly better funded than those for blacks, but the "separate but equal" legacy of the *Plessy v. Ferguson* case in 1896 probably contributed to the overall poor quality of the schools for all children.[10]

Perhaps one of the largest bodies of literature relevant to the improvement of educational opportunities for mountain people focuses on the missionary movement in the Appalachian region. There are conflicting views about how this movement came about and how it influenced education. Some argue that it began prior to the Civil War and was focused primarily on an antislavery campaign. Most writers agree that the major thrust for education came from the American Missionary Association, which helped found the school that eventually became Berea College in Kentucky. Several denominations, including Methodists, Southern Baptists, various Presbyterian bodies, Episcopalians, Seventh-Day Adventists, and Disciples of Christ, all supported mountain schools by the early 1920s. Most of these schools were of the grammar-school variety, and the curriculum was not only somewhat evangelical but also designed to "save the mountain child from the errors of his background. His ignorance, his accent and his values were seen as things to be 'corrected'; his view 'broadened' under the guidance of books . . . and worthwhile things dignified by admission to the curriculum tended to be things of value brought from the outside and imposed paternalistically."[11]

In addition to grammar schools, the missionary movement also took the form of settlement schools, modeled after those in Britain, the Northeast, and, in particular, Jane Addams's Hull House in Chicago. For the most part, the people who led the missionary movement in the development of settlement houses were women. Perhaps one of the best known of these institutions is the

Hindman Settlement School, which was established in 1902. Although Katherine Pettit was a native of Kentucky, she was not from the mountains in eastern Kentucky, and she had received a significant part of her own education in the Northeast. As she came to work in eastern Kentucky, first to develop summer programs for young children and later to develop the settlement school, she implemented the patterns of education that she had seen in the Northeast. The settlement school was designed to be community based and to provide cultural and educational activities for the entire community, not just the children.[12]

Although settlement schools sought to preserve mountain culture, some analysts have accused missionaries of modifying reality to make it more worthy, in their minds, of being preserved. At the time of the schools' development, for example, the banjo was a highly popular instrument, yet in the music classes at the settlement houses, the mountain dulcimer was introduced and promoted as more appropriate to the highly romanticized image of Appalachian people as speakers of archaic English and lovers of fine crafts. As Whisnant claims, settlement schools were "based upon a flawed reading of local culture, as well as upon a naïve analysis of the relationship between culture, political and economic power, and social change."[13] While Addams's Hull House became an advocate for confronting important social and economic issues, the founders of the Appalachian settlement schools ignored these issues, seemingly almost deliberately. For example, negative consequences of the industrialization of Appalachia by entrepreneurs outside the region were never dealt with by the founders. In fact, settlement schools were often supported by the coal companies and therefore could not be openly critical of the injustices imposed on the workers in the mines. Whisnant concludes, however, that the settlement schools probably did a good job of providing academic training for children in the region. Schools were provided for kindergarten children initially, then boarding schools were provided for older children who came from farther distances in the region. Settlement schools claimed to have promoted education for children who would return to their homes to live and work, but in fact, they were the best escape route for young people who wished to leave the region. As public schools became more prevalent in the 1920s and 1930s, the educational functions, for children, of the mission and settlement schools were largely discontinued, and activities centered more on adult education, crafts and mountain culture, and recreation.

By the late 1800s, all states had legislative documentation to indicate that public schools must be provided.[14] Almost all states report that the Civil War had a disastrous effect on public education, and states that had made progress prior to the 1860s were faced with a mammoth task of rebuilding the schools after the war. With all of the factors involved in reconstruction, education for all students was not systematically implemented until the early part of the twentieth century. Even though the Kalamazoo case in 1874 set the precedent for using taxes to fund secondary education, high schools in the Appalachian region were not common until well after the 1900s.[15] In addition, the school terms may have varied from as little as four months a year to a more standard eight or nine months of the year. Tennessee implemented a compulsory school law in 1913 and was one of the first southern states to do so. By the 1920s, all states in the United States had compulsory school laws on the books.[16]

Because so much negative publicity was given to the educational level of the people in the region and the quality of the school facilities and resources, education was a focus of national efforts. As early as 1895, the National Education Association appointed the Committee of Twelve to examine the quality of education in Appalachia and to make recommendations about what should be done. Philander P. Claxton, a native of Tennessee and commissioner of education, focused attention on the type of education that would be most appropriate for the people. On one hand, outsiders bemoaned the state of education in the region and advocated that everyone should have the same quality and type of education that was provided in other areas of the country. With the appointment of the Country Life Commission in 1908 and 1909, some observers noted, however, that providing traditional education experiences, which focused primarily upon the basics and the classics, would result in making people dissatisfied with their lives in the region and would thus contribute to migration from the region. The overwhelming concern seemed to be that such a migration would reduce food production and diminish supply to more urban areas.[17]

Claxton had traveled to Denmark and was familiar with the folk schools there, which focused not only on the basics in education but also on vocational and craft training. He once said of the educational needs of the region, "Their greatest need is good schools adapted to their conditions—schools that will make them intelligent about the life they live; that will teach them what they need to know to enable them to adjust themselves to their environment and to conquer it; schools that will appeal to children and grown people alike; schools with courses of study growing out of their daily life as it is and turning back into it a better and more efficient daily living."[18]

Claxton began to promote the idea of vocational education as being exceptionally important for the region, not only to remedy adult illiteracy but also to provide training for high school students. The Campbell Folk School of North Carolina resulted from Claxton's introduction of the folk school notion to John C. Campbell, who with his wife, Olive Dame Campbell, established the well-known school that exists to this day. The school continues to be open to a wide range of ages and ability levels, and its focus is on the development of skills for enriching one's life. Claxton was intrigued with the notion of incorporating this type of education into all schools in the region and hoped that vocational education experiences in the public schools would reflect the philosophy of his school.[19]

In addition to focusing on the curriculum that might be most appropriate for people in the region, the Committee of Twelve soon concluded that one of the problems with the school systems was that there were simply too many schools to fund at a level that would be beneficial to the residents of the region. Thus the committee recommended that schools be consolidated to improve the buildings and to offer a wider range of course offerings. Although most people think of school consolidation as a phenomenon occurring in the latter part of the twentieth century, the beginning of the end of the stereotypical one-room schoolhouse, the community school, and the small high school began as early as 1910.[20]

Although much had already been written qualitatively about educational dilemmas in the region, one of the earliest systematic studies of education was published in 1937 by the U.S. Department of the Interior's Office of Education, titled *Education in the Southern Mountains.* The specific intent of this study was to determine if the quality of education in six southern states (Georgia, Kentucky, North Carolina, Tennessee, Virginia, and West Virginia) differed for white students who lived in mountainous areas versus those who lived in more densely populated areas. The percentage of students attending school in the most mountainous regions was reported to be consistently lower than that of students in more urban parts of the states. In every state, students from nonmountainous areas were more likely to attend high school. In some mountain communities, it appeared that no high school was available, and while the area's students may have been in school after age sixteen, they were attending an elementary school. With the exception of West Virginia, schools of more mountainous counties seldom retained more than a fourth of their students through high school. One factor that seemed to be associated with higher school attendance rates in West Virginia was simply the proximity of the school to the children, especially for elementary-aged children; if a school was nearby, children were more likely to attend.[21]

The comparison of the length of the school term also revealed that children in nonmountainous communities were in school approximately two months longer than were students in mountainous communities. Illiteracy rates for all of the six states were higher than for the nation as a whole. A higher percentage of students in mountain communities were over age for their grade level. With the exception of West Virginia, teachers were better trained and more experienced in the nonmountain regions. In all states, teachers in the nonmountain communities were more highly paid. Money expended for schools in general was significantly less in mountain communities; in some cases, such as Georgia, funding for schools was nearly 300 percent higher for nonmountain communities than for those in the mountains. Buildings were much less valuable in the mountainous communities. In nonmountainous communities, there was a higher proportion of taxable adults in the general population. Transportation was less likely to be provided in the mountainous areas, and the rate of attendance dropped as schools were located farther from homes. In communities where school attendance was low, children had to travel farther to reach the school.[22]

The Gaumnitz and Cook study also reported on the availability of denominational and independent nonpublic schools. At the time of the study in 1937, there were 162 nonpublic schools, and 44 were elementary schools. Fifteen schools offered junior college work, and 12 were four-year college institutions. Due to accessibility problems, some of these schools were boarding schools. In some cases, these private schools were better able to provide for the residents than the public schools. However, as public schools were becoming more available, independent schools were either likely to work cooperatively with the public school system or to be phased out.[23]

Education in the Southern Mountains was significant in that it pointed toward themes that would emerge throughout the study of education in the Appalachian region: discrepancies between the educational experiences of children living in mountainous and nonmountainous regions; the low income levels of families in the mountainous regions, which contributed to a low level of funding for public schools; poor attendance rates; high illiteracy rates; and poor qualifications of teachers in the mountainous areas. Although the study was relatively dismal in terms of its findings, the authors were quick to note that the situation in all of the southern states seemed to be improving, particularly in the mountainous regions, and especially in the educational experiences provided for the younger children of the region.[24]

As the country became engrossed in World War II, attention in the media seemed to shift, and for more than a decade, not much was written about the poor educational conditions of people in Appalachia. But Appalachia was rediscovered with a vengeance in the 1960s. Article after article appeared in both the educational and popular literature, most telling the same story. Some of the commonly reported statistics were that 70 percent of the adult population had completed fewer than eight years of school, the school dropout rate was as high as 65 percent, and the construction needs of the thirteen states identified as

Appalachian by the Appalachian Regional Commission accounted for 42 percent of the construction needs of the entire country.[25] Articles about the region acknowledged that "the average mountaineer is fully committed to the idea of education for his children, but often he does not know, and cannot know, what effective education is, or how it can be achieved."[26] Writing took on what now seems to be an especially condemning and blaming tone: "Applying every yardstick of social well being, their Appalachian homeland emerges a sordid blemish on the balance sheet of the wealthiest nation in history. You name it—school, health services, housing, per capita income—and the Appalachian south stacks up as an underdeveloped region which produces citizens incapable of realizing their human potential in the complex twentieth century. Their stunted growth not only saps the vitality of the mid-South, but also weakens the nation."[27]

As the negative statistics and images continued to proliferate in the media, analysts began to focus on factors that contributed to the situation. Of primary concern was the way school systems were funded. As is described in other chapters of this book, much of the wealth of the region was, and continues to be, controlled by individuals and corporations outside of the region. States had failed to develop tax structures that would tap into the wealth that was flowing from Appalachia. Because schools were funded through taxes on individuals residing within the region, and because most of the jobs were relatively low paying, property and income taxes netted little for school funding. Exploitation of the region had become a vicious cycle—resources were largely controlled outside of the region, jobs were low paying in the region, and motivation and resources to complete higher forms of education were lacking. Without appropriate education, workers could not move beyond low-level jobs. Those who completed higher levels of education and were capable of earning higher incomes were forced to leave in order to find work. Hence, resources for schools continued to stay low.[28]

Some writers again began to question the relevance of public school curricula. Following the models and patterns that had developed in the earliest days of public schooling, in which curricula and instructional strategies were imported from outside the region, little attention was devoted to helping students understand the issues of their own region or develop a sense of place. Few teachers were provided information that would help them do so.[29]

Complicating the problem with schools in the region was the ongoing press toward consolidation of schools in order to be more economically efficient and provide a broader range of educational offerings, particularly to college-bound students, in the areas of advanced science, math, and foreign languages. This strategy is one that the educational establishment in the country at large had embraced, but within the communities of the Appalachian region, resistance to consolidation was evident. Nonetheless, by the end of the 1970s, practically every county system within the Appalachian region had been consolidated to permit one central high school with only a few feeder elementary and middle schools.[30]

With the formation of the Appalachian Regional Commission (ARC), attention focused on improving education, with once more the concept of vocational education being touted as the solution to the region's economic and educational problems. Although the journal *Appalachia,* published by ARC, includes numerous examples of positive changes effected in education through the ARC, including school construction and instructional innovations, most analysts conclude that funding has always been too low, and the political processes too entangled, to have effected significant change in the educational climate, and subsequently the economic conditions, of the region.[31]

The most prolific writing about education in Appalachia occurred during the late 1960s and early 1970s, as researchers attempted to understand the dynamics of the region's educational needs.[32] The field of rural education blossomed, and educators and researchers within the region began to study the issues in education from an insider perspective. For the first time in the history of education within Appalachia, it was not outside investigators who were doing the bulk of the writing about the region. Although numerous articles discuss a variety of factors that affect the inclination of young Appalachians to continue in school, the relationship between the economic health of the region and the overall quality of education continued to be the major focus.

With the publication of *A Nation at Risk* in 1983 by a commission appointed by President Ronald Reagan to assess the quality of America's schools, the overall quality of education in the United States was deemed to be so poor that it posed a security risk. Although there are those who question the validity of the findings, poor test scores of students in the United States as compared to those in other countries have commanded mass media attention. For once, the Appalachian region was not singled out for its educational failures. A wave of educational reform has swept the country since 1983, with calls for higher standards for students in all areas of the country. Goals 2000, developed first in the George H. W. Bush administration and continued through the Clinton administration, focused attention on improving education throughout the country. At the heart of educational reform are calls for higher standards and more rigorous curricula for all students and better preparation of teachers. As studies of effective schools have become more widespread, calls for broad reform of school structures in order to incorporate more locally governed schools have been a major part of the picture. Funding made available through Goals 2000 to the states, although still inadequate, has encouraged the development of education reform at the local level.

Interestingly enough, as the educational reform movement has progressed from the 1980s through the end of the century, leadership has been provided by some of the states in the region. Although not without its critics, the Kentucky Education Reform Act (KERA) has received considerable positive attention for its sweeping changes and innovations in the state. Tests scores and other measures of achievement have improved in Kentucky as the new systems have been implemented, and school systems are being encouraged to find ways to involve parents more actively in schools and to create smaller school communities, a feature of schooling that has much appeal to families in the Appalachian region.[33] In the 2000 issue of the *Quality Counts* report on technology, published by *Education Week,* West Virginia was deemed to be "a bright spot."[34]

A review of the 2000 statistics about the dropout rate for students in the Appalachian states is still somewhat discouraging. The only Appalachian states that rank in the top half of the country are Virginia and West Virginia, and when the figures for the percentage of children living in poverty are examined, only Virginia is in the top half of the national rankings. Kentucky and West Virginia both have 25 percent of their children living in poverty.[35] The latter statistic is perhaps the most significant, for while educational researchers report that schools have actually improved nationwide since the implementation of reform efforts, improvements are not evident in the poorest communities.[36] Many of the same patterns that existed in the early 1937 Department of Interior study seem to persist: lower funding and resource allocation for the most remote and poorest areas of the Appalachian states.

Colleges and Universities in the Region

Although education for children in grades K–12 (kindergarten to twelfth grade) is the one most universally experienced, the development and impact of colleges and universities cannot be ignored. When one thinks of the Appalachian region's colleges, certain names, such as Berea College, Berry College, and Alice Lloyd College, automatically come to mind.[37] These private and/or denominationally affiliated institutions had their early beginnings as outgrowths of the missionary movement; they started as grammar schools and progressed to serving college-aged students. For example, Warren Wilson College in North Carolina had its beginnings as one of the better-known missionary schools.[38] The school began in 1896 as the Asheville Farm School, then merged with the Dorland-Bell School to become the Warren Wilson Vocational Junior College. As one of the longest running missionary efforts, Warren Wilson graduated its last mission high school class in 1957 and became a four-year liberal arts college in 1966. Berea, established in 1855, has long had the tradition of serving the region's youth, providing free tuition and work opportunities for students, both black and white, who otherwise could not attend college.[39] The Augusta Academy was established in 1749 in Lexington, Virginia. It went through several transformations and, as Liberty Hall Academy, became a college in 1796, and finally went on to become Washington and Lee University.[40] Other colleges followed shortly, including Greeneville College in Greeneville, Tennessee, in 1784 (later Tusculum College), and the University of Tennessee, founded in 1794 as Blount College. Many private colleges were founded by Presbyterians, but Methodists, Disciples of Christ, and Baptists also supported the development of colleges in the region. As early as 1850, there were at least twelve denominationally affiliated colleges in the region.[41]

The establishment of large, public universities in the region was boosted by the passage of the Morrill Land Grant College Acts in 1862 and 1890. Virginia Polytechnic Institute, Clemson, West Virginia University, West Virginia State, and the University of Tennessee all became beneficiaries of the Land Grant College Acts. The establishment of these universities greatly expanded the professional development opportunities for students in the region, particularly as curricula were expanded to include graduate and other professional programs.

Still other colleges and universities evolved to serve the need for competent teachers for the increasing number of public schools. Beginning in the late 1800s and early 1900s, several institutions were developed specifically as normal schools for the training of teachers, most of whom came from the region and had little or no more education than that received in the local mountain grammar schools. Institutions such as East Tennessee State University, Appalachian State University and Western Carolina University in North Carolina, Fairmont State University in West Virginia, Morehead State University in Kentucky, and Radford University in Virginia are among those institutions established specifically for the training of teachers. These colleges evolved to become comprehensive universities with specializations in many different curricular areas, offering graduate as well as undergraduate programs.

Again mirroring national patterns, the region's colleges and universities seem to have reached a higher level of quality and esteem than the public schools for children in the K–12 grades. It is not uncommon to see many of the institutions highly ranked in national polls. Some of the same criticisms leveled at the K–12 institutions are also aimed at colleges and universities; too often, colleges and universities have neglected to instill an appreciation for the region in which they are located. And too often, as Loyal Jones states, the curriculum of some of the finest regional institutions seem to be elitist. As an example, Jones notes that even at Berea College, which is specifically devoted to serving students from Appalachia, the music program focuses exclusively on classical music, paying no attention to traditional mountain music.[42]

On the other hand, scholars at colleges and universities throughout the region have been the impetus for the development of the Appalachian studies movement, and journals such as *Appalachian Journal, Journal of the Appalachian Studies Association, Now and Then,* and *Appalachian Heritage* have done much to raise awareness of issues in the region. Several institutions provide specific programs focusing on the uniqueness of the region. For example, Radford University began to offer a minor in Appalachian studies in 1981. Today the curricular program continues to operate out of the Appalachian Regional Studies Center, along with extensive outreach activities in the public schools of southwest Virginia. East Tennessee State University offers an Appalachian studies minor, has a program of study in bluegrass and country music, and provides a Center for Appalachian Studies that archives numerous items relevant to the study of the region. Berea College has long been known for its Appalachian Studies Center, which also includes extensive archives. Other colleges and universities, such as Emory and Henry College, have become known for providing opportunities in the curriculum to help students develop the skills for activism in the region. A recurring issue is, of course, that graduates of institutions will only stay in the region if they can find ways to earn a living.

Summary

A number of patterns and issues about education in Appalachia have emerged:

1. Although not unique to Appalachia, there is an integral linking of education and economics. Because resources have flowed from the region, and tax structures have not been altered significantly to tap into those resources, the mountainous regions of Appalachia, in particular, have suffered economically. The availability of funding for education and the jobs available for graduates of educational institutions are perhaps the two greatest factors in determining the quality of education in the region.

2. From the earliest settlement of the region, ideas about education and what was appropriate for the people of the region came from experts outside the region rather than from those within the region.

3. Again not totally unique to Appalachia, educational institutions have focused on curriculum and instructional strategies that have often been insensitive to the cultural context of the region.

4. Consolidation of schools has further isolated the people of the region from the educational experiences that can be provided for the youth of the region. Whereas parent and community support of a local high school might have been high, the placement of that high school to a more remote, central locale

has diminished parent involvement and ownership of their children's educational experiences.

5. Institutions of higher education and K–12 schools can be considered almost to have a codependent relationship. Because many of the colleges and universities draw their students from the region, the quality of the students coming to colleges will depend upon the quality of education received in the K–12 schools. On the other hand, because most teachers in K–12 schools attend schools within the region, the quality of educational experiences provided in K–12 settings depends largely on the quality of the teachers who graduate from the institutions of higher education in the region.

6. With the emphasis upon educational reform nationally since the 1980s, and the publication of effective school research, the region is in the position to reassert some of the qualities that strengthened schools in the past (such as maintaining small schools and parent involvement).

These issues and patterns will likely continue to affect education in the region.[43] Policy makers and educators who attempt to improve the quality of education will undoubtedly have to address these issues before the overall quality of education can be improved significantly. This might seem to be a somewhat dismal prospect, given the nature of the economic picture in the Appalachian region. Given the available income, however, there are things that can be done to maximize the quality of education received by individuals within the region.

To close, one approach to education that was actually developed in the region and has shown past success and future promise is the Foxfire approach. It is rooted in the thirty-year history of the production of *Foxfire,* a student-produced magazine, and the series of *Foxfire* books documenting Appalachian traditions. *Foxfire* began in a high school English class in Rabun County, Georgia, when the teacher, Eliot Wigginton, encountered repeated failure to motivate students to engage in meaningful learning activities. Out of frustration, the teacher and students launched a student magazine, named *Foxfire,* which was edited and expanded into the popular *Foxfire* book series documenting Appalachian traditions.[44] In spite of their commercial success, the *Foxfire* books have received mixed reviews for their contribution to the folklore literature. However, since the late 1980s, perhaps the most valuable contribution of *Foxfire* has been in the modeling of an approach to teaching. Initial efforts to replicate *Foxfire's* success resulted in some two hundred short-lived magazine projects, and it was not until twenty years after the founding of *Foxfire* that training to "do *Foxfire*" focused not on magazines and books but on the approach to teaching used in the process of producing the magazine and book series. The Foxfire mission is now ". . . to teach, model, and refine an active, learner-centered approach to education which is academically sound and promotes continuous interaction between students and their communities, so that students will find fulfillment as creative, productive, critical citizens."[45]

The approach is used not only in the Appalachian region but also across the nation by teachers of students from preschool through the college years, as documented in the Foxfire Fund's early magazine for teachers, *Hands On,* and its more recent publication, *The Active Learner.* Much of what was documented in the early days of implementation of the approach by teachers other than Wigginton took the form of descriptions of projects completed in classrooms. In order to articulate the essential elements of the Foxfire approach more clearly, a list of core practices was devised, based on the reflections of students and teachers on the qualities of good teachers and memorable learning activities from their own past educational experiences. Beginning originally with nine core practice statements, with an admission that the refinement process is continuous, the list (in abbreviated form) includes the following: (1) the work teachers and learners do together is infused from the beginning with learner choice, design, and revision; (2) the role of the teacher is that of facilitator and collaborator; (3) the academic integrity of the work teachers and learners do together is clear; (4) the work is characterized by active learning; (5) peer teaching, small group work, and team work are all consistent features of classroom activities; (6) connections between the classroom work, the surrounding communities, and the world beyond the community are clear; (7) there is an audience beyond the teacher for learner work; (8) new activities spiral gracefully out of the old, incorporating lessons learned from past experiences and building on skills and understanding that can now be amplified; (9) imagination and creativity are encouraged in the completion of learning activities; (10) reflection is an essential activity that takes place at key points throughout the work; and (11) the work teachers and learners do together includes rigorous, ongoing assessment and evaluation.[46]

When teachers use Foxfire core practices to guide the ways in which they teach, they begin first with the state- and/or locally mandated curricular objectives. They share the objectives with the students in their classrooms, and they try to find ways in which the knowledge, attitudes, and skills implied in the objectives are used in the world outside the classroom. Students make decisions about how they will meet the objectives by designing activities and projects that have some application beyond the classroom. Students and teachers in the region have completed an array of projects, all, like the original *Foxfire* books, infused with student decision making, but with a great variety of end results: developing nature trails, managing school stores, producing orientation manuals for new students coming into middle schools, initiating recycling programs in schools, and on and on. Although current reform and research-based movements in education advocate many of the same ideas articulated in the core practices, it is the element of student decision making and empowerment that seems to be, if not a unique contribution, at least one of the most outstanding contributions that the approach has made to the field of education. Once students and teachers begin to make decisions together, the entire atmosphere in the classroom changes, and students and teachers alike testify to the fact that the empowerment spills over into other aspects of their lives beyond the classroom. The approach, if used faithfully and over time, has the real potential to empower the youngest citizens of the Appalachian region to become increasingly decisive about how their lives will be led.

This chapter has highlighted some of the historical patterns of education in Appalachia that have shaped the ways in which educational experiences are currently provided. Although economic considerations are still of grave concern, at least the locus of control seems to be shifting back to the people of the region. With more emphasis upon school reform that invites participation by both students and parents, and with greater emphasis upon the uniqueness of the region at the college level, the potential for positive change appears to be greater than at any other time.

Wahoo School, Indian Valley, Virginia, c. 1928. From the collection of Ricky Cox.

SHARON TEETS

John C. Campbell Folk School, Brasstown, North Carolina. By Katherine A. Combiths.

Pulaski County High School, Pulaski, Virginia, constructed during the peak of the school consolidation movement. By Pete Huber.

Students and staff picnicking on the grounds of the Christiansburg Institute, c. 1908.
Courtesy of Ann S. Bailey.

Appalachian School of Law, Grundy, Virginia. By John C. Nemeth.

Notes

1. Kevin Ryan and James M. Cooper, *Those Who Can, Teach,* 10th ed. (New York: Houghton Mifflin, 2001).

2. Lincoln David Kelsey and Cannon Charles Herne, *Cooperative Extension Work* (Ithaca, N.Y.: Comstock Publishing Association, 1963).

3. Jim B. Pearson and Edgar Fuller, eds., *Education in the United States: Historical Development and Outlook* (Washington, D.C.: National Education Association of the United States, 1969).

4. Myra P. Sadker and David M. Sadker, *Teachers, Schools, and Society,* 6th ed. (Boston: McGraw-Hill, 2003).

5. Ina W. Van Noppen and John J. Van Noppen, *Western North Carolina Since the Civil War* (Boone, N.C.: Appalachian Consortium Press, 1973).

6. Sadker and Sadker, *Teachers, Schools, and Society.*

7. Ronald D Eller, *Miners, Millhands, and Mountaineers: Industrialization of the Appalachian South, 1880–1930* (Knoxville: Univ. of Tennessee Press, 1982).

8. W. K. McNeil, *Appalachian Images in Folk and Popular Culture,* 2d ed. (Knoxville: Univ. of Tennessee Press, 1995), 171.

9. Ibid., 244.

10. Sadker and Sadker, *Teachers, Schools, and Society.*

11. Richard B. Drake, "The Mission School Era in Southern Appalachia: 1880–1940," *Appalachian Notes* 6 (1978): 5.

12. Henry D. Shapiro, *Appalachia on Our Mind: The Southern Mountains and Mountaineers in American Consciousness, 1870–1920* (Chapel Hill: Univ. of North Carolina Press, 1978).

13. David E. Whisnant, *All that Is Native and Fine: The Politics of Culture in an American Region* (Chapel Hill: Univ. of North Carolina Press, 1983), 11.

14. Charles W. Dabney, *Universal Education in the South,* vols. 1 and 2 (Chapel Hill: Univ. of North Carolina Press, 1936).

15. Sadker and Sadker, *Teachers, Schools, and Society.*

16. Van Noppen and Van Noppen, *Western North Carolina.*

17. Shapiro, *Appalachia on Our Mind.*

18. James Watt Raine, *The Land of the Saddle-Bags* (Lexington: Univ. Press of Kentucky, 1924), 162.

19. Shapiro, *Appalachia on Our Mind.*

20. Ibid.

21. Walton H. Gaumitz and Katherine M. Cook, *Education in the Southern Mountains: Bulletin 1937,* No. 26 (Washington, D.C.: Dept. of the Interior, Office of Education, 1937).

22. Ibid.

23. Ibid.

24. Ibid.

25. Jim G. Branscome, "Annihilating the Hillbilly: The Appalachians' Struggle with America's Institutions," in *Colonialism in Modern America: The Appalachian*

Case, ed. Helen M. Lewis, Linda Johnson, and Donald Askins (Boone, N.C.: Appalachian Consortium Press, 1978), 213–27.

26. Peter Schrag, "The School and Politics," in *Appalachia in the Sixties: Decade of Reawakening,* ed. David S. Walls and John B. Stephenson (Lexington: Univ. Press of Kentucky, 1972), 223.

27. Harry W. Ernst and Charles H. Drake, "The Lost Appalachian," in *Appalachia in the Sixties: Decade of Reawakening,* ed. David S. Walls and John B. Stephenson (Lexington: Univ. Press of Kentucky, 1972), 8.

28. Branscome, "Annihilating the Hillbilly."

29. David N. Mielke, ed., *Teaching Mountain Children: Towards a Foundation of Understanding* (Boone, N.C.: Appalachian Consortium Press, n.d.).

30. Tom Boyd, "Progress Is Our Most Important Product: Decline in Citizen Participation and the Professionalization of Schooling in an Appalachian Rural County," in *Appalachia: Social Context Past and Present,* ed. Bruce Ergood and Bruce E. Kuhre, 3d ed. (Dubuque, Iowa: Kendall/Hunt, 1991), 337–44.

31. Branscome, "Annihilating the Hillbilly."

32. Alan J. DeYoung, *The Life and Death of a Rural American High School* (New York: Garland, 1995).

33. Annie E. Casey Foundation, http://www.aecf.org/kidscount/index.htm.

34. Craig D. Jerald and Bess Keller, "The State of the States: West Virginia," in *Quality Counts 2000: Who Should Teach? Education Week* 19 (Jan. 2000): 161.

35. Annie E. Casey Foundation, http://www.aecf.org/kidscount/index.htm.

36. National Center for Education Statistics, *Condition of Education, 2005.* Http:// nces.ed.gov.

37. P. David Searle, *A College for Appalachia: Alice Lloyd on Caney Creek* (Lexington: Univ. Press of Kentucky, 1995).

38. Warren Wilson College web site, http://www.warren-wilson.edu/history.

39. Richard Sears, *A Utopian Experience in Kentucky: Integration and Social Equality of Berea, 1866–1904* (Westport, Conn.: Greenwood, 1996).

40. Edgar Wallace Knight, ed., *Private and Denominational Efforts,* vol. 4 of *A Documentary History of Education in the South before 1860* (Chapel Hill: Univ. of North Carolina Press, 1953).

41. Richard B. Drake, *A History of Appalachia* (Lexington: Univ. Press of Kentucky, 2001).

42. Loyal Jones, *Faith and Meaning in the Southern Uplands* (Urbana: Univ. of Indiana Press, 1999).

43. Phillip J. Obermiller and Michael E. Maloney, *Appalachia: Social Context Past and Present* (Dubuque, Iowa: Kendall/Hunt, 2002).

44. Eliot Wigginton, *Sometimes a Shining Moment* (Garden City, N.Y.: Anchor Press/Doubleday, 1985).

45. Sarah D. Hatton, ed., *The Active Learner* 4 (1992).

46. Ibid, 7.

140

Suggested Readings

Adams, Frank. *Unearthing Seeds of Fire: The Idea of Highlander.* Winston-Salem, N.C.: John F. Blair, 1975.

Annie E. Casey Foundation. Http://www.aecf.org/kidscount/index.htm.

Barker, Garry. *Notes from a Native Son: Essays on the Appalachian Experience.* Knoxville: Univ. of Tennessee Press, 1995.

Boyd, Tom. "Progress Is Our Most Important Product: Decline in Citizen Participation and the Professionalization of Schooling in an Appalachian Rural County." In *Appalachia: Social Context Past and Present,* edited by B. Ergood and B. E. Kuhre, 337–44. 3d ed. Dubuque, Iowa: Kendall/Hunt, 1991.

Bradshaw, Michael. *The Appalachian Regional Commission: Twenty-five Years of Government Policy.* Lexington: Univ. Press of Kentucky, 1992.

Branscome, Jim G. "Annihilating the Hillbilly: The Appalachians' Struggle with America's Institutions." In *Colonialism in Modern America: The Appalachian Case,* edited by Helen M. Lewis, Linda Johnson, and Donald Askins, 213–27. Boone, N.C.: Appalachian Consortium Press, 1978.

Clark, Mike. "Education and Exploitation." In *Colonialism in Modern America: The Appalachian Case,* edited by Helen M. Lewis, Linda Johnson, and Donald Askins. Boone, N.C.: Appalachian Consortium Press, 1978.

Clark, Mike, Jim Branscome, and Bob Snyder. *Appalachian Miseducation.* Huntington, W.Va.: Appalachian Press, 1974.

Cornett, William Terrell. "Untying Some Knots in Knott County: Two Educational Experiments in Eastern Kentucky." In *Appalachia/America: Proceedings of the 1980 Appalachian Studies Conference,* edited by Wilson Somerville. Johnson City, Tenn.: Appalachian Consortium Press, 1981.

Couto, Richard A. *An American Challenge: A Report on Economic Trends and Social Issues in Appalachia.* Dubuque, Iowa: Kendall/Hunt, 1994.

Cunningham, Rodger. *Apples on the Flood: Minority Discourse and Appalachia.* Knoxville: Univ. of Tennessee Press, 1987.

Dabney, Charles W. *Universal Education in the South.* Vols. 1 and 2. Chapel Hill: Univ. of North Carolina Press, 1936.

DeYoung, Alan J. *The Life and Death of a Rural American High School.* New York: Garland, 1995.

Drake, Richard B. *A History of Appalachia.* Lexington: Univ. Press of Kentucky, 2001.

———. "The Mission School Era in Southern Appalachia: 1880–1940." *Appalachian Notes* 6 (1978).

Eller, Ronald D. *Miners, Millhands, and Mountaineers: Industrialization of the Appalachian South, 1880–1930.* Knoxville: Univ. of Tennessee Press, 1982.

———. *Ron Eller's Lecture Notes for Appalachian History.* Http://www.uky.edu/RGS/AppalCenter/eller2.htm.

Ergood, Bruce, and Bruce E. Kuhre, eds. *Appalachia: Social Context Past and Present.* 3d ed. Dubuque, Iowa: Kendall/Hunt, 1991.

Ernst, Harry W., and Charles H. Drake. "The Lost Appalachian." In *Appalachia in the Sixties: Decade of Reawakening,* edited by David S. Walls and John B. Stephenson, 3–10. Lexington: Univ. Press of Kentucky, 1972.

Forderhase, Nancy. "Settlement School Goes to the People: Pine Mountain School's Community Centers at Big Laurel and Line Fork, 1919–1940." In *The Impact of Institutions in Appalachia: Proceedings of the 8th Annual Appalachian Studies Conference,* edited by Jim Lloyd and Anne G. Campbell, 88–99. Boone, N.C.: Appalachian Consortium Press, 1986.

Gaumnitz, W. H., and K. M. Cook, eds. *Education in the Southern Mountains: Bulletin 1937,* No. 26. Washington, D.C.: Dept. of the Interior, Office of Education, 1937.

Glen, John M. *Highlander: No Ordinary School, 1932–1962.* 2d ed. Knoxville: Univ. of Tennessee Press, 1996.

Hatton, Sarah D., ed. *The Active Learner* 4 (1992).

Jerald, Craig D., and Bess Keller. "The State of the States: West Virginia." In *Quality Counts 2000: Who Should Teach? Education Week* 19 (Jan. 2000): 161.

Jones, Loyal. *Faith and Meaning in the Southern Uplands.* Urbana: Univ. of Illinois Press, 1999.

Kelsey, Lincoln David, and Cannon Charles Hearne. *Cooperative Extension Work.* Ithaca, N.Y.: Comstock Publishing Association, 1963.

Knight, Edgar W., ed. *Private and Denominational Efforts.* Vol. 4 of *A Documentary History of Education in the South before 1860.* Chapel Hill: Univ. of North Carolina Press, 1953.

———. *Toward Educational Independence.* Vol. 2 of *A Documentary History of Education in the South before 1860.* Chapel Hill: Univ. of North Carolina Press, 1950.

LeMaster, J. R., ed. *Jesse Stuart on Education.* Lexington: Univ. Press of Kentucky, 1992.

McNeil, W. K. *Appalachian Images in Folk and Popular Culture.* 2d ed. Knoxville: Univ. of Tennessee Press, 1995.

Mielke, David N., ed. *Teaching Mountain Children: Towards a Foundation of Understanding.* Boone, N.C.: Appalachian Consortium Press.

National Center for Education Statistics. *Condition of Education, 1998.* Http://nces.ed.gov.

National Commission on Excellence in Education. *A Nation at Risk: The Imperative for Educational Reform.* Washington, D.C.: GPO, 1983.

Obermiller, Phillip J., and Michael E. Maloney. *Appalachia: Social Context Past and Present.* Dubuque, Iowa: Kendall/Hunt, 2002.

Pearson, Jim B., and Edgar Fuller, eds. *Education in the United States: Historical Development and Outlook.* Washington, D.C.: National Education Association of the United States, 1969.

Puckett, John L. *Foxfire Reconsidered: A Twenty-year Experiment in Progressive Education.* Chicago: Univ. of Illinois Press, 1989.

Raine, James Watt. *The Land of the Saddle-Bags.* Lexington: Univ. Press of Kentucky, 1924.

Ryan, Kevin, and James M. Cooper. *Those Who Can, Teach.* 10th ed. New York: Houghton Mifflin, 2003.

Sadker, Myra P., and David M. Sadker. *Teachers, Schools, and Society.* 6th ed. Boston: McGraw-Hill, 2003.

Schrag, Peter. "The School and Politics." In *Appalachia in the Sixties: Decade of Reawakening,* edited by David S. Walls and John B. Stephenson. Lexington: Univ. Press of Kentucky, 1972.

Searle, P. David. *A College for Appalachia: Alice Lloyd on Caney Creek.* Lexington: Univ. Press of Kentucky, 1995.

Sears, Richard. *A Utopian Experience in Kentucky: Integration and Social Equality of Berea, 1866–1904.* Westport, Conn.: Greenwood, 1996.

Shapiro, Henry D. *Appalachia on our Mind: The Southern Mountains and Mountaineers in American Consciousness, 1870–1920.* Chapel Hill: Univ. of North Carolina Press, 1978.

Stokely, Jim. "To Make a Life: Settlement Institutions of Appalachia." In *Appalachia: Social Context Past and Present,* edited by Bruce Ergood and Bruce E. Kuhre. 3d ed. Dubuque, Iowa: Kendall/Hunt, 1991.

Stuart, Jesse. *The Thread that Runs So True.* New York: Charles Scribner's Sons, 1949.

Turner, William H., and Edward J. Cabbell, eds. *Blacks in Appalachia.* Lexington: Univ. Press of Kentucky, 1985.

Van Noppen, Ina W., and John J. Van Noppen. *Western North Carolina Since the Civil War.* Boone, N.C.: Appalachian Consortium Press, 1973.

Walls, David S., and John B. Stephenson, eds. *Appalachia in the Sixties: Decade of Reawakening.* Lexington: Univ. Press of Kentucky, 1972.

Warren Wilson College. Web site. Http://www.warren-wilson.edu/history.

Whisnant, David E. *All that Is Native and Fine: The Politics of Culture in an American Region.* Chapel Hill: Univ. of North Carolina Press, 1983.

———. *Modernizing the Mountaineer.* Boone, N.C.: Appalachian Consortium Press, 1980.

Wigginton, Eliot. *Sometimes a Shining Moment.* Garden City, N.Y.: Anchor Press/ Doubleday, 1985.

Williamson, Jerry W., and Edwin T. Arnold. *Interviewing Appalachia: The Appalachian Journal Interviews, 1978–1992.* Knoxville: Univ. of Tennessee Press, 1994.

APPALACHIAN FOLKLIFE

DEBORAH THOMPSON AND IRENE MOSER

Folk Beginnings

The diversity of immigrants to the Appalachian region over time has resulted in a rich and complex folklife. Storytelling, food preservation techniques, traditional building designs, fiddle tunes, banjo "licks," basketry, wood carving, dance steps, and the use of native plants contribute to the active and distinctive expression of mountain culture. Scholars commonly use the term "folklife" to refer to such informally learned behaviors, customs, and artifacts, especially when they have elements that reappear across generations or in other parts of the region, country, or globe. Important contributions to folklife in the southern mountains have been made by a wide variety of groups, including Native American, Scots-Irish, Jewish, German, French Huguenot, Welsh, English, African American, Slavic, and southern European peoples. Hmong immigrants from the mountains of Southeast Asia as well as Latinos from Mexico and Central America added their traditions to the mix around the turn of the twenty-first century.

To Appalachians of today, as in the past, urban and trade centers bring new ideas and neighbors, academic researchers, cultural revivalists, and changing markets and audiences for cultural products. Our exploration of this folklife reveals a panorama of artistic and technological creativity linking people through informal networks of kinship, trade and transportation, and shared historical experiences. Networks centered on the family have especially encouraged the continuous learning of traditional arts, crafts, and technologies as well as the individual creativity and variety that signals a living folk culture.

The many artifacts left by generations of Native Americans before European colonization attest to the folklife of the region's earliest settlers. Newly plowed fields in springtime regularly yield ancient treasures of arrow and spear points, pottery shards, and grinding stones. When observed with the knowledge provided by cultural tradition and archaeological study, such objects can explain attitudes, traditions, and beliefs. A lively part of the region's folklore reflects a mystique centered on the region's first peoples. The disputed origin of such place names as Swannanoa, Cullowhee, Kanawha, Kentucky, and Tennessee; legends of the Cherokee "Little People"; such ballads as "The Little Mohee" (even though "Mohee" probably refers to a Pacific Islander, most people think of her as Indian); questions concerning Melungeon origins; and such fiddle tunes as "Lost Indian"—all of these reflect the ongoing strong interest in the region's earliest settlers.

With the discovery of gold on Cherokee lands came the forced removal of 1838, called the Trail of Tears, resulting in over four thousand American Indian deaths. The Cherokee who went west (the "darkening land" in Cherokee belief) said goodbye to their homelands, but a few hid in remote areas of the Smoky Mountains and became the parents and grandparents of the Eastern Band of the Cherokee. Despite this great tragedy, the Eastern Cherokee have returned from near extinction to create a lively community on the Oconaluftee River and elsewhere in the Great Smoky Mountains. Additionally, about one-third of mountain people, like other southerners both black and white, trace part of their ethnic heritage to Native Americans, most often to a Cherokee ancestor. At their annual Fall Festival, the Cherokee people celebrate and share their living heritage with native peoples from as far away as Canada and Florida, as well as with their non-Indian neighbors. Storytellers such as Freeman Owl, Lloyd Arneach, and Kathi Littlejohn; traditional foods including chestnut bread and bean bread; Walker Calhoun's dancers; the stick-ball game; and such fine crafts persons as basket maker Emma Taylor celebrate these earliest roots of mountain culture and maintain them for the next generations.

Folk Beliefs, Healing, and Foodways

European pioneers learned how to survive in their new environment from Indian neighbors, relatives, and enemies. Knowledge of edible plants and medicinal herbs was especially important. Settlers needed to know, for example, when the native chestnuts, hickory nuts, butternuts, hazelnuts, and chinquapins ripen, which berries are edible, and where to find ramps (wild garlic) and ginseng. Native peoples shared their expertise in cultivating beans, squash, tobacco, tomatoes, and maize with their new neighbors. How to prepare the versatile maize by boiling, roasting, or grinding into meal for nutritious bread, hominy, and grits was another critical part of that learning.

The Scots-Irish extended the use of this new kind of corn by adapting a medieval European tradition of pot still liquor. By substituting maize corn for the original barley grain ("John Barley Corn"), they developed a highly prized product, one more profitably hauled to market in its liquid form than in bushel baskets. Due to the whiskey tax levy in the nineteenth century, distilleries were often hidden and operated only at night. Thus mountain "moonshine" corn whiskey was born. Much folklore centers around this brew, its proper production, ways to check its potency, and stories of still locations and encounters with revenue agents, or "revenuers."

Euro-Americans adapted their own planting traditions to their new environment and created new Appalachian folk beliefs. Today, perhaps unknowingly using a Cherokee sacred number system, they may sow four bean, squash, or corn seeds in evenly spaced mounds of soil, commonly known as hills. At the same time, they draw authority from the Old Testament, especially the book of Ecclesiastes, to plant by the signs, interpreted astrologically. The almanac provides information on the moon's phases and the position of the zodiac signs. Root crops (e.g., carrots and potatoes) grow best if planted on the dark or waning of the moon; plants harvested above ground, like beans and corn, grow bigger when planted on a waxing moon or in the light of the moon. The position of the stars can also predict when it's best to pull teeth, cut hair, or perform surgery.

Christian belief in healing through the laying on of hands remains active. Other fusions of Christianity and secular traditions also persist. Some people continue to plant their potatoes on Good Friday, regardless of the weather. The power to stop blood flowing from a wound simply by reciting a certain Bible verse is passed down from female to male in a family line. The right person can heal certain illnesses; for example, the seventh son of the seventh son can blow into a baby's mouth to cure thrush. Wart removal is another problem that has many folk cures, including simply being in the presence of a "wart witch."

Due to environmental damage, less than half of the over four hundred medicinal plants used by the Cherokee are readily available today. Though much knowledge is now lost, for generations Cherokee medicine persons as well as white and black "herb doctors" and "granny women" (respected healers in the community experienced in childbirth and home remedy preparation) maintained an active knowledge of plants and their healing powers. A few still remember that tea from the root of goldenseal soothes the stomach, that the poisonous mayapple eases childbirth pains, and that wild cherry bark makes an excellent cough syrup. Spring tonics, poultices, and salves are made from herbs, and other traditional remedies come from turpentine, sulfur, baking soda, and animal tallow. Traditional wild herb gathering techniques often included the planting of the ginseng berries when the root was harvested to ensure future crops. Such traditional practices are critical while the commercial herb market remains active in the region.

While much herbal lore has been lost with the improvement and availability of medicines, traditions related to foodways have remained strong. Across America, the pace of twenty-first-century life, with its accompanying packaged and fast foods, has radically changed our diets. Yet here in the mountains, local farmers' markets, potluck suppers, the church "dinner on the grounds," family reunions, spring ramp festivals, street fairs, and fiddlers' contests are held regularly and still offer a taste of traditional foods. Like southern cooking in general, mountain foodways include both cultivated crops and wild plants rich in vitamins and minerals. Among the most common wild delicacies are sassafras bark and root, morel mushrooms (also known as hickory chicks or mountain oysters), and such wild greens as lamb's-quarters, pokeweed (poke salad or "sallet"), and various cresses. Abundant wild berries have always been important seasonal food: blackberries, blueberries, strawberries, and raspberries (*yona-ugisdi,* "what the bear likes to eat," in Cherokee).

Mountain women have been rightly proud of their skills in preserving foods in root cellars and by drying, salting, canning, pickling, and freezing. Summer beans strung up to dry, known as shuck beans or "leather britches," are valued in the winter, cooked all day with pork seasoning. Dried blueberries make delicious pies at Old Christmas (January 6). From German and French traditions come recipes for making wine, outstanding relishes and sauerkrauts, and delicious sausages and head cheese. Perhaps the most common traditional meal consists of a bowl of soup beans seasoned with pork and served with cornbread, greens, and fried potatoes. Chicken and dumplings grace the table for company and for special events. Vegetable oils have recently replaced lard and pork fat, due to health concerns, but many people still express their preference for the taste of foods cooked with a little "fat back." Favorite family recipes for jam-cakes, stack cakes made with dried apples, fried pies, apple butter, and chow chow are treasured ties to earlier generations and sources of pride for Appalachian cooks and their communities.

Folk beliefs concerning weather predictions linger, although they are not usually taken too seriously. Weather predictions mostly have to do with determining how hard the winters will be, with clues determined by the width of stripes on wooly worms or height of wasp and hornet nests. "Thunder out of season, soon there'll be a freezin'" is but one of many weather-related rhymes and sayings.

Nearly all important events in life, especially those which entail risk and danger, like courtship, marriage, and childbirth, were surrounded by customs ensuring success. The "shivaree" was a good-natured harassment of a newly married couple, which has modern equivalents in soaping the windows of the getaway car and tying tin cans and other noisemakers to the rear. Placing an axe under the childbirth bed for cutting the pain has been replaced by hospital births and pain-killing drugs or natural childbirth under the care of a certified midwife. One thing that has not changed is the importance of visiting with family and friends, spending time and sharing meals.

Various ethnic groups contributed traditions about death and dying to the region. Scots-Irish and Irish immigrants brought with them the belief that the cry of the banshee (in Irish, *bean sidhe*) announces a death. These Celtic peoples may also have been the source of the belief that a bird in the house foretells a death. However, the owl's foretelling a death, an idea common to white and black residents of the region, comes from Native American tradition. In some homes, the clocks are covered on a death or the bees are told so they will not leave. These practices show change in response to technological changes in the society, as do other aspects of folk life. With the advent of the camera in the 1800s, a photograph taken of a family patriarch in his coffin, surrounded by his respectful family, was commonly hung on the house or cabin wall. Today, with the widespread use of funeral homes and the fact that most people die in the hospital, perhaps the most persistent custom surrounding death is to bring food to the family of the deceased.

Material Culture

In the creation of many necessary items, the art and the work are tied together. Whenever possible, doing something necessary meant it should be done well and be pleasing to behold. Thus the aesthetic underpinnings of such practical activities as basket making, weaving and quilting, blacksmithing, stone and wood work, and home building become clearer as these skills become rarer in the community.

Basketry was important for containers of all kinds. The Cherokee, master basket makers, continue to use river cane, honeysuckle vine, hickory and other barks, and splits from the white oak. Non-Cherokee basket makers use all of the above, as well as rounded rods from white oak and synthetic materials. Today's basketmakers, instead of preparing their materials completely by hand, often rely on imported or factory-prepared reed and other nontraditional sources and have incorporated shapes and techniques from other cultures as well.

Of the numerous fiber arts practiced in the region, the best-known forms are the patchwork quilt and the overshot woven coverlet. Before the availability of store-bought blankets, everyday quilts had to be sturdy and serviceable and were often made without attention to pattern. Patterned quilts frequently served as gifts and on guest beds. The common quilt fillers of wool batting, old blankets, and the infrequent homegrown cotton made these items warm for sleeping, but they were also used as insulation hung along the walls or were hung from the ceiling or in doorways to create privacy. Since cotton does not grow well in the mountains, most hand-woven fabric traditionally was linen, wool, or a combination called linsey-woolsey, with a linen warp and wool weft. Printed cottons were out of reach for most farm families but became more available when grain distributors used colorfully printed feed and flour sacks as an incentive for purchase. Synthetics, blends, and factory mill ends have generally replaced rags and leftover scraps as low-cost materials of choice for some crafters, and quilting machines are viewed as laborsaving devices by many today. Some quilters however, still insist on 100 percent cotton fabrics and hand stitching. Despite the rivalry of inexpensive imported bedcovers, the handmade quilt remains a vibrant art form in the mountains.

Like the fiber arts, metalworking and woodworking were skills that were common, at least in a basic form, to every farm and settlement. As populations grew, crafters could specialize more to provide a wider variety of skills and choices to the community. Until the early twentieth century, traveling crafters were common, bringing their skills from community to community, whether they were jacquard weavers, stonemasons, blacksmiths, or clockmakers. Materials used were usually those available in the local area. People in clay-producing areas made pottery for cooking or storage vessels; otherwise, bark, wood, or metal containers served these purposes. Iron was wrought into hinges, locks, tools, wagon wheel rims, and horse and mule shoes.

Stones, though plentiful, make for hard work, so wood traditionally was used for most buildings, and even for some early chimneys. Dry masonry (without mortar) was common. Stonework typically formed foundations, fireplaces and chimneys, retaining walls, and small rock outbuildings such as springhouses and root cellars. Most larger stone buildings in rural areas date from the Depression era of the 1930s; the abundance and availability of stone allowed many people who could not otherwise afford building materials to build homes.

Wood, being readily available and easily worked, in skilled hands yields a wide variety of useful items, from gee-haw whimmydiddles to barns and houses.

Whittling remains an important pastime, resulting in a beautiful animal sculpture, a child's toy or a pile of shavings and a toothpick. Along with creating a carving, it is a productive activity while sitting, visiting, or sharing stories. Essential tools and tool handles, split-rail fences, furniture, toys, walking sticks, musical instruments, and buildings were generally made to last. For traditional craftspeople, art and function join to create a classic design or, through innovation and experimentation, a unique piece of folk art.

Wood has from earliest settlement times provided the basic building material in Appalachia. Common types of vernacular or folk architecture in the region include log structures for barns and outbuildings as well as houses, the framed "I" house (a two-story house, one room deep, with a center hallway), and the "box" house, constructed of sawmill lumber without a conventional frame. Traditional home-building skills involve log hewing and notching, splitting shingles, knowing the proper dimensions for each type of structure, and building without a blueprint. The knowledge of which woods are good for which purpose, their general qualities, and how they will behave are other important aspects of traditional woodworking. Oak, poplar, and, until the killing blight of the early twentieth century, chestnut were generally the materials of choice. All this information would be traditionally passed down through the informal teaching of family groups or neighbors. Homes were often built by local networks of kin and neighbors. When the work was completed, the participants would celebrate.

Music and Dance

Traditionally a potluck or covered-dish supper, accompanied by games, dances, and "play party" activities rewarded the work of house and barn raisings, corn shuckings, molasses stir-offs, and other gatherings where work and pleasure combined. In some areas, Christian traditions frowned on social dancing and fiddle music—after all, the fiddle was known as the devil's instrument. People responded creatively to such proscriptions with play parties, where participants provided their own vocal musical accompaniment for games similar to dancing. These games fulfilled the need for social connection and entertainment, especially for the young unmarried people in the community.

But dancing was a very popular activity in most communities. The figures of the Appalachian square dance, which involve small sets of only two couples, or four people, occur in a large circle, thus differing from the western square dance with its stand-alone eight-person sets (four couples each). Favorite figures performed with a smooth running step or clogging step include the grapevine, do-si-do, star, birdie-in-the-cage, chase the squirrel, take a little peek, and Georgia rang-tang. The folk school movement in the 1920s and 1930s introduced English and Danish country dances into some local traditions. Two contemporary national trends that have also gained hold in the Appalachian region are modern western square dancing, since the 1950s, and New England contra dancing, starting in the 1980s.

Although barn dances have gained currency through radio programs, dances in people's homes were also common. Folklore from some areas contains stories of moving out all the furniture, even red-hot stoves, to make room for a house dance. The solo fiddler became the archetypal musician for house dances, but in reality, dancers were inspired by the accompanying music of whatever musicians were handy. Today, some older people describe how dancing fell out of favor in their communities as it became associated with drinking and fighting. Dances today often ban alcohol, but many communities simply no longer hold the dances that were once so prevalent. On the other hand, contra dancing and western square have developed active followings, especially around population centers such as Asheville and Knoxville.

Other types of dance traditionally performed solo are variously called clogging, flat-footing, or buck dancing. These dance forms incorporate varieties of earlier British and Irish clog steps as well as African American "buck 'n' wing" steps from the Deep South. The European tradition discourages upper body motion; the main motion, in the leg below the knee, involves elaborate chugs and shuffles supplemented by kicks, slides, and taps. As in tap dancing, the human feet become percussive instruments, especially in African American communities. Since the folk revival of the 1960s, clogging has become a team dance performance, especially among children and youth. Team members wear matching costumes, and a more vigorous style of dance incorporating upper body movement is often employed. Recorded music—often rock or pop music— as well as old-time or bluegrass string bands can accompany the dancers.

The music of the region is especially illustrative of the flexibility, richness, hardiness and creativity of folk tradition. String bands remain vital in the region, although their genesis, the square dance, has less vitality. The homemade or store-bought violin or fiddle, brought first by European immigrants, remains the primary instrument and has often been played alone for dances. Hundreds of distinctly different melodies, from German, French, and especially British and Celtic roots, are found today in the repertoires of mountain fiddlers. The solo fiddle tradition produced many different tunings, including open or cross-tuning.

The banjo is a truly African American instrument. Adapted from a similar instrument in West Africa, it was at first connected mainly with slave culture and used for accompanying dancing and singing. It spread widely during the nineteenth century, becoming associated with minstrel shows. After emancipation, many blacks turned instead to the guitar, and the banjo, associated for a short time with classical music, became popular with white mountaineers. Older banjo picking styles include minstrel, clawhammer or frailing, and finger picking using two or three fingers. The Dixieland tradition of the plectrum banjo never really took hold in the region. The rolling, three-finger picking style using steel finger picks, popularized by Earl Scruggs and others in the 1940s and 1950s, has become standard and is a mainstay of the contemporary fast-paced bluegrass tradition. The folk revival of the 1960s, however, ensured that old-time banjo would continue to ring.

The earliest accompaniment to the banjo was often a drum, but banjo and fiddle combinations became popular in the twentieth century, later to be joined by the flat-top or Spanish guitar, mandolin, and upright bass to create a string band. At times, the ukulele and Hawaiian or steel guitar would be added, these being brought back by servicemen stationed in the Pacific during the Spanish-American War and World War II. The pedal steel is an occasional addition, more commonly found in country music than in the string band. In both old-time and bluegrass bands, acoustic rather than electric instruments are preferred.

The dulcimer, sometimes erroneously viewed as the only true Appalachian instrument, actually has its roots in northern Europe, though not in the British Isles. Until the folk revival of the late twentieth century, the dulcimer appeared infrequently in the mountains, although it is documented in what is now West Virginia, Virginia, and Tennessee in the mid-nineteenth century. Two areas now well known for this instrument are Perry County, Kentucky, and Watauga County, North Carolina. One of the dulcimer's ancestors, the German scheitholt, sometimes existed alongside the newer version, especially in the Great Valley of Virginia, where many Germans settled. The dulcimer's simple construction, in true folk tradition, resulted in the many variations we find today in size, shape, and number of strings. Its ease of playing and beautiful simplicity has made it a favorite among folk revivalists, and the soft tones of the dulcimer make it an effective accompaniment for vocal music.

The rich vocal music traditions in the mountains, along with storytelling, have until recently been the performances of greatest interest to folklorists and other outsiders with cultural interests. Except for the play-party songs and religious hymnody, most vocal music was sung solo or in small groups. The English and Scottish narrative ballads found by Cecil Sharp and other collectors are known for their oral poetry and spellbinding accounts of tragic lovers, conflicts between family members, and adventures with supernatural beings.

The exploits of lords and ladies in the past ("Lord Randall," "Lady Margaret," "Sweet William," and "Fair Eleanor," etc.), like those of the movie stars of today, excited the imaginations of ordinary people who sang about them, and the ballads sometimes offered humorous and even bawdy revelations about the ancient conflicts between men and women.

The older British ballads are but a portion of the continuing song tradition that developed in the twentieth century into the national phenomenon of country music. Popular ballads of American origin tell stories of heroes and villains, war, local accidents, murders, and other events in American history. An important thread in the musical texture of Appalachia comes from African American tradition. Blues and work songs created by gandy dancers on the railroad lines and by laborers in mines, lumber camps, and prisons have become standard to repertoires of black and white musicians alike. The call-and-response form embodied by many African American songs has also worked its way into other folk music traditions; perhaps the best-known example is the instrumental "Dueling Banjos."

Vocal music associated with religious traditions formed another large repertory. Many popular religious tunes were taken directly from the earlier ballad tradition or other secular songs. An example is "Amazing Grace," which borrowed the tune of the ballad "Lord Thomas and Lady Margaret," an ancient ghost story. John Wesley, the founder of Methodism and a hymn composer, reportedly asked, "Why should the Devil have all the good tunes?" Such religious borrowings have helped preserve the tunes of some very old "Devil's ditties."

Dominant in this early hymn tradition was the group singing of hymns in four-part harmony, unaccompanied, using a system of shaped notes. The name of this musical style developed from the belief that the human voice is "the Sacred Harp" and that, therefore, no instruments are needed. First developed by New England singing teachers before the American Revolution, shape-note singing spread across the Southeast during the Great Awakening of the mid-eighteenth century and is still practiced in a number of rural communities. When combined with a covered dish dinner on the grounds, such musical celebrations may last an entire day. The traditional method of learning shape-note singing was for an itinerant singing teacher to spend a week or two living in a community and teaching the children. Shape-note singing experienced a revival in the late twentieth and early twenty-first centuries, and most people now learn through monthly or yearly singing conventions or festival workshops. Many hymnals retain the shaped-note notation, but a relatively small number of people know how to sing the shapes; most singers treat them like regular round notes.

Storytelling, Speech, and Narrative

The often-noted verbal skills of the mountain people are well cultivated. Along with singing and storytelling sessions, the school yard, workplace, barber shop, bar, local convenience store, and street offer many opportunities to hone one's riddling, word play, proverb, and joke-telling skills. Word games, riddles, and counting and alphabet rhymes enhance both verbal and "critical thinking" skills. Sermons and prayers delivered in traditional mountain churches often reflect distinctive rhetorical styles. This varied and dynamic swapping of oral forms has provided an important creative environment for Appalachia's many poets and novelists.

Storytelling and traditional speech patterns have been of special interest to folklorists and linguists as well as to writers. Observers of the tale-telling tradition now realize that the communication achieved between storyteller and audience goes well beyond entertainment. Storytelling creates a social bond between and among teller and audience members. Some stories, for example, those of the trickster Jack, model such socially accepted behavior as cleverness, generosity, and hard work and deride such antisocial and foolish behaviors as selfishness, dishonesty, and egotism. Listeners and storytellers alike can explore the intricacy of relationships, the difficulties of growing up, or other psychological issues through following the characters in traditional stories.

Storytelling offers ordinary people a chance to exercise their verbal skills and vivid imaginations, to entertain family and neighbors, and to reassert emotional and symbolic ties to earlier generations of storytellers. Doug Stanley of Beckley, West Virginia, is always willing to tell one of his uncle's "Jack" tales. And the audience always loves to hear him, whatever their backgrounds. A favorite subject for storytelling since the earliest exploration has been the interaction between the human and animal world. Mountaineers especially enjoy astounding newcomers and young people with accounts of bears and rattlesnakes of prodigious size, the "hoop" snake which can roll up hill, hunting dogs of unparalleled toughness, and the time twelve turkeys succumbed to a single shot.

Appalachian stories often parallel stories found in other regions of America and even throughout the world. "Vanishing hitchhikers" have appeared in Appalachia as well as in California and New York. The trickster hero, Jack, and his female counterpart, Mutsmag, have long histories in the British Isles, and their adventures share plot lines with similar folktale characters in Africa, Russia, and other parts of Europe. Many stories and legends are unique, of course, like that of the Greenbrier Ghost (of West Virginia), the only ghost in American history whose testimony has been used at an actual murder trial.

A rich repertoire of storytelling forms is an especially important inheritance for the region's talented writers. Appalachian story forms include personal narratives, the myths of the Cherokee, psychologically complex ballads, wonder or "set" tales of northern Europe, and tall tales and exaggerated hunting stories. Legends about local residents are also popular. Mary Draper Ingles in Virginia, explorer Daniel Boone in Kentucky, Davy Crockett in Tennessee, Jesse James in West Virginia, and John Henry working on the Chesapeake and Ohio rails were real people with extraordinary stories. Before the advent of radio and television, storytelling took place in the home and in local trade and business situations, often accompanying everyday activities.

Today, storytelling and related sayings may be the most common (and unconscious) form of traditional folklore still engaged in by regular folks in their daily lives. Even so, many people today enjoy professional storytellers such as Ray Hicks, Sheila Kay Adams and Don Davis, who have captivated audiences both in and outside the region with their spellbinding and often hilarious tales. Storytelling clubs and networks (e.g., the Asheville, North Carolina, Storytelling Circle) provide a contemporary environment for an ancient art form. Many Appalachian storytellers are featured at the National Storytelling Festival, held in early October each year in Jonesborough, Tennessee, with tellers and listeners from all over the world.

Traditional storytellers enhance their style through the use of traditional speech patterns common to the region before the days of radio and television. Appalachian speech, with its Anglo-Saxon verb forms, double negatives, and unique pronunciation, still offers the linguist and tourist alike insight into the development of the English language. The use of the "a" prefix for some verbs ("a-huntin," "a-fishin"), the lack of "g" on the present participle (added much later), and the double or triple negative were common in Anglo-Saxon England. The Scots-Irish retained such correct forms and taught their children and their new friends from other parts of Europe and America to use these forms. Along with sometimes vivid metaphorical phrases, that speech still enriches the region's spoken and written expression.

Folk Revivals and the Future

In the early industrial period of the nineteenth and early twentieth centuries, factory-produced goods and professional entertainment generally replaced the more time-consuming handmade, traditional arts in the region as family members sought regular wages in mines, mills, factories, and commercial establishments. We are presently in the midst of a revival of interest in the old-time ways; a similar revival has occurred in virtually every generation since the industrialization of the region: in the late nineteenth century, the 1930s, the 1960s, and the 1990s. Interest in herbal lore, gardening, and traditional foodways has accompanied a national rise in the popularity of natural foods and alternative healing methods. The fact that storytelling, music, dance, and handcrafts are now found throughout the region at a host of local and regional festivals attests to the strength of both traditions and revivals. The limitations of postmodern life, especially the frequent loss of community and neighborhood, have led urban residents to search for meaningful ties to past communities. Folk traditions in Appalachia and elsewhere respond to that need.

Folk artists are now recognized as national treasures, and most state and regional arts organizations have folklife sections. Skilled artisans and craftspersons remain, although the traditions do change with the times and each generation is lamented as the last to know the "real" traditions. In many cases, family networks have been essential to the learning and preservation of artistic and craft traditions. Some families, like the Ritchies of Viper, Kentucky, the Harmon-Hicks family of western North Carolina, and Everette Lilly and his sons in Beckley, West Virginia, continue to serve as informal schools of the arts. Informal teaching on the community level, the reintroduction of crafts as an economic development tool, and the establishment of folk schools and craft centers has continually replenished the numbers of people involved in the folk revival. Berea College students no longer pay their tuition in coverlets, but they can choose to learn the skills required for a craft and work at that craft for their required labor hours. The Augusta Heritage Center and the John C. Campbell Folk School both offer extensive and varied hands-on workshops for the general public. Information on such programs and the many large and small festivals and street fairs throughout the region is available from local chambers of commerce and state folklore societies.

In the last half of the twentieth century, folklorists shifted attention from an exclusive focus on the "items" of folklore—stories, songs, games, riddles, jokes, tunes, and so on—to the situations or context in which folklore is performed or created. Since this puts an emphasis on the "folk process," folklorists, grants agencies, and artists have become more concerned about the method and context in which folk artists learned their skills. Today, many folk artists develop their arts in various ways. Books, video and audio recordings, and being "self-taught" are the most frequently cited ways people learn their skills today, although learning directly from other people still occurs.

The distance many modern Appalachians feel from their folk heritage may be revealed by changes in the perceived function and identity of the folk artist within his or her community. The once common assumption that most people in the culture shared many of these skills has yielded to a belief that only a few exceptional, widely scattered folk artists are worthy of recognition. In our age of specialization and performance, many folk artists and performers become professionals and gain status through preserving or practicing a skill once considered ordinary.

In this context, understanding the role such families as the Couches, Ritchies, Harmons, and Gentrys have played in their children's artistic and musical development has become increasingly important. Their own stories of their upbringing as well as folklorists' studies of these families may bring to life the folk context of previous generations. A sense of the historical context of folklife and material culture may also be gained by visiting such folklife exhibits and museums as those at Cherokee, Biltmore Homespun Crafts, the Southern Highland Handicraft Guild, and Penland School, all in North Carolina; the Museum of Appalachia in Norris, Tennessee; and Wolf Creek Indian Village and the Museum of American Frontier Culture, both in Virginia.

Folk culture typically has been described as changing slowly, but even this defining quality has become less valid as the rate at which change occurs accelerates. Some Appalachian scholars have suggested that traditional culture is increasingly threatened by America's growing dependence on electronic media—in colloquial terms, becoming "road kill" on the information highway. Certainly, with each new cable network, satellite link, cell phone, and Internet connection, the region becomes more exposed to mainstream commercial culture. In some ways, this homogenizes Appalachian culture with the rest of America, but it also allows for more influences to create more diversity. The future of folklore in the region is difficult to predict with the challenges of commercial interests and the tourist industry. However, the burgeoning eco-tourism industry and such cultural projects as the Blue Ridge Heritage Initiative may encourage and reinforce the region's still rich and active folklife. The recurring appeal of Appalachian folklore lies not only in its intrinsic beauty or usefulness but also in the sense of heritage and stability it offers. At the same time, the human need to create and to invest our daily lives with meaning will continue to bring about new traditions. As long as old or young "folk" apply their shared or individual creativity and ingenuity to their activities, there will be folklore and folklife.

Trula Craig Aust of Pulaski, Virginia, with three blue ribbons from the county fair for her preserves. By JoAnn Asbury.

The I-House, a typical architectural design through the early twentieth century. By Ricky Cox.

The "log cabin" pattern, as pieced and quilted by Susan Marshall Quesenberry of Willis, Virginia.
By Ricky Cox.

Chair caner Junior Lyle. By Ricky Cox.

Friday Nite Jamboree, Cockram's General Store, Floyd, Virginia. By Grace Toney Edwards.

Dancing at the Carter Fold, Hiltons, Virginia. Photograph by Ricky Cox.

Suggested Readings

Adams, Sheila Kay. *Come Go Home with Me.* Chapel Hill: Univ. of North Carolina Press, 1995.

Chase, Richard. *Grandfather Tales.* Boston: Houghton Mifflin, 1976.

———. *Jack Tales.* Boston: Houghton Mifflin, 1971.

Cheek, Pauline Binkley. *Appalachian Scrapbook: An A, B, C of Growing Up in the Mountains.* Boone, N.C.: Appalachian Consortium Press, 1988.

Conway, Cecelia. *African Banjo Echoes in Appalachia: A Study of Folk Traditions.* Knoxville: Univ. of Tennessee Press, 1995.

Duncan, Barbara R. *Living Stories of the Cherokee.* Chapel Hill: Univ. of North Carolina Press, 1998.

Duncan, Barbara R., and Brett H. Riggs. *Cherokee Heritage Trails Guidebook.* Chapel Hill: Univ. of North Carolina Press, 2003.

Eaton, Allen H. *Handicrafts of the Southern Highlands.* New York: Dover Press, 1973.

Farr, Sidney Saylor. *More than Moonshine: Appalachian Recipes and Recollections.* Pittsburgh: Univ. of Pittsburgh Press, 1983.

Gillespie, Paul F., ed. *Foxfire 7.* Garden City, N.Y.: Anchor Press/Doubleday, 1982.

Hill, Sarah H. *Weaving New Worlds: Southeastern Cherokee Women and Their Basketry.* Chapel Hill: Univ. of North Carolina Press, 1997.

Jackson, George Pullen. *White Spirituals in the Southern Uplands: The Story of the Fasola Folk, Their Songs, Singings, and "Buckwheat Notes."* New York: Dover Press, 1965.

Jones, Loyal. *Laughter in Appalachia: A Festival of Southern Mountain Humor.* Little Rock, Ark.: August House, 1987.

Lambert, Walter N. *Kinfolks and Custard Pie: Recollections and Recipes from an East Tennessean.* Knoxville: Univ. of Tennessee Press, 1988.

Law, Rachel Nash, and Cynthia W. Taylor. *Appalachian White Oak Basketmaking: Handing Down the Basket.* Knoxville: Univ. of Tennessee Press, 1991.

Lopes, Danielle, Joan Moser, and Annie Louise Perkinson. *Appalachian Folk Medicine: Native Plants and Healing Traditions.* Swannanoa: Warren Wilson College Press, 1996.

Malone, Bill C. *Country Music, U.S.A.* Austin: Univ. of Texas Press, 1968.

Milnes, Gerald. *Play of a Fiddle: Traditional Music, Dance, and Folklore in West Virginia.* Lexington: Univ. Press of Kentucky, 1999.

Montell, William Lynwood. *Ghosts along the Cumberland: Deathlore in the Kentucky Foothills.* Knoxville: Univ. of Tennessee Press, 1975.

Mooney, James, ed. *History, Myths and Sacred Formula of the Cherokee Indians.* Asheville, N.C.: Historical Images, 1992.

Musick, Ruth Ann. *The Telltale Lilac Bush and Other West Virginia Ghost Tales.* Lexington: Univ. Press of Kentucky, 1965.

Neely, Sharlotte. *The Snowbird Cherokees.* Athens: Univ. of Georgia Press, 1991.

Olson, Ted. *Blue Ridge Folklife.* Jackson: Univ. Press of Mississippi, 1998.

Page, Linda Garland, and Hilton Smith, eds. *The Foxfire Book of Toys and Games: Reminiscences and Instructions from Appalachia.* New York: E. P. Dutton, 1985.

162

Patterson, Daniel W., and Charles G. Zug III. *Arts in Earnest: North Carolina Folklife.* Durham, N.C.: Duke Univ. Press, 1990.

Ritchie, Jean. *Singing Family of the Cumberlands.* New York: Oxford Univ. Press, 1955.

Roberts, Leonard. *Sang Branch Settlers: Folksongs and Tales of a Kentucky Mountain Family.* Pikeville, Ky.: Pikeville College Press, 1980.

Spalding, Susan Eike, and Jane Harris Woodside, eds. *Communities in Motion: Dance, Community, and Tradition in America's Southeast and Beyond.* Westport, Conn.: Greenwood Press, 1995.

White, Newman Ivey et al. *The Frank C. Brown Collection of North Carolina Folklore.* Durham, N.C.: Duke Univ. Press, 1952–64.

Wigginton, Eliot, ed. *Foxfire 2–6.* Garden City, N.Y.: Anchor Press/Doubleday, 1972–80.

———. *The Foxfire Book.* Garden City, N.Y.: Doubleday, 1972.

Wigginton, Eliot, and Margie Bennett, eds. *Foxfire 8–9.* Garden City, N.Y.: Anchor Press/Doubleday, 1984–86.

Williams, Cratis D. *Southern Mountain Speech.* Edited by Jim Wayne Miller and Loyal Jones. Berea, Ky.: Berea College Press, 1992.

Williams, Michael Ann. *Great Smoky Mountains Folklife.* Jackson: Univ. Press of Mississippi, 1995.

———. *Homeplace: The Social Use and Meaning of the Folk Dwelling in Southwestern North Carolina.* Athens: Univ. of Georgia Press, 1991.

APPALACHIAN MUSIC: EXAMINING POPULAR ASSUMPTIONS

TED OLSON AND AJAY KALRA

With the growth of mass-market print media across the United States during the second half of the nineteenth century and the advent of such newer media as phonograph records, radio, and motion pictures during the first half of the twentieth century, the image of Appalachian culture in the American popular mind has evolved in marked contrast to American mainstream culture. Whether extolled for its authentic "folk" qualities or derided for its rustic "hillbilly" characteristics, Appalachian culture has long been represented as distinctly different from American culture. The stereotype-infused representation of the region's culture has not only affected popular conceptions of Appalachian people but also has had a considerable impact on the region's music.

In fact, mainstream audiences tend to value Appalachian music for the distinctiveness of some of its musical genres and styles. Such valuation has led to the selective promotion of certain Appalachian musical genres and styles within the national mainstream. This has been part of a larger pattern among promoters of American regional music traditions. Folklorists and folk revivalists, for instance, have long been interested in finding distinctly regional "folk" musics; thus, many such people have tended to associate a given region with a specific type of music—for instance, the Mississippi River Delta and the Carolina Piedmont with the blues, New Orleans with jazz, and Appalachia with white European folk music. In the latter case, this tendency has led to widespread neglect of other significant musical influences within Appalachia, such as the African

American contribution to Appalachian traditional and popular music. Similarly, given the general privileging of the region's "folk" music, scholars have neglected many of the region's commercial and elite music heritages, despite the fact that a wide variety of American music genres—including jazz, blues, rock, and classical music—have been furthered by important contributions from musicians born and/or raised in Appalachia. While some of these latter musicians have been widely recognized as important American musicians, their association with their native region has been ignored.

Three recent movies, *O Brother, Where Art Thou?* (2000), *Songcatcher* (2000), and *Cold Mountain* (2003), have drawn much attention to the rural "roots" music of the South in general and of the southern Appalachian region in particular. All three yielded popular soundtrack albums containing interpretations of that "roots" music. The *O Brother* soundtrack was released to spectacular sales unprecedented in non-mainstream music circles. Even without significant airplay on commercial radio, the album sold over seven million copies. Previous roots music anthologies had rarely sold more than a few thousand copies. For instance, Folkways Records' long-influential *Anthology of American Folk Music,* when reissued on CD by the Smithsonian Folkways label in 1997 as an award-winning expanded package, sold only in the low thousands. Two well-known tributes to Appalachian music by prominent rock groups—the Nitty Gritty Dirt Band's *Will the Circle Be Unbroken* (1972) and Old and In the Way's eponymous debut album—have not officially achieved platinum sales (i.e., sales of a million copies). The *O Brother* soundtrack even inspired successful spin-off projects, among them *Down from the Mountain* (2001), which yielded a nationwide tour by acts associated with the *O Brother* soundtrack along with a number of other related musicians, as well as a number of album compilations that continue to tout a connection with *O Brother.*

The popularity of the *O Brother* and *Songcatcher* soundtracks spawned a groundswell of media pronouncements proclaiming a surge of national interest in American roots music. Many such pronouncements asserted that those soundtracks' success signaled the triumph of a more "pure," more "authentic" type of music over "commercial" country music. In many instances, the media have directly suggested that much of the roots music recently capturing the nation's attention has been Appalachian music. For example, in a 2001 *Washington Post* article, novelist Lee Smith, after praising the *O Brother* and *Songcatcher* soundtracks and other recent media projects (specifically, several novels and movies set in Appalachia), contended that "mainstream American culture is becoming 'Appalachianized.'"[1] In identifying the music on the *O Brother* soundtrack as Appalachian, Smith overlooks the fact that much of the music on that soundtrack reflects the musical repertoire of the broader South and not necessarily of Appalachia. Other writers acknowledging the growing popularity of roots music have espoused romanticized perspectives on Appalachia's musical heritage. In a 2001 *USA Today* article entitled "O Country Music, Where Art Thou?" Brian Mansfield suggested that the banjo was an instrument brought to Appalachia by "British, Scottish, and Irish settlers," despite that instrument's well-documented African origins.[2] Such an inaccurate perspective from a music journalist indicates the widespread persistence of erroneous and monolithic conceptions of Appalachian music as being essentially a continuation of British folk music traditions, a supposition that ignores the defining role of African American music in shaping Appalachia's musical identity. Through the presence of African Americans, living, working, or traveling in the region, and through the pervasive influence of the blues, black gospel, rhythm and blues, and jazz on contemporary popular music, African American music has become an integral part of Appalachian music, including some of the most traditional-sounding Appalachian folk music. Oversight of this important aspect of Appalachian musical culture constitutes but one of the many fallacies regarding the region's music.

The application of the terms "roots" and "folk" to recent Appalachian-influenced music, whether that of musicians associated with the *O Brother* and *Songcatcher* soundtracks or that of other acts associated with the Americana music movement, has a longstanding history. For over a century, non-natives have been fascinated by the relative distinctiveness of Appalachian music, and producers and musicians have sought to amplify this difference to make their music seem more fascinating and attractive to non-native audiences. Depending upon the type of audience, the purposes of the promoters, and the medium of such promotion, presentations of Appalachian musicians to specific non-native audiences have veered to one of two extremes: the exalted "folk" musician depicted as the keeper of a disappearing heritage or the unrefined "hillbilly" musician stuck in another time and place.

Academics, folklorists, and their audiences have long been enamored of the "authentic folk" image of the Appalachian musician and have done much to promote it. During the World War I years, English song collector Cecil Sharp and his assistant Maud Karpeles traveled through the southern Appalachians and collected over one hundred Old World ballads that were still being sung in Appalachia with remarkably little variation from their earlier British versions. Sharp and Karpeles confirmed for subsequent music collectors, folklorists, and folk music revivalists the importance of Appalachia as a haven for older forms of folk music and culture. Thenceforth, during four different folk music revivals (in the 1930s, the 1940s, the late 1950s–1960s, and in the late 1990s–early 2000s), Appalachian traditional music has been both revered and romanticized, not only in academic circles but also by the media and among mainstream audiences.

While some portrayals of Appalachian music have been complimentary, albeit monochromatic, other depictions have been overtly derogatory—manifesting an attitude visible in the early years of "hillbilly" music (the prevailing label for what later became known as country music). Although the country music industry by the late 1950s had largely discarded the early strategies by northern producers to market the music with hillbilly stereotypes, a struggle against the unrelenting grip of such stereotypes on the mainstream American mind has continued to define both the nature and the iconography of subsequent country music. In the 1950s and 1960s, the country music industry, by then centered in Nashville, promoted a music and iconography that downplayed references to the hillbilly or Appalachian origins of the music and many of its performers. Guitarist-producer Chet Atkins, from East Tennessee, was one of the chief architects of this urbane "countrypolitan" music and image, and such Appalachian natives as Patsy Cline and Don Gibson found mainstream success with that sound. In the late 1970s and early 1980s, Appalachian-born country-pop musicians Dottie West, Crystal Gayle, and Ronnie Milsap were among the country music acts who reached wider audiences by deemphasizing their Appalachian connections. By the late 1980s, an Appalachian identification had become attractive to mainstream audiences, encouraging Appalachian musicians to embrace, and even exaggerate, the regional roots of their music. As part of country music's neotraditionalist movement, Ricky Skaggs, Keith Whitley, and Dwight Yoakam all achieved mainstream success through linking their music with traditional Appalachian music. In the late 1990s, several musicians who had formerly attained stardom in mainstream country music, including Ricky Skaggs, Patty Loveless, and Dolly Parton, embraced the acoustic roots of Appalachian music on their recordings and in concerts, to considerable critical acclaim.

Since the advent of radio and the growth of the recording industry in the 1920s, Appalachian music has been widely judged as being different from mainstream musical fare. Media and record labels have often exaggerated this difference in order to ensure that Appalachian music would stand out as a distinctive product in the mainstream market. Producers have manipulated both the sound and the presentation of performers to suit certain well-defined images deemed commercially viable; through repetition, though, such images have become intractable stereotypes, whether derogatory or complimentary. The numerous local and regional radio barn dances, nationally televised music shows such as *Hee Haw,* and such television series as *The Beverly Hillbillies* are examples of negative stereotyping; positive stereotyping was inherent in the celebration of early country music acts as master folk musicians by 1950s- and 1960s-era urban folk revivalists.

Appalachian musical history dates back to the first arrival of Native Americans in the region. However, the music of Appalachia's predominant tribe, the Cherokee, has not been well documented. Antecedents of better-known Appalachian regional musics were present in the region over two centuries ago, from the days of the first European settlement. To understand the distinctiveness of Appalachian music and its image, however, one need only go back to the 1920s, when the advent of the recording industry and the radio brought into focus the contrast between northern popular music and southern hillbilly music.

Since the end of World War I, the expanding recording industry had been searching for new potential markets to tap. Recordings of black music—made in makeshift field recording studios in Atlanta and New Orleans starting around 1918 and marketed as "race" records—represented the earliest of such attempts. In the early 1920s, competition with a new technology—the radio—compelled commercial record companies to intensify the search for additional markets and musical products, leading to the "discovery" of rural white southern music. The beginnings of this hillbilly record industry can be traced back to June 1922 to studio recordings made in New York City by Texas fiddlers Eck Robertson and Henry Gilliland for the Victor label. In June 1923, Ralph Peer, who in 1920 had produced a number of race recordings for the OKeh label, traveled to Atlanta to make the first commercial "field recordings" of old-time Appalachian music. While initially distributed only in regional markets, these recordings— featuring performances by Fiddlin' John Carson—were surprisingly successful, encouraging record labels to circulate the recordings in other markets. Finding it most profitable to restrict their field recording sessions in the South to talent-scouting trips, record companies often invited "discovered" musicians to their established studios in northern cities for subsequent recordings. Often, commercial labels encouraged locally available talent to make recordings in a simulated Appalachian style; for example, in 1925, Texas-born but New York–based light operatic pop singer Vernon Dalhart became the first act to record a million-selling country music single. Yet even at this early stage of contact with Appalachian musicians, northern producers and promoters had decided which qualities made music distinctly southern or Appalachian and hence were worth emphasizing. The music was being molded into hillbilly music, and the hillbilly image and iconography soon followed.

In 1925, Ralph Peer, after recording one Appalachian string band, asked the musicians the name of their group; the musicians responded, "We're nothing but a bunch of hillbillies from North Carolina and Virginia. Call us anything."[3] And so the producer named them "The Hill Billies." According to scholar John Solomon Otto, "The band's records sold widely, and 'The Hill-Billies' [sic] even toured the vaudeville circuit. Dressed in overalls and ragged hats and playing mountain music before urban audiences, 'The Hill-Billies' did much to popularize the hillbilly stereotype."[4] Soon Appalachian music, theretofore marketed variously as "old familiar tunes" and "old-time music," came to be known as hillbilly music.

The term "hillbilly" did not always have derogatory connotations. It possibly first circulated in the oral tradition of lowlanders and urban people in the late nineteenth century, though the term was not committed to print until the early twentieth century. Appalachian people did not use the term when referring to themselves until the 1920s; traditionally, they called themselves by such descriptions as "just plain folks."[5] Otto has speculated that the term "hillbilly" stems from the British slang term "billy," meaning "fellow" or "comrade"; a hillbilly is thus a "fellow from the hills."[6] The first printed use of the term appeared in the *New York Journal* in 1900, when an anonymous reporter claimed that "a Hill-Billie is a free and untrammeled white citizen who lives in the hills . . . has no means to speak of, dresses as he can, talks as he pleases, drinks whiskey when he gets it, and fires off his revolver as the fancy takes him."[7] Moreover, the term was not used exclusively to refer to Appalachian residents. The second printed use of the term dates from 1902, from a travel narrative written about the Ozarks in which the narrator uses the term to ridicule the Arkansas hill folk for the inefficiency of their train system.[8] These two print appearances suggest how quickly the connotations of the word were changing. The spread of hillbilly stereotyping increased dramatically in 1903, when Thomas W. Jackson published *On a Slow Train Through Arkansaw* [sic], a best-selling collection of jokes about Ozark railroads; here, Jackson further popularized the myth of the laziness and ineptitude of hillbillies, the same myth that author John Fox Jr. had recently propagated through his best-selling novels.[9]

Jackson's jokebook spawned a flurry of imitations by authors unfamiliar with the southern upland way of life. As Otto explains, "Several of these jokebooks contained crude caricatures of Arkansas mountain folk. Urban artists depicted the mountain men in wool hats, homespun trousers that had one suspender, and brogans. They portrayed mountain women in ragged shifts, barefooted, and smoking corncob pipes. And finally, artists showed mountain families living in tumble-down log cabins, which were surrounded by skinny hounds and razorback hogs. In other words, they created the classic cartoon hillbillies."[10]

It was not long before such fictional representations began to depict hill dwellers overtly as hillbillies in avowedly nonfictional pieces, including several in major national periodicals. One such piece was "Hobnobbing with Hillbillies" by William Bradley, which appeared in *Harper's Magazine* in December 1915. Depicting Appalachian people by utilizing many of the stock characteristics found in the jokebooks, such articles had the unfortunate effect of legitimizing the hillbilly stereotype to sophisticated urban audiences across the United States. The aforementioned Appalachian string band's reference to itself as "nothing but a bunch of hillbillies" came from a position of self-deprecation and from a sense of regional identity, but it also reflected the group's having accepted hillbilly stereotyping. For decades, continuing into the present, Appalachian musicians have repeatedly found themselves compelled to conform to, and even promote, stereotypes initially levied on them by outsiders. At the other end of this spectrum are musicians who reject not only such stereotypes but also Appalachian identities. Yet few Appalachian musicians are able to escape the compulsion to react strongly to such stereotypes, whether through conforming to them or through rejecting them.

Radio was a new technology in the early 1920s, and the significant drop in commercial record sales after its appearance was one of the incentives compelling northern-based recording companies to look for additional musics and markets, thus leading to the beginnings of the country music recording industry. Both the radio and the record industry stressed that Appalachian and southern musicians should "keep it country," encouraging them to play material that sounded like "old familiar tunes" and to dress to emphasize their regionality.

A number of southern radio stations, such as WSB in Atlanta, played the new phonograph records and broadcasted live performances of hillbilly music. One type of live performance was particularly successful: the radio barn dance. Popular in the South and the Midwest, two American regions still clinging to their nineteenth-century rural identities despite enormous twentieth-century economic and social changes, the "radio barn dances . . . were designed to recreate the atmosphere of wholesome family fun and entertainment associated with village or rural life."[11] The exaggeratedly rural format of the barn dance, however, advanced a one-dimensional view of Appalachian music and culture and resulted in the firm entrenchment of the hillbilly image as an intractable stereotype.

Most barn dances were hosted by radio stations outside of Appalachia but featured a number of Appalachian musicians. The musical traditions they drew upon—ballads, fiddle tunes, blues, string band music, and gospel music—were shared among audiences across the rural South and Midwest as well as across Appalachia; such a repertoire was also favored by city-dwelling expatriated rural audiences from those same regions. The first barn dance of importance, dating from April 19, 1924, was the *National Barn Dance,* produced by WLS, a Chicago radio station then owned by the Sears-Roebuck Company. This was followed by WSM Nashville's *Grand Ole Opry,* produced by pioneer disc jockey "Judge" George D. Hay. Initially called the *WSM Barn Dance* when first presented on November 28, 1925, the *Grand Ole Opry* prospered in Nashville despite the fact that "there was a rather strong bias against rural music among the Nashville upper crust."[12] According to music historian Bill C. Malone, "Hay zealously worked to preserve the informal, down-home atmosphere of the shows, and he constantly admonished the musicians to keep things 'down to earth,' while he also gave the string bands names that seemed appropriate to the rustic image: Possum Hunters, Clod Hoppers, Fruit Jar Drinkers, etc."[13]

Producers from record companies based in the urban North, who set up field recording sessions in the 1920s and early 1930s in southern cities—including such Appalachian locations as Asheville, North Carolina, and Bristol, Johnson City, and Knoxville, Tennessee—similarly encouraged Appalachian musicians to record traditional, or more specifically, traditional-sounding, material. Ralph Peer, who conducted the seminal Bristol recording sessions in 1927 for the Victor Talking Machine Company (the so-called "Big Bang of Country Music"), in media interviews tried to make his acts seem like unrefined hillbillies. From the start, Appalachian music was marketed nationally as a regional novelty music, and there was no expectation that those records would compete with the more polished popular music industry then thriving in the North. A few decades later, however, Nashville's country music industry (by then comprising hundreds of Appalachian musicians and songwriters) would begin attempts to cross over to the mainstream national market and find success with nonrural audiences. In those attempts, country music as well as its image would be tweaked to reach a commercially saleable balance between "rural" simplicity and authenticity and "urban" pop glitz.

Commercial means of disseminating music—recordings and the radio barn dance—were soon complemented by another, less overtly commercial way to present Appalachian music to a wider audience: the folk music festival. Folksong collector Jean Thomas, noting the swift sales of recordings by Appalachian musicians in the 1920s, organized the American Folk Song Festival, which differed from the barn dances in that it was staged not in a major urban center but in the small town of Ashland in rural eastern Kentucky. Unlike the blatantly commercial barn dances, which thrived because of corporate sponsorship, Thomas's festival—begun in 1930—was organized by scholars and supported largely by philanthropists and state agencies. The American Folk Song Festival and the slightly earlier Asheville, North Carolina–based Mountain Dance and Folk Festival (the latter organized by Bascom Lamar Lunsford in 1928) were significant manifestations of the first of several twentieth-century folk revivals. The American Folk Song Festival purported to be a celebration of traditional Appalachian music and dance; yet, desiring a wide reception, the organizers insisted that the festival be carefully orchestrated. Hence, they encouraged local people to don costumes depicting various periods in regional history. Some locals dressed like frontiersmen, some like Cherokee; others, because of the widespread assumption that Appalachian people were strictly of English descent, dressed in Elizabethan-era costumes. Despite the fact that its interpretation of Appalachian culture was highly romanticized, that festival was a major success: twenty thousand people attended in 1938, its peak year. The national media fueled the festival's popularity, in part through drawing attention to the stereo-typed "mountain" characters.

Recording companies and folk music enthusiasts were more interested in promoting specific aspects of Appalachian music than in documenting or understanding the true diversity of the region's music. Outsiders stood to gain little from acknowledging the African American influences on this complex musical hybrid. Blues, jazz, and black gospel music, however, were inextricably entwined with European influences in much of the early hillbilly music. "Hill-billy blues" or "mountain blues," for example, was a common song form in early country music, and several white country musicians from Appalachia, including Frank Hutchison, Cliff Carlisle, and the Carter Family, borrowed from the blues and learned from African American mentors. Subsequent major re-gional music styles have continued to borrow from African American sources. In the 1940s, two major country music stylists regarded as founders of their respective styles—finger-picking guitarist Merle Travis and the "Father of Blue-grass Music," Bill Monroe—learned from a legendary African American itiner-ant musician, Arnold Shultz. Travis and Monroe were both natives of western Kentucky, yet their music is often viewed today as Appalachian, thematically as well as stylistically. Both musicians were strongly influenced by black music, yet their music has most often been associated with the perceived "white" music of Appalachia. Only in the last three decades, since the rise of academic interest in Appalachian cultural history and in country music, have some of these misper-ceptions been corrected.

Religious music, a significant component of Appalachian life, similarly fea-tures intertwinings of white and black musical influences. Again, while the dom-inant image of Appalachian sacred music is that of white southern gospel groups or white Protestant church congregations, African American contributions to the region's religious music repertoire and singing styles often go unacknowledged. Indeed, some of the most influential musicians in the history of black gospel music came from the southern margins of Appalachia, in Alabama, Georgia, Mississippi, and South Carolina. A short list of important African American gospel musicians from this region includes "the Father of Gospel Music," Thomas A. Dorsey, the Five Blind Boys of Alabama, the Dixie Hummingbirds, and the Rev. Gary Davis. Claude Jeter, who formed the popular gospel group the Swan Silvertones in West Virginia, also was a northern Alabama native. Even in areas with a comparatively small black population, white musicians were influenced by African American gospel music, whether through direct contact with black gospel singing or through recordings. From Roy Acuff's and Tennessee Ernie Ford's classic recordings of Thomas A. Dorsey's famous gospel composition "Precious Lord, Take My Hand" to Ralph Stanley's recent rendition of the public domain song "O Death," the influence of black gospel songs and spirituals infuses white southern gospel. Stanley's version of the latter song, which appeared on the *O Brother, Where Art Thou?* soundtrack, drew attention to his harrowing "mountain" singing style, yet the song has African American origins and was likely popularized among white Appalachian musicians in the early twentieth century by itinerant black musicians traveling in Appalachia to find work.

The enormous popularity of the *O Brother* soundtrack and its being widely viewed as containing bluegrass music also brings into focus the problematic relation of bluegrass music with Appalachia, a commonly perceived connection that bears clarification. Perhaps because of the predominance on that soundtrack of musicians with backgrounds in bluegrass, many music journalists have described the popularity of *O Brother* as a triumph for bluegrass music and have at the same time associated that genre with Appalachia. This perspective contradicts the understanding among older bluegrass enthusiasts who primarily associate bluegrass with western Kentucky, the birthplace of Bill Monroe. While Monroe was responsible for the initial innovations that made his group's music distinct from other country music styles, a number of Appalachian musicians whose musical and cultural backgrounds were not markedly dissimilar from Monroe's helped him define the ensemble sound of bluegrass. Three-finger-style banjoist Earl Scruggs and lead vocalist and guitarist Lester Flatt, both Appalachian natives, were integral contributors to the sound that in the mid-1950s, nearly a decade after it emerged in the classic 1946 lineup of Monroe's group, became widely known as "bluegrass" (honoring Monroe's group, the Blue Grass Boys, which featured Scruggs and Flatt in 1946 and 1947). Many other Appalachian musicians who had grown up playing acoustic string band music had to make only minor adjustments to their music to emulate the more popular sound that Monroe's ensemble was crafting. The Stanley Brothers, Reno and

APPALACHIAN MUSIC

Smiley, the Osborne Brothers, Mac Wiseman, Jimmy Martin, and Jim and Jesse were some of the better-known Appalachian acts that helped define and popularize the early bluegrass sound. With the dominant presence of such Appalachian-based bluegrass stalwarts as Ralph Stanley and Norman Blake on the *O Brother* soundtrack, it is understandable that the movie's music has been linked with bluegrass and Appalachia, even though the producer and musicians on the project in actuality were attempting to evoke a 1930s-era pre-bluegrass, rural Mississippi (as opposed to Appalachian) musical heritage.

While the current revival of Appalachian music among urban Americana musicians and audiences has favored the relatively raw, folklike sound of such early country and bluegrass performers as the Carter Family and the Stanley Brothers, other smoother, more polished Appalachian singing styles have in the past had even stronger influence on mainstream popular music. Appalachian brother-duo harmony singing, as represented by the Blue Sky Boys, the Delmore Brothers, and the Louvin Brothers, entered the pop field in the 1950s through the vocal harmony style of the Everly Brothers, who during their early years as performers were based in Knoxville, Tennessee. Through the influence of the Everly Brothers on the Beatles and countless other pop and rock groups, Appalachian duo harmony singing became a significant influence on popular music across the Western Hemisphere.

Two other important, overlapping music genres strongly associated with Appalachia are coal-mining music and protest music. From the late nineteenth century, when industrialization displaced many Appalachian people from their familiar subsistence agricultural ways of life, working classes have protested through song (as through their participation in strikes) the increasing social and environmental abuse within the region. Many of these protest songs are strongly linked in the mainstream American consciousness with compelling visual images from Appalachia's coal-mining areas. Songs such as Florence Reece's "Which Side Are You On?" Sarah Ogan Gunning's "Come All You Coal Miners," Billy Edd Wheeler's "Coal Tattoo," Merle Travis's "Dark as a Dungeon" and "Sixteen Tons," Jean Ritchie's "The L&N Don't Stop Here Anymore" and "Blue Diamond Mines," and Hazel Dickens's "Black Lung" and "Coal Mining Woman" are some of the songs that transcend their topical concerns. Even with the decreasing number of coal-mining-related jobs within Appalachia, musicians from the region, as well as from elsewhere, have continued to write coal-mining songs set in Appalachia; notable among these are Appalachian natives Dwight Yoakam's "Miner's Prayer" (1985) and Darrell Scott's "You'll Never Leave Harlan Alive" (1997), as well as non-natives Steve Earle's "Hillbilly Highway" (1986) and "Harlan Man" (1999) and Gillian Welch's "Miner's Refrain" (1998). Granted the preponderance of coal-mining songs in the Appalachian protest music repertoire, people across the region have utilized the protest song to address other injustices. Some noteworthy examples are Blind Alfred Reed's "How Can a Poor Man Stand Such Times and Live"; the Bentley Boys' "Down on Penny's Farm," which decried the exploitation of tenant farmers; Fiddlin' John Carson's "The Farmer Is the Man Who Feeds Them All"; and perhaps the most renowned protest song worldwide, "We Shall Overcome," which was reworked at the East Tennessee–based Highlander Center for utilization by striking textile and tobacco workers and which was later adopted by Martin Luther King Jr. as the official theme song of his March on Washington in 1963.

Most popular conceptions of Appalachian music are based primarily on a very small number of regional music genres, and such notions exclude many other aspects of Appalachia's musical life. Many musicians and musical communities in the region are devoted to musical genres that are not widely considered as Appalachian. Exemplifying an overlooked Appalachian musical community, Chattanooga, Tennessee, yielded early jazz singer Bessie Smith as well as jazz bass innovator Jimmy Blanton. Yet many Appalachian-based musicians, working in such regionally underrecognized musical genres as classical, rock, pop, rhythm and blues, and jazz, do draw upon Appalachia's ostensibly European American folk music legacy to give their works a distinctive regional flavor. For instance, several rock and pop music acts from Appalachia—including the Marshall Tucker Band, Dave Loggins, and Goose Creek Symphony—have incorporated diverse aspects of Appalachian music into their music, creating amalgams ranging from country rock and country pop to progressive country. Internationally celebrated flat-pick guitar innovator Doc Watson, multi-instrumentalist Darrell Scott, and double bass virtuoso Edgar Meyer have not only tread a line between musical genres but also have performed in both regional and nonregional styles. Several Appalachian-based classical music composers, such as Kenton Coe of Johnson City, Tennessee, have drawn heavily on regional themes.

The choice by some Appalachian-based classical music school programs to not focus on the region's folk music legacy, on the other hand, represents another face of Appalachia's multifaceted musical life—a nonregional approach to musical expression. Similarly, many rock musicians from Appalachia (including guitarist-singer Warren Haynes of the groups Gov't Mule and the Allman Brothers Band, and industrial metal innovator Trent Reznor of Nine Inch Nails) do not draw from the folk/country musical roots most often associated with Appalachia. A comprehensive understanding of any region's people requires recognition of not only the well-known facets of their culture but also those aspects of culture that underscore the diversity and possibilities within that region. If myths are punctured and stereotypes are dismantled in the process of presenting a more accurate portrayal of Appalachia's culture, so be it.

Music making at home, c. 1940. Courtesy of Versie Hollandsworth Phillips.

The singing school in Floyd County, Virginia, popular in the mountains through the 1930s.
From the collection of Ricky Cox.

Maple Shade Inn musicians of Pulaski, Virginia, c. 1900. From the collection of Gary Hancock. Courtesy of the Raymond Ratcliffe Memorial Museum.

Janette Carter, daughter of A. P. and Sarah Carter and founder of the Carter Fold in Hiltons, Virginia. Courtesy of the Carter Family.

Nat Reese, mountain blues musician, Princeton, West Virginia. Courtesy of Nat Reese, Sr.

The Appalkids, carrying on the tradition. Courtesy of the Radford University Appalachian Regional Studies Center.

Notes

1. Lee Smith, "Mountain Music's Moment in the Sun," *Washington Post,* August 12, 2001: G 1.
2. Brian Mansfield, "O Country Music, Where Art Thou?" *USA Today Home Page,* July 9, 2001, http://www.usatoday.com/life/music/2001-07-09-country-usat. htm#more (July 25, 2003).
3. John Solomon Otto, "Plain Folk, Lost Frontiersmen, and Hillbillies: The Southern Mountain Folk in History and Popular Culture," *Southern Studies: An Interdisciplinary Journal of the South* 26, no.1 (1987): 11.
4. Ibid.
5. Ibid., 5.
6. Ibid., 9.
7. Ibid., 8.
8. Ibid., 9.
9. Ibid.
10. Ibid., 9–10.
11. Ibid., 10.
12. Bill C. Malone, *Country Music, U.S.A.* Rev. ed. (Austin: Univ. of Texas Press, 1985), 68.
13. Ibid., 70.

Suggested Readings

Burton, Thomas G. *Some Ballad Folks.* Johnson City: East Tennessee State Univ. Press, 1978.

Carawan, Guy. *Voices from the Mountains.* Athens: Univ. of Georgia Press, 1996.

Conway, Cecilia. *African Banjo Echoes in Appalachia: A Study of Folk Traditions.* Knoxville: Univ. of Tennessee Press, 1995.

Green, Archie. *Only a Miner: Studies in Recording Coal-Mining Songs.* Urbana: Univ. of Illinois Press, 1972.

Irwin, John Rice. *Musical Instruments of the Southern Appalachian Mountains.* West Chester, Pa.: Schiffer, 1979.

Lilly, John. *Mountains of Music: West Virginia Traditional Music from Goldenseal.* Urbana: Univ. of Illinois Press, 1999.

Malone, Bill C. *Country Music, U.S.A.* Austin: Univ. of Texas Press, 1968.

McGee, Marty. *Traditional Musicians of the Central Blue Ridge: Old Time, Early Country, Folk and Bluegrass Label Recording Artists, with Discographies.* Jefferson, N.C.: McFarland, 2000.

Patterson, Beverly B. *Sound of the Dove: Singing in Appalachian Primitive Baptist Churches.* Urbana: Univ. of Illinois Press, 1995.

Ritchie, Jean. *Singing Family of the Cumberlands.* Lexington: Univ. Press of Kentucky, 1988.

Romalis, Shelly. *Pistol Packin' Mama: Aunt Molly Jackson and the Politics of Folksong.* Urbana: Univ. of Illinois Press, 1998.

Rosenberg, Neil V. *Bluegrass: A History.* Urbana: Univ. of Illinois Press, 1985.

———. *Transforming Tradition: Folk Music Revivals Examined.* Urbana: Univ. of Illinois Press, 1993.

Sharp, Cecil J. *English Folk Songs from the Southern Appalachians.* London: Oxford Univ. Press, 1917.

Smith, Betty N. *Jane Hicks Gentry: A Singer Among Singers.* Lexington: Univ. Press of Kentucky, 1998.

Titon, Jeff Todd. *Powerhouse of God: Speech, Chant, and Song in an Appalachian Baptist Church.* Austin: Univ. of Texas Press, 1988.

Warner, Anne. *Traditional American Folk Songs from the Anne and Frank Warner Collection.* Syracuse, N.Y.: Syracuse Univ. Press. 1984.

Wolfe, Charles K., and Ted Olson. *The Bristol Sessions: Writings About the Big Bang of Country Music.* Jefferson, N.C.: McFarland, 2005.

RELIGION IN APPALACHIA

MELINDA BOLLAR WAGNER

What do the controversies concerning school textbook content in Kanawha County, West Virginia, in 1974; the United Mine Workers of America (UMWA) strike of Pittston Coal Company in 1989–90; and the labeling of school break periods (Winter/Spring vs. Christmas/Easter) in Montgomery County, Virginia, in the mid-1990s have in common? They are examples of struggles in which strong religious beliefs have played a large part. Conservative Christian parents in Kanawha County objected to their children's textbooks, fearing that they perpetuated an antireligious secular humanism. A National Education Association official said that the Kanawha County protestors "represented a true conflict between a truly old mountain culture and an urban one. They were true believers, those mountain men."[1] One of the major issues precipitating the strike of Pittston Coal was that the company wanted to change the UMWA contract so that miners would work on Sundays. When miners confronted Pittston officials at a stockholders' meeting in Greenwich, Connecticut, one official "suggested that miners resisting the company's demand that they work on Sunday were using religion as a crutch. A miner replied, 'I use church to get through work during the week. That's my crutch in life, the whole meaning of it, because I hope to go to a better place when this is over.'" A company official retorted, "Come to Greenwich," while other Pittston personnel laughed.[2] These few examples portray the importance of religion in daily life in the Appalachian region, adhered to, in these cases, even in the face of strong opposition.

Appalachian Diversity

The Appalachian region contains as much variety in types of religion practiced, and degrees to which they're practiced, as other regions of the country. Virtually every religion found in the United States is represented in Appalachia. On the other hand, some religious groups are unique to the region and to places Appalachian migrants have carried them. In the United States, religious families that have been identified include Judaism, Liturgical (Catholic), Eastern Orthodox, Anglican (Episcopalian), Lutheran, Reformed-Presbyterian, Liberal (Unitarians and so on), Pietist-Methodist, Holiness, Pentecostal, Free-Church (Mennonites and Brethren), Baptist, Independent Fundamentalist, Adventist, New Thought, Psychic, and Magical, plus growing manifestations of the world religions of Islam, Hindu, and Buddhist.[3] All of these are found in Appalachia.

Statistically, people in the region, especially in what the Appalachian Regional Commission labels central and southern Appalachia, are affiliated more often than not with conservative Christian churches and carry a type of religion that is not easily compartmentalized to Sunday mornings. In the United States, the largest Christian groups are the Catholics, Baptists, and Methodists. Of churchgoers in the United States, 39 percent are Catholic, 22 percent Baptist, and 8 percent Methodist. In Appalachia, the rankings of these three large denominations are turned around a bit, with Baptist being first, the Catholic Church second, and Methodists third. Twenty-one percent of the Appalachian population, as defined by the Appalachian Regional Commission, is Baptist; 13 percent is Catholic, and 9 percent is Methodist.[4]

These statistics themselves hide a good deal of diversity, since the Baptist category includes 11,584 different churches, some conservative Southern Baptist, others more liberal American Baptist, and still others "Old Time" Baptist groups; the myriad of purely independent Baptist churches are not included in these statistics, which are largely derived from reports made to national denominational organizations. For the same reason, nondenominational churches and independent charismatic churches are not counted in the statistics.

Appalachian Difference

Denominational labels can be misleading in other ways as well. For example, it has been said that if a person wanted to see what an early Presbyterian church—newly transplanted from Ulster (Northern Ireland) in the 1700s—looked like, she would get a truer picture by visiting an Appalachian Baptist church than by visiting a current-day Presbyterian church in the region.[5]

Indeed, the knowledge the reader already has about denominations in other regions may not be helpful in understanding the religions of Appalachia. A recent history of religion in the region uses the label "Appalachian mountain religion" to signify that it is a unique form, not the same as denominations in other regions. The history of this religious tradition can ultimately be traced to the Protestant Reformation, with the strands that particularly forged mountain religion being German Pietism, which emphasized Christian piety, purity, sanctification and perfection; the Scots-Irish immigrants' Calvinism, emphasizing conversion and renewal of conversion; and the Baptist culture of immersion baptism and revival meetings.[6]

Groups unique to the region or to places mountain people have settled include the various types of Old-Time Baptist churches: Primitive Baptist, Old Regular Baptist, Regular Baptist, Missionary Baptist, and Free Will Baptist, to name a few.[7] The most conservative of the Old-Time Baptist churches retain a belief that salvation is gained strictly by predestination: a person's after-death fate is set, and no human action is required to, nor is able to, change it. This was a part of the Calvinism that the Scots-Irish brought with them to the Appalachian Mountains when they emigrated from Ulster; it is supported by Bible verses such as these:

> Blessed be the God and Father of our Lord Jesus Christ, who hath blessed us with all spiritual blessings in heavenly places in Christ:
> According as he hath chosen us in him before the foundation of the world, that we should be holy and without blame before him in love:
> Having predestined us unto the adoption of children by Jesus Christ to himself, according to the good pleasure of his will. . . .
> In whom we have redemption through his blood, the forgiveness of sins, according to the riches of his grace.[8]

Nationwide, the numbers of adherents in the various Old-Time Baptist groups are small, ranging from 172 General Six Principle Baptists to 293,000 Free Will Baptists. For each Old-Time Baptist group, the proportion of its adherents residing in the Appalachian region ranges from one-third to the total number.[9]

There is some variety in the perspective on salvation among various churches in Appalachia. For example, the evangelical Presbyterian Church in America (different from the more mainline Presbyterian Church USA) holds to a Calvinistic doctrine of total depravity of humans and unconditional election by God to a saved state, sharing their view of salvation with some Old-Time Baptists. Baptists who do not believe in predestination believe at least in eternal salvation or the security of salvation: once a person has taken on a personal relationship with Jesus, he is saved, and nothing he can do will prevent him from going to heaven. Holiness churches have a different view of salvation, teaching that a believer's behavior can backslide to the point that she would again become lost. Holiness beliefs allow for humankind's fall from grace as well as its perfectibility. Holiness Pentecostal churches add belief in the gifts of the Spirit:

> But the manifestation of the Spirit is given to every man to profit withal.
>
> For to one is given by the Spirit the word of wisdom; to another the word of knowledge by the same Spirit;
>
> To another faith by the same Spirit; to another the gifts of healing by the same Spirit;
>
> To another the working of miracles; to another prophecy; to another discerning of spirits; to another divers kinds of tongues; to another the interpretation of tongues.[10]

Much has been made of snake-handling congregations in Appalachia and in cities that house Appalachian migrants, although they number no more than "3,000 people at most."[11] Snake-handling churches are Holiness Pentecostal churches, but by no means are all Holiness Pentecostal churches snake-handling churches.

The snake-handling congregations add to the gifts of the Spirit the handling of snakes and, sometimes, the drinking of poison and the handling of fire, harking generally to Mark 16:16–18 and Isaiah 43:2:

> He that believeth and is baptized shall be saved; but he that believeth not shall be damned.
>
> And these signs shall follow them that believe; In my name shall they cast out devils; they shall speak with new tongues;
>
> They shall take up serpents; and if they drink any deadly thing, it shall not hurt them; they shall lay hands on the sick, and they shall recover.[12]
>
> When thou passest through the waters, I will be with thee; and through the rivers, they shall not overflow thee: when thou walkest through the fire, though shalt not be burned; neither shall the flame kindle upon thee.[13]

History has it that snake handling was added to some Pentecostal services through the work of George W. Hensley in the early 1900s in Tennessee. (See Birckhead 1997, Burton 1993, Kane 1979, Kimbrough 1995, Morrow 2005 for more on snake handling.)

Characteristics of Appalachian Religion

Although religion in Appalachia can be described as diverse, several authors have come to similar conclusions regarding certain characteristics of religion in the region. These characteristics include fundamentalism; Puritanism; an emphasis on a personal relationship with God and on otherworldly salvation rather than on social problems; fatalism and an ability to withstand hardship and privation; an experiential and emotional expression of religious faith that includes rituals such as homecomings, memorial days, and graveyard decoration days that symbolize the connection between the history of the church (reaching back to Christ's day) and departed loved ones; management by God of the temporal world and everyday life; and humility and simplicity in belief, ritual, and church architecture.[14] Many of these characteristics require some explanation.

"Fundamentalist" has come to signify the most conservative end of the liberal-to-conservative continuum for those who map and categorize religions in the United States. Other conservative churches are those labeled "evangelical" and "charismatic"; they include independent Baptists, Wesleyan churches, the Presbyterian Church in America, Holiness churches, and Pentecostal churches. The Unitarian Universalist Church would be on the most liberal end, while mainline Presbyterian USA, American Baptist, Methodist, and Lutheran churches would be somewhere in the middle. Even within the fundamentalist category, there is a good deal of variety in belief and practice. Usually fundamentalism is associated with a literal interpretation of the Bible. The word "fundamentalist" was not used until the 1900s, following the publication from 1909 to 1915 of a set of twelve books containing ninety articles titled "The Fundamentals." They delineated the elements of traditional doctrine, at that time being threatened by the teaching of evolution, the restructuring of the family, and the kind of scholarship that challenges the inerrant nature of the Bible. These elements included the beliefs that (1) the Bible was created from divine inspiration and is authentic and unerring, (2) following the Bible is absolutely sufficient for man's redemption, and (3) Christ is the savior, born of a virgin, who died for humans' sins and was miraculously resurrected.[15]

Puritanism has been jokingly referred to as the fear that someone somewhere is having a good time. The jokesters are referring to the rules that churches make to govern the behavior of their adherents. The more conservative churches, the fundamentalists, are likely to hold rules against drinking alcohol, playing cards, dancing, and the like. Holiness churches and some Baptist churches are likely to add regulations with regard to dress and hairstyle.

Puritanism brings with it the connotation of fear of eternal damnation, made famous in cleric Jonathan Edwards's "Sinners in the Hands of an Angry God" sermon, delivered in 1741 in Connecticut. Fear is not missing from the pulpits of Appalachian churches as a motivation for becoming saved and living a Christian life as defined by the church. For example, a signboard in front of a church recently proclaimed, "No Fear, No God." (Yet not all Appalachian churches believe in the eternal damnation of those not saved; see Dorgan 1997 concerning Primitive Baptist Universalists.)

The importance of a personal relationship with God is made clear in conversations in which people try to discern the religion of another. "Is she a Christian?" "Well, I know she goes to church, but I don't know if she has a personal relationship with Jesus." As the charismatic conservative Christians put it, "If a person believes in his heart and confesses with his mouth that Jesus Christ is Lord and that God has raised Him from the dead, that person shall be saved." The alternative is the lake of fire in hell. Church membership and salvation come about through each individual's acceptance of an invitation: "Christ is knocking—will you answer?" Christ and the individual are not seen as equals, but Christ is spoken of as a "friend" and a "personal savior" as well as a Holy Spirit. The verses of hymns sung in the churches of Appalachia celebrate this relationship

There are days I'd like to be
All alone with Christ, my Lord,
I can tell Him of my troubles
All alone, all alone.
Do you know Him, know my Savior,
Do you know his wondrous love
And mighty power?
You would make my Savior yours
This very hour,
If you knew Him,
As I know Him
You would make my Savior yours
This very hour.[16]

The otherworldly salvation is achieved, most adherents of mountain religion believe, through God's grace. In this ideology, when God brought Jesus Christ to earth and allowed him to die to atone for the sins of humankind, he offered salvation, by his grace, to all who would choose it—or, for those who affirm predestination, those who are chosen. This choice, it is thought, is proffered by God's grace, and no amount of good deeds or works people might do can ever make them good enough for heaven. Here the conservative Christians say they differ from mainline liberal Protestantism, which, they say, uses a balance-scale approach—weighing people's good and bad attributes and behavior—to determine their after-death fate.

Fatalism could be transformed into a much more positive-sounding word. Folklorist Emma Bell Miles joined it with "courage" in her description of Appalachian religion. It has also been called "realism." Fatalism implies an acceptance of fate, of God's will, as conservative Christians see it. The personal relationship with Christ allows a person to handle life's adversities. An often-heard homily in Appalachia is "God doesn't give a person more than he can handle." But we go astray when we see fatalism as leading to a "There's nothing I can do" attitude throughout the region. If fatalism prevented doing anything about social problems, how would labor union activity, for example, be explained? In fact, the union activist and the ardent churchgoer is the same person in Appalachia.

The experiential and emotional expression of faith derives from the personal relationship with God. Appalachian churches, especially of the Holiness and Pentecostal persuasion, tend not to be highly formalized in the order of worship. Calling out by the congregation is common, for example. Individual congregants have much control over the worship service, as the Spirit leads them to sing and to testify about what their faith has wrought in their lives.

Religion in Appalachia indeed touches all aspects of people's lives. Sociologist Max Weber long ago made a distinction among kinds of religions that may help to describe this aspect of Appalachian religion.[17] As Geertz explains, "rationalized" religion is "apart . . . above . . . outside" of ordinary life. In "traditional" religion, on the other hand, as is more common in Appalachia, the sacred is found everywhere—in the "rooftrees, graveyards, and road-crossings of everyday life." In traditional religion, ties between humans and the sacred are maintained through "numberless concrete, almost reflexive gestures done in the general round of life."[18]

In Appalachia, as in the South in general, when a person moves in, a new neighbor is likely, more so than in other regions of the country, to hand her a small business card with information about his church printed on it. A newcomer may be disappointed if he sets out to shop on Sunday, buy beer at baseball games, or order mixed drinks at every restaurant. Blue laws prohibit these activities in many localities. In community newspapers, correspondents' columns, birth and wedding announcements, birthday notices, obituaries, memorials, and even advertisements are more likely to contain explicitly religious language.[19] Several Christian stations will be found on the radio dial and in the local cable television network's lineup, and a patron is likely to see a family bowing their heads to say grace before partaking of a meal in a fast-food restaurant. "Praise God" may be scattered throughout a conversation. Drivers will often see cars whose bumper stickers proclaim the occupants' faith. "To the Christian all things are sacred" are words conservative Christians live by.

Religion in Appalachian Cultures

If Appalachian religion is to fit with the rest of Appalachian life, it should contain characteristics that are intertwined with other aspects of Appalachian cultures. Several authors have found in Appalachia a "collective" orientation as opposed to the "individualistic" one more common in middle America. The preferred social character in the region is embodied in one who is modest and not comfortable standing out, one who communicates in indirect, nonconfrontational modes, avoiding rancor and giving advice carefully and in a roundabout way.[20]

Yet Appalachian churches have been said to be individualistic. They have been characterized this way because (1) their major concern is with the individual soul and not social reform, (2) church services include the religious experience of the individual, and (3) there is a proliferation of small churches in the region. But these indicators of individualism are muted by other, more collective attributes of Appalachian religion. Indeed, it could be said that religion reflects submerging the self in the family of Christ, just as secular life reflects submerging the self to some degree in the collectivity. It seems that a native understanding of the religion would not focus on individualism, world rejection, or fatalism. It would, instead, focus on the central belief tenet: a personal relationship with God.[21]

In Protestant denominations, in particular, this relationship is incarnated in the social structure of the church, in the church service itself, and in beliefs about salvation and conversion. Belief in a personal relationship with Christ implies that every member of a congregation is in direct communion with the Holy. Thus, formal leadership in the church is sparse. To have it otherwise would be interposing a humanly devised hierarchy between the individual and God. Within congregations, decisions are often reached by consensus. "The focus appears to be less on the efficient conduct of business than on maintaining and exhibiting the solidarity of the church," notes F. Carlene Bryant.[22] This parallels secular life, where "it is more important to us to get along and have a good relationship with other persons than it is to make our true feelings known."[23]

The individual's relationship with a personal savior results in a church service that is more often informal and spontaneous. Individual congregants can participate. But individuals are not doing whatever they like; they are doing whatever they are called upon by the Spirit to do: "Be obedient. Just let the Spirit take control." Preachers act as mouthpieces for the Lord.[24]

Salvation and conversion are seen as a separation from a preconversion life. To be born again is to take on a new life with a self that has a new relationship with Christ. Churches that practice immersion baptism may view it as a washing away of the old self. Some Holiness churches use an analogy that describes a sinner as a vessel or tub of dirty water. When the sinner is saved, the dirty water is dumped out of the tub; when he is sanctified, the tub is scrubbed out. When he is baptized in the Holy Spirit, signified by the gifts of the Spirit, clean water is poured into the tub.[25] The "individual is reborn through voluntary submission to the will of the Holy Spirit."[26] He then sees himself as part of the family of Christ with others who have been saved in the same way.

Thus religious life compels not an acting out of a person's individual characteristics but a submerging of that self while seeking a relationship with Christ. In the same way, life virtues in the region include humility and a repudiation of the individual spotlight.

To conclude, let us hark back to the original point: that diversity characterizes religion in Appalachia. The diversity in the region indeed lies at the heart of the controversies listed at the beginning of this chapter. If everyone in the region were "singing out of the same hymn book," there would be no question whether a school break should be called Christmas Break or Winter Break. If everyone believed alike, there would be no question whether textbook contents were controversial. Nationwide, religious affiliation is becoming less an ascribed characteristic—highly predictable by a family's longstanding affiliation—and more a matter of personal choice and life-cycle change. As more of Appalachia becomes urban and suburban, that trend will affect this region, too. The picture of religion in Appalachia—never easy to visualize clearly—promises to become more intricate in the future.

Baptizing in southwest Virginia. Courtesy of Timothy Boone.

Oriskany Church, Craig County, Virginia. Arcadia series © 1999 M. Anna Fariello.

Praying before a foot-washing service. By Angela V. Clevinger.

Eternity. By Jack Jeffers.

Religious expression through yard art. By Ricky Cox.

Church sign, Pulaski County, Virginia. By JoAnn Asbury.

Notes

I would like to thank the following readers for their comments and suggestions for revisions: Christi Leftwich Boone, Howard Dorgan, Loyal Jones, Sharon Heller, Rev. Jimmie Lee Price, Carolyn Quinn, and Radford University's Anthropology 411 Appalachian Cultures Class, Fall 2002.

1. Stephen Bates, *Battleground: One Mother's Crusade, The Religious Right, and the Struggle for Control of Our Classrooms* (New York: Poseidon Press, 1993), 303–4.

2. Richard A. Couto, "The Memory of Miners and the Conscience of Capital: Coal Miners' Strikes as Free Spaces," in *Fighting Back in Appalachia: Traditions of Resistance and Change,* ed. Stephen L. Fisher (Philadelphia: Temple Univ. Press, 1993), 165–94.

3. J. Gordon Melton, *A Directory of Religious Bodies in the United States* (New York: Garland, 1977, 1992).

4. Martin B. Bradley, et al., *Churches and Church Membership in the United States 1990: An Enumeration by Region, State, and County Based on Data Reported for 133 Church Groupings* (Atlanta: Glenmary Research Center, 1992); Bennett D. Poage, *The Church in Central Appalachia, 1990–2000* (Berea, Ky.: Appalachian Ministries Educational Resource Center, 2004).

5. Richard A. Humphrey, "The Scotch-Irish and Religion in the Southern Appalachian Mountains," in Course Packet for Appalachian-Scottish Studies Program, East Tennessee State Univ. and Univ. of Edinburgh, 1993.

6. Deborah Vansau McCauley, *Appalachian Mountain Religion: A History* (Urbana: Univ. of Illinois Press, 1995).

7. Loyal Jones, "Old-Time Baptists and Mainline Christianity," in *An Appalachian Symposium: Essays in Honor of Cratis D. Williams,* ed. J. W. Williamson (Boone, N.C.: Appalachian State Univ., 1977), 120–30.

8. Ephesians 1:3–5, 7 (KJV).

9. Clifford A. Grammich Jr., *Maps of the Churches and People of the Appalachian Region* (Knoxville: Commission on Religion in Appalachia, 1994).

10. 1 Corinthians 12:7–10 (KJV).

11. Jim Birckhead, "Snake Handlers: Heritage, Salvation, and Celebrity in the '90s," *Appalachian Journal* 23 (Spring 1996): 261.

12. Mark 16:16–18 (KJV).

13. Isaiah 43:2 (KJV).

14. Bruce Ergood and Bruce E. Kuhre, "Religion 'Just a Closer Walk with Thee,'" in *Appalachia: Social Context Past and Present,* ed. Bruce Ergood and Bruce E. Kuhre, 3d ed. (Dubuque, Iowa: Kendall/Hunt, 1991), 353–54.

15. Stewart G. Cole, *The History of Fundamentalism* (New York: Harper and Row, 1931).

16. F. Carlene Bryant, *We're All Kin: A Cultural Study of a Mountain Neighborhood* (Knoxville: Univ. of Tennessee Press, 1981), 95–96.

17. Max Weber, *The Sociology of Religion,* trans. Ephraim Fischoff (1922; reprint, Boston: Beacon Press, 1963).

18. Clifford Geertz, *The Interpretation of Cultures* (New York: Basic Books, 1973), 171–75.

19. Jerusha Brooks, Julia Everett, and Melinda Bollar Wagner, "Producing the Sacred in Community Newspapers" (paper presented at the Society for the Scientific Study of Religion meetings, Nashville, Tenn., Nov. 8–10, 1996).

20. Kai T. Erikson, *Everything in Its Path* (New York: Simon and Schuster, 1976); George L. Hicks, *Appalachian Valley* (New York: Holt, Rinehart, and Winston, 1976); Loyal Jones, *Appalachian Values* (Ashland, Ky.: Jesse Stuart Foundation, 1994); David H. Looff, *Appalachia's Children: The Challenge of Mental Health* (Lexington: Univ. Press of Kentucky, 1971); Melinda Bollar Wagner, "A Cross-Cultural Study of Ethnopersonality: The Scottish and Appalachian Sense of Self," *ALCA-Lines: Journal of the Assembly on the Literature and Culture of Appalachia* 6 (1994): 6, 16; Melinda Bollar Wagner, *God's Schools: Choice and Compromise in American Society* (New Brunswick, N.J.: Rutgers Univ. Press, 1990).

21. Bryant, *We're All Kin.*

22. Ibid., 98.

23. Loyal Jones, "Appalachian Values," in *Appalachia: Social Context Past and Present,* ed. Bruce Ergood and Bruce E. Kuhre, 3d ed. (Dubuque, Iowa: Kendall/Hunt, 1991), 171.

24. Bryant, *We're All Kin,* 107.

25. J. Gordon Melton, personal communication to author, November 7, 1992.

26. Bryant, *We're All Kin,* 111.

Suggested Readings

Bates, Stephen. *Battleground: One Mother's Crusade: The Religious Right and the Struggle for Control of Our Classrooms.* New York: Poseidon Press, 1993.

Birckhead, Jim. "Snake Handling: Critical Reflections." In *Anthropology of Religion: A Handbook,* edited by Stephen D. Glazier. Westport, Conn.: Praeger, 1997.

———. "Snake Handlers: Heritage, Salvation, and Celebrity in the '90s." *Appalachian Journal* 23 (Spring 1996): 260–74.

Bradley, Martin B., et al. *Churches and Church Membership in the United States 1990: An Enumeration by Region, State, and County Based on Data Reported for 133 Church Groupings.* Atlanta: Glenmary Research Center, 1992.

Brooks, Jerusha, Julia Everett, and Melinda Bollar Wagner. "Producing the Sacred in Community Newspapers." Paper presented at the Society for the Scientific Study of Religion Meeting, Nashville, Tenn., Nov. 8–10, 1996.

Bryant, F. Carlene. *We're All Kin: A Cultural Study of a Mountain Neighborhood.* Knoxville: Univ. of Tennessee Press, 1981.

Burton, Thomas. *Serpent-Handling Believers.* Knoxville: Univ. of Tennessee Press, 1993.

Cole, Stewart G. *The History of Fundamentalism.* New York: Harper and Row, 1931.

Couto, Richard A. "The Memory of Miners and the Conscience of Capital: Coal Miners' Strikes as Free Spaces." In *Fighting Back in Appalachia: Traditions of Resistance and Change,* edited by Stephen L. Fisher. Philadelphia: Temple Univ. Press, 1993.

Dorgan, Howard. *Giving Glory to God in Appalachia: Worship Practices of Six Baptist Subdenominations.* Knoxville: Univ. of Tennessee Press, 1987.

———. *In the Hands of a Happy God: The "No-Hellers" of Central Appalachia.* Knoxville: Univ. of Tennessee Press, 1997.

———. *The Old Regular Baptists of Central Appalachia: Brothers and Sisters in Hope.* Knoxville: Univ. of Tennessee Press, 1987.

Ergood, Bruce, and Bruce E. Kuhre. "Religion 'Just a Closer Walk with Thee.'" In *Appalachia: Social Context Past and Present,* edited by Bruce Ergood and Bruce E. Kuhre. 3d ed. Dubuque, Iowa: Kendall/Hunt, 1991.

Erikson, Kai T. *Everything in Its Path.* New York: Simon and Schuster, 1976.

Geertz, Clifford. *The Interpretation of Cultures.* New York: Basic Books, 1973.

Grammich, Clifford A., Jr. *Maps of the Churches and People of the Appalachian Region.* Knoxville, Tenn.: Commission on Religion in Appalachia, 1994.

Hicks, George L. *Appalachian Valley.* New York: Holt, Rinehart, and Winston, 1976.

Humphrey, Richard A. "The Scotch-Irish and Religion in the Southern Appalachian Mountains." In Course Packet for Appalachian-Scottish Studies Program, East Tennessee State Univ. and Univ. of Edinburgh, 1993.

Jones, Loyal. *Appalachian Values.* Ashland, Ky.: Jesse Stuart Foundation, 1994.

———. "Appalachian Values." In *Appalachia: Social Context Past and Present,* edited by Bruce Ergood and Bruce E. Kuhre. 3d ed. Dubuque, Iowa: Kendall/Hunt, 1991.

———. "Appalachian Religion." In *Encyclopedia of Religion in the South,* edited by Samuel S. Hill. Macon, Ga.: Mercer Univ. Press, 1984.

———. "Old-Time Baptists and Mainline Christianity." In *An Appalachian Symposium: Essays in Honor of Cratis D. Williams,* edited by J. W. Williamson. Boone, N.C.: Appalachian State Univ., 1977.

Kane, Steven M. "Snake Handlers of Southern Appalachia." Ph.D. diss., Princeton Univ., 1979.

Kimbrough, David L. *Taking Up Serpents: Snake Handlers of Eastern Kentucky.* Chapel Hill: Univ. of North Carolina Press, 1995.

Looff, David H. *Appalachia's Children: The Challenge of Mental Health.* Lexington: Univ. Press of Kentucky, 1971.

Marsden, George M. *Fundamentalism and American Culture: The Shaping of Twentieth-Century Evangelicalism: 1870–1925.* New York: Oxford Univ. Press, 1980.

Maurer, Beryl. "Religion." In *Mountain Heritage,* edited by Beryl Maurer. Parsons, W.Va.: McClain, 1975.

McCauley, Deborah Vansau. *Appalachian Mountain Religion: A History.* Urbana: Univ. of Illinois Press, 1995.

Melton, J. Gordon. *A Directory of Religious Bodies in the United States.* New York: Garland, 1977, 1992.

Miles, Emma Bell. *The Spirit of the Mountains.* Reprint Facsimile Edition. Knoxville: Univ. of Tennessee Press, 1975.

Morrow, Jimmy, with Ralph W. Hood Jr., ed. *Handling Serpents: Pastor Jimmy Morrow's Narrative History of His Appalachian Jesus' Name Tradition.* Macon, Ga.: Mercer Univ. Press, 2005.

Peacock, James L., and Ruel W. Tyson Jr. "Pilgrims of Paradox: Calvinism and Experience among the Primitive Baptists of the Blue Ridge." *Smithsonian Series in Ethnographic Inquiry* 17. Washington, D.C.: Smithsonian Institution Press, 1989.

Piepkorn, Arthur Carl. *Profiles in Belief: The Religious Bodies of the United States and Canada.* New York: Harper and Row, 1978–79.

Poage, Bennett D. *The Church in Central Appalachia, 1990–2000.* Berea, Ky.: Appalachian Ministries Educational Resource Center, 2004.

Sandeen, Ernest R. *The Roots of Fundamentalism: British and American Millenarianism, 1800–1930.* Chicago: Univ. of Chicago Press, 1970.

Wagner, Melinda Bollar. "A Cross-Cultural Study of Ethnopersonality: The Scottish and Appalachian Sense of Self." *ALCA-Lines: Journal of the Assembly on the Literature and Culture of Appalachia.* National Council of Teachers of English (1994): 6, 16; (1996): 16–17, 23.

———. *God's Schools: Choice and Compromise in American Society.* New Brunswick, N.J.: Rutgers Univ. Press, 1990.

Weber, Max. *The Protestant Ethic and the Spirit of Capitalism.* Translated by Talcott Parsons. 1921–21. Reprint, New York: Scribner's, 1948.

———. *The Sociology of Religion.* Translated by Ephraim Fischoff. 1922. Reprint, Boston: Beacon Press, 1963.

Additional Recommended Resources

Bruce, Dickson D., Jr. *And They All Sang Hallelujah: Plain-Folk Camp-Meeting Religion, 1800–1845.* Knoxville: Univ. of Tennessee Press, 1974.

In the Good Old Fashioned Way. Directed by Herb E. Smith. 29 min. Appalshop Film and Video. Videocassette.

Jones, Loyal. *Faith and Meaning in the Southern Uplands.* Urbana: Univ. of Illinois Press, 1999.

Leonard, Bill J. *Christianity in Appalachia: Profiles in Regional Pluralism.* Knoxville: Univ. of Tennessee Press, 1999.

McCauley, Deborah Vansau, and Laura A. Porter. *Mountain Holiness: A Photographic Narrative.* Knoxville: Univ. of Tennessee Press, 2003.

Melton, J. Gordon. *Encyclopedia of American Religions.* New York: Gale Group, 2002.

Patterson, Beverly Bush. *The Sound of the Dove: Singing in Appalachian Primitive Baptist Churches.* Urbana: Univ. of Illinois Press, 1995.

Photiadis, John D., ed. *Religion in Appalachia: Theological, Social, and Psychological Dimensions and Correlates.* Morgantown: Center for Extension and Continuing Education, Division of Social and Economic Development, Office of Research and Development, West Virginia Univ., 1978.

Reid, Melanie Sovine. "On the Study of Religion in Appalachia: A Review/Essay." *Appalachian Journal* 6 (Spring 1979): 239–44.

Sovine, Melanie L. "Studying Religious Belief Systems in Their Social Historical Context." In *Appalachia and America: Autonomy and Regional Dependence,* edited by Allen Batteau. Lexington: Univ. Press of Kentucky, 1983.

Titon, Jeff Todd. *Powerhouse for God: Sacred Speech, Chant, and Song in an Appalachian Baptist Church.* American Folklore Recordings. Chapel Hill: Univ. of North Carolina Press, 1982.

———. *Powerhouse for God: Speech, Chant, and Song in an Appalachian Baptist Church.* Austin: Univ. of Texas Press, 1988.

Tyson, Ruel W., Jr., James L. Peacock, and Daniel W. Patterson. *Diversities of Gifts: Field Studies in Southern Religion.* Urbana: Univ. of Illinois Press, 1988.

APPALACHIAN LITERATURE

DANNY MILLER, SANDRA BALLARD, ROBERTA HERRIN, STEPHEN D. MOONEY, SUSAN UNDERWOOD, AND JACK WRIGHT

The Appalachian region has been the setting and source of a significant body of written literature. Appalachian writing is distinguished from the more general designation of southern literature, which is more Gothic and more concerned with North-South conflicts, among other differences. As is true of all literature, the best fiction, poetry, nonfiction, and drama by and about the people of Appalachia deals with universal truths as revealed through the lives of specific individuals in localized settings. Appalachian literature, however, is sometimes distinguished from other literatures by its strong emphasis on setting, or "place," as an influence upon the values and motivations of characters. On the one hand, this quality has made it easier for critics to devalue Appalachian writing, based, in part, on the assumption that "regional" art of any kind, from any region, is necessarily inferior. This tendency is compounded by some critics' acceptance of unflattering stereotypes of the Appalachian region, many of which, ironically, were created and continue to be perpetuated by writers who choose to accentuate and exaggerate the most exotic or romantic components of Appalachian history and culture. On the other hand, the willingness, particularly among writers native to the region, to incorporate local and regional beliefs and values into their work has resulted in a literature that offers insight into the distinguishing values of a particular place and time, even as it exposes the common threads linking lives lived in all places at all times.

Fiction

Short stories and novels about Appalachia did not become a staple of the literary scene until after the Civil War, when the interest of the reading public was captured by what was perceived as the oddity (sometimes picturesque, sometimes strange) in the Appalachian people. The local colorists created and often relied upon stereotypes of the people they had usually only observed from a respectable distance: the moonshiner, often drunk and abusive; the feudist, taking matters into his own hands; the beautiful, unappreciated mountain girl often longing to escape the restrictions of mountain isolation; the tired wife and mother, old before her time from endless work and childbearing; the aged grandmother; the barefoot urchin; and the "idiot," to name a few.

Mary Noailles Murfree is credited with catapulting the Appalachian mountaineers into the American consciousness in her extremely popular stories about the East Tennessee mountains which began to appear in the literary magazines in the 1870s and were collected into the best-selling *In the Tennessee Mountains* in 1884. John Fox Jr., a native of the Kentucky Bluegrass region, succeeded Murfree as the next best-selling author to write about Appalachia. His most popular novels were *The Little Shepherd of Kingdom Come* (1903) and *The Trail of the Lonesome Pine* (1908).

Though mountain people were often negatively portrayed in the works of local colorists, who relied heavily on negative stereotypes such as feuding and violence or lack of education and sophistication (in Fox's *Trail of the Lonesome Pine*, for example, the mountain girl Maggie Tolliver is too unsophisticated to marry the outsider Jack Hale until she has inherited money and gone East to a finishing school), there was withal a romantic haze enshrouding them. Many of the individual characters we find in these works are admirable and heroic, intelligent if not educated, sincere and unpretentious. The focus in these works was often on their setting, the sublime natural beauty of the Appalachian mountains, and local colorists felt a nostalgic regret at the loss of much of the nobility and hopefulness of American life as a result of the Civil War, which they seemed to find in some aspects of Appalachian life. These romantic depictions gave way in the first quarter of the twentieth century, however, to mostly negative and disturbing portrayals.

Spurred by national interests in social betterment, many writers of the first quarter of the century portrayed the mountaineers as disgusting rather than picturesque, deranged and degraded rather than merely peculiar, mysterious and malign in their isolated hollows. Incest, illegitimacy, drunkenness, abusiveness of women and children, violence—all of these became familiar in depictions of the Appalachian people as writers turned to what they perceived as the need for "reform" in the mountains. One of the subplots of Anne W. Armstrong's *This Day and Time* (1930), for example, involves incest. Will Allen Dromgoole wrote several stories for *The Youth's Companion* aimed at attracting social reformers and Christian missionaries to the region. These novels also tackled issues of labor and politics through proletarian themes dealing with communism, socialism, and unionism in the coal mines and textile mills (such as in Gastonia, North Carolina). Among these are Sherwood Anderson's *Kit Brandon* (1936), Grace Lumpkin's *To Make My Bread* (1932), Ellen Glasgow's *Vein of Iron* (1935), and Olive Tilford Dargan's *Call Home the Heart* (1932).

For many reasons, including the lack of educational opportunities and the leisure time required to cultivate a literary tradition, Appalachian people did not begin to write novels and stories about themselves until the second quarter of the twentieth century. Thomas Wolfe's *Look Homeward, Angel* (1929) was one of the first novels written by a native Appalachian, but even at its publication (and still today) this novel was not specifically identified as "Appalachian," perhaps because it does not deal with the typical Appalachian backwoods people and is set in the more urban area of Asheville, North Carolina. A serious misconception of the Appalachian region is its homogeneity of experience, with the rural stereotyped as the norm.

In their 1962 essay "Literature Since 1900," W. D. Weatherford and Wilma Dykeman pointed out that "one of the distinctive virtues of contemporary mountain literature as opposed to that of an earlier day [is that] it has grown from within the Region."[1] In the late 1930s and early 1940s, native Appalachian literature blossomed in the works of native authors who, because of their personal backgrounds, wrote with a greater sense of authenticity and balanced realism in their portrayals of the mountain people. The three most prominent of these were Jesse Stuart, James Still, and Harriette Simpson Arnow.

A native of Greenup County, Kentucky, Jesse Stuart's first best seller was *Taps for Private Tussie* (1943), a satire of the welfare system which conveyed the serious message that private land ownership (which many Appalachian sharecroppers had lost over the years) and hard work could restore a sense of dignity and personal honor to the disenfranchised who had come to rely on government assistance. Although the Tussie clan is satirically and comically presented as the epitome of all the worst of the welfare system, their zest for life and their submerged desire for betterment are undiminished, and they come across to the reader not as negative stereotypes but as victims of a supposedly benevolent but actually debilitating system.

James Still's novel *River of Earth* (1940) is often compared to Steinbeck's *Grapes of Wrath* because it recounts the hardships of a struggling family during the Depression. The novel is told from the innocent-eye first-person point of view of an unnamed boy narrator who tells about his family's, the Baldridges', removal from the sustenance of the land and capitulation to the coal industry as the father moves the family from one coal camp to another. Although the lives of the Baldridge family are bleak and their poverty is at times crushing, Still, like Stuart, does not see them as defeated or merely victims of fatalism. Through all their hardships, the Baldridges maintain a dignity comparable to the heroes of Greek tragedy.

Harriette Arnow is perhaps the most widely known Appalachian writer in academic literary circles today. The first of her Appalachian trilogy of novels, *Mountain Path* (1936), belongs in some respects to an earlier literary tradition, focusing on moonshining and feuding. Similarly, the central plot of a young woman who comes from outside the region to teach school and learns to discard her preconceptions and value and respect the mountain people, echoes the works of Murfree and Fox. Arnow is better able than they, however, to show the dignity and humanity of the mountain people. Her second novel, *Hunter's Horn* (1949), is a naturalistic tragedy of the Ballew family; again, she depicts the hill people as essentially admirable and sympathetic, despite the mistakes they make. *The Dollmaker* (1954), Arnow's exploration of the out-migration of the Appalachian people to urban centers, is perhaps the most highly acclaimed Appalachian novel. It is often used in college and university classes and is one of the few Appalachian novels finding its way into the American literary canon.

Since the advent of native portrayals of the Appalachian region, there has been a tremendous amount of fiction written by Appalachian authors. Some of these have achieved national recognition, though many often have not been identified as specifically "Appalachian" or have been seen as somehow "transcending" the regionalism of Appalachian literature. For example, James Agee's classic *A Death in the Family* (1957), set in Knoxville, Tennessee, and the mountains just north of it, is often seen as defying its regionalism. Gail Godwin, likewise, writing about Asheville, North Carolina, in several of her novels (such as *A Southern Family* 1987), has been identified as "southern" rather than Appalachian. Lisa Alther, who has also written about the East Tennessee mountains and the Knoxville area, specifically in *Kinflicks* (1976), is not often identified in literary circles as an Appalachian author. Neither are Dorothy Allison, Jayne Anne Phillips, or Annie Dillard, among others.

Other writers in the last half-century, however, have been identified nationally as Appalachian, and therefore many of these are barely known outside Appalachian studies. Some of these writers have focused on the negative and disturbing aspects of the culture. Mildred Haun, for example, in a collection of connected stories, *The Hawk's Done Gone* (1940), depicted some of the worst aspects of mountain life, including infanticide, murder, the negative effects of superstition, and racial prejudice. Breece D'J Pancake (*The Stories of Breece D'J Pancake* 1983), Pinckney Benedict (*The Dogs of God* 1994), and Chris Offutt (*Kentucky Straight* 1992), talented writers assuredly, have returned to the gloomiest depictions of the region, focusing on modern characters in the negative mode of such earlier writers as Haun, Armstrong, and Dromgoole, and depict the mountain culture as primitive, depraved, and elemental. Perhaps the most damning portrayal (though now over thirty years old) was outsider James Dickey's *Deliverance* (1970), which remains one of the worst pictures of the mountain people as inbred, suspicious, violent, and bestial.

Still, other writers have presented a more positive picture, showing the dignity, strength, and virtues of the Appalachian people. In *The Tall Woman* (1962), Wilma Dykeman portrayed Lydia McQueen as "tall" in character as well as stature. In her later two novels, *The Far Family* (1966) and *Return the Innocent Earth* 1973), Dykeman explores outside exploitation of the region, environmental issues, and family ties. Earl Hamner's *Spencer's Mountain* (1961) and *The Homecoming* (1970), on which the popular TV series *The Waltons* was based, likewise examines the positive virtues of the mountaineers. Gurney Norman, in his short story collection *Kinfolks* (1977) and his "novel of the counter culture" *Divine Right's Trip* (1972), presents characters who value family ties and a return to the sustenance of the land and who have a reverence for the past as they struggle for personal identity in the present. Others writers in this vein include Mary Lee Settle, John Ehle, Fred Chappell, Jim Wayne Miller, David Huddle, Charles Frazier, Robert Morgan, Chris Holbrook, George Ella Lyon, Meredith Sue Willis, Elaine Fowler Palencia, Ron Rash, and Silas House.

Three of the most popular and best-selling authors of recent years are Lee Smith, Denise Giardina and Sharyn McCrumb. Smith's novels, including *Black Mountain Breakdown* (1980), *Oral History* (1983), *Family Linen* (1985), and *Fair and Tender Ladies* (1988), while perhaps relying on some stereotypes, nevertheless reveal much of the history and cultural change of the region. *Fair and Tender Ladies* is one of the most beautiful portrayals of an Appalachian mountain woman's life ever written.

Denise Giardina's two Appalachian novels, *Storming Heaven* (1987) and *The Unquiet Earth* (1992), depict the economic exploitation of the region by outside forces and the struggle of the people to control their own destiny. *Storming Heaven* culminates with the Battle of Blair Mountain in 1921, in which federal troops were called in to squelch the unionized coal miners' march on Logan, West Virginia. *The Unquiet Earth* has as its central climax an episode based on the Buffalo Creek disaster of 1972.

Sharyn McCrumb has reintroduced a genre of Appalachian fiction with her mysteries set in the mountains. Like Smith, who has relied on oral history and Appalachian sources for her fiction, McCrumb is introducing a different audience to Appalachian ballads, folklore, and locales. McCrumb's "ballad series," *If Ever I Return, Pretty Peggy O* (1990), *The Hangman's Beautiful Daughter* (1993), *She Walks These Hills* (1994), *The Rosewood Casket* (1996), *The Ballad of Frankie Silver* (1998), *The Songcatcher* (2001), and *Ghost Riders* (2003), juxtapose the region's cultural history reflected in old-time ballads with such timeless, contemporary problems as poverty, lost loves, greed, class struggles, and the environment. With *St. Dale* (2005), she explores grassroots heroism by introducing a road trip/quest dedicated to NASCAR's Dale Earnhardt.

Coal mining is arguably the single most influential force in the lives and culture of late-nineteenth-century and early-twentieth-century central Appalachians, precipitating a regional shift from a local-based subsistence agriculture and trade and-barter lifestyle and economy to a cash wage lifestyle and economy linked directly to national patterns of industrial production and consumption.

There have been many novels about the coal-mining industry in Appalachia, including John Fox Jr.'s *Trail of the Lonesome Pine* (1908), James Still's *River of Earth* (1940), Myra Page's *Daughter of the Hills: A Woman's Part in the Coal Miners' Struggle* (1950), Davis Grubb's *Barefoot Man* (1971), John Knowles's *Vein of Riches* (1978), Mary Lee Settle's *Scapegoat* (1980), and Denise Giardina's *Storming Heaven* and *The Unquiet Earth*. Those novels of coal-mining life appearing in the 1980s and 1990s, including Settle's, Giardina's, John Yount's *Hardcastle* (1980) and Loletta Clouse's *Wilder* (1990), are "revisionist histories." Written primarily by native Appalachians who intend to speak for themselves and to provide their own interpretations of the industrialization of their region, they tend to offer harsh criticism of the absentee capitalists who helped transform the mountain region. These novels also present rich and satisfying depictions of central Appalachians and their coal-mining culture, depictions that counterbalance the simplistic, superficial, and stereotypical representations offered in the works of fiction mentioned as well as numerous others.

One of the first full-length collections of Appalachian literary criticism (fiction, poetry, and drama) was published in 2005. *An American Vein: Critical Readings in Appalachian Literature,* edited by Danny L. Miller, Sharon Hatfield, and Gurney Norman, seeks to position the region's literature in the American canon.

Poetry

An important facet of contemporary Appalachian literature is the emergence of a large body of work by native Appalachian poets in the last twenty or so years. Just as the writing of novels and short stories in Appalachia burgeoned during the 1960s and 1970s, so did the creation of the region's poetry.

Although it is only within the past fifteen years that Appalachian poetry has received true critical attention and classroom discussion, the genesis of the body of this poetry began with resounding talents in the 1930s. Those early poets important in vocalizing the Appalachian experience in verse included Jesse Stuart, Don West, Byron Herbert Reece, James Still, and Louise McNeill.

Many individual regional poets have risen to renown within the Appalachian literary community and in the national literature. Perhaps the most widely known among contemporary regional poets, Fred Chappell has written prolifically, publishing nearly a dozen volumes of poetry. Like Chappell, the region's best known and loved poets have inspired and influenced not only through numerous publications but also through their diligent teaching and lecturing. Jim Wayne Miller, Jeff Daniel Marion, George Scarbrough, Robert Morgan, Kathryn Stripling Byer, Rodney Jones, Charles Wright, George Ella Lyon, Bettie Sellers, Jo Carson, Marilou Awiakta, Irene McKinney, and Maggie Anderson have created a rich and strong tradition on which the next generation of poets may build. In recent years African American poets have begun to dispel the myth of white homogeneity among Appalachian writers. Frank X Walker, who coined the term "Affrilachian," is the chief of those writers, who include poet Nikky Finney and fiction writer Crystal Wilkinson. Other African American poets include Effie Waller Smith, who is being reclaimed by scholars, and Nikki Giovanni.

Because of the efforts of these poets and others, there is quite a community of poets in Appalachia and a collective vision of the region's poetry. During the 1970s, the work of groups such as the Soupbean Poets and individuals such as Jeff Daniel Marion, who edited *The Small Farm*, brought great attention to the region's poets. In the late 1970s, the work of several individuals concerning the Appalachian Poetry Project culminated in *Old Wounds, New Words*, an anthology of poetry edited in the early 1980s by George Ella Lyon, Bob Henry Baber, and Gurney Norman, fourteen years before its publication in 1994. *Her Words: Diverse Voices in Contemporary Appalachian Women's Poetry*, a collection of poetry by Appalachian women writers and essays on their work, edited by Felicia Mitchell, appeared in 2002.

Along with *Old Wounds, New Words* and *Her Words*, two scholarly projects by poet Rita Quillen round out the trio of thorough quality resources for the study of Appalachian poetry. Quillen's *Looking for New Ground: Contemporary Appalachian Poetry,* the only comprehensive full-length scholarly discussion of Appalachian poetry today, is a study of four Appalachian poets, Jim Wayne Miller, Robert Morgan, Jeff Daniel Marion, and Fred Chappell. Also most beneficial to future scholarship concerning Appalachian poetry is Quillen's comprehensive bibliography of "Modern and Contemporary Mountain Poetry," published in *Appalachian Journal* in 1986. Though rapidly becoming dated, this compilation of primary and secondary sources provides scholars, teachers, students, and readers with a glimpse of the history of Appalachian poetry and assures us of its powerful future.

Literature for Youths and Young Adults

Like its adult counterpart, early Appalachian children's literature conformed to the local color tradition of the age, a tradition which, for children, at least, may have begun with Robert Montgomery Bird's 1837 publication of *Nick of the Woods,* set on the Kentucky frontier after the Revolutionary War. Highly stereotypical views of Native Americans and the usual frontier adventure made it one of the most successful juvenile books for a male audience. Another book classified as juvenile is Sterling King's *Wild Rose of Cherokee,* published in 1895. Like *Nick of the Woods,* by today's standards this book would hardly qualify as juvenile; its stilted dialogue and long descriptive sentences make this story of Nancy Ward and the Cherokees in northeast Tennessee inaccessible to a contemporary young audience, but its very existence is proof that early in the history of Appalachia, writers were producing literature about the region for young readers.

William Altsheler (*Forest Runners,* 1908) and Erskine Payne (*The Mountain Girl,* 1912) produced fiction typical of the early 1900s. In the 1920s, the number of juvenile titles began to increase. The work of May Justus first appeared in the twenties, followed by more than fifty titles through the next five decades; typical titles include *Children of the Great Smoky Mountains* (1923), *The House in No-End Hollow* (1938), *Lizzie* (1944), and *The Complete Peddler's Pack* (1957). The 1920s also gave us Elizabeth Madox Roberts's *Under the Tree* (1922), whose title echoes the classic *Under the Window,* by British poet and illustrator Kate Greenway. For all its local color, its poetry is so highly readable and accessible to today's readers that it was reissued in 1985 by the University Press of Kentucky.

From the 1930s to the 1960s, the number of Appalachian children's books continued to grow, though with little variety of theme and character. Under the pseudonym of Maristan Chapman, John Stanton Chapman and Mary Isley

Chapman produced many juvenile books, including a highly popular series about a Tennessee mountain town called Glen Hazard. Begun in 1928 with *The Happy Mountain,* the series continued well into the 1940s. Rebecca Caudill's work spans four decades: *Happy Little Family* (1947) introduced Bonnie Fairchild, who appeared in a series of books; *Tree of Freedom* (1949) and *The Far-Off Land* (1964) are both set in the 1780s Kentucky wilderness; but her classics are *A Certain Small Shepherd* (1965) and *Did You Carry the Flag Today, Charlie?* (1971). Ruth and Latrobe Carroll gave us titles such as *Beanie* (1952) and *Tough Enough and Sassy* (1958). Ellis Credle's *Down, Down the Mountain* (1934) was followed by titles well into the 1950s, such as *Big Doin's on Razorback Ridge* (1956) and *Tall Tales from the High Hills* (1957). Other significant authors from this period are Charlie May Simon, Hubert Skidmore, and Lois Lenski.

Two additional writers who made their appearance in the fifties and sixties are Jesse Stuart and Billy Curtis Clark, both of whom produced stories about Kentucky mountaineers for the middle grades. Stuart wrote more than a dozen titles for this age group, notably *The Beatinest Boy* (1953), *A Penny's Worth of Character* (1954), *Red Mule* (1955), *Andy Finds a Way* (1961), *A Ride with Huey the Engineer* (1966), and *Old Ben* (1970). Clark's first novel, *Song of the River* (1956), established him in the Stuart tradition and was followed by such titles as *Useless Dog* (1961), *Goodbye Kate* (1964), and *The Trail of the Hunter's Horn* (1957). Clark and Stuart produced local color at its best, adventuresome, rural, fun-filled, but somber at times.

A contemporary of Stuart and Clark is William O. Steele, who from the 1950s to the 1970s produced more than one hundred historical fiction titles about frontier themes which depict highly stereotypical attitudes toward Native Americans. In spite of their predictability, many of these titles remain in print today in paperback form: *Buffalo Knife* (1968), *Flaming Arrows* (1957), *The Perilous Road* (1958), and *Winter Danger* (1954). William O. Steele's wife, Mary Q. Steele, writing under the pseudonym Wilson Gage, produced excellent fiction for children, most notably *Big Blue Island* (1964).

Beginning in the 1930s, a number of juvenile biographies appeared; *Stonewall* (1931) by Julia Adams, *Six Feet Six: The Heroic Story of Sam Houston* (1931) by Bessie and Marquis James, and *Davy Crockett* (1934) by Constance Rourke are typical. Davy Crockett, Daniel Boone, Andrew Johnson, Andrew Jackson, Stonewall Jackson, Rachel Jackson, Sam Houston, Sequoyah, Nancy Ward—biographies about these individuals set the tone and offered little variety. It was not until the 1960s that biographers began to explore the lives of other notable Appalachians in fiction, such as Mother Jones (*Labor's Defiant Lady,* 1969) and John Brown (*John Brown: One Man Against Slavery,* 1993).

Appalachian children's literature shows very little change in themes, attitudes, characterization, setting, and style until the 1960s and 1970s, when the Great Society and the War on Poverty made their way into Appalachian children's fiction. Vera and Bill Cleaver's classic *Where the Lilies Bloom* (1969) and its sequel *Trail Valley* (1977) are among titles which depicted for the first time a self-awareness among characters of the "outsider's" perceptions of mountain people. Margaret Wise Shull's *Children of Appalachia* (1969) is a fictionalized photo essay about government programs, isolation, deprivation, and strip mining. Beverly Courtney Crook's *Fair Annie of Old Mule Hollow* (1978) introduced the theme of strip mining and mountaineer activism in young adult Appalachian fiction. Books like Lillie Chaffin and Conrad Stein's *World of Books* (1971), Gail Hardin's *Road from West Virginia* (1971), and Charles Geary's *What I'm About Is People* (1971) dealt with nonfiction accounts of "hillbillies" who migrated to northern urban centers and their struggles as minorities trying to fit into the majority culture.

Also during this period attention to folklore, folkways, and the oral tradition in literature grew. A host of titles followed the *Foxfire* magazine and book series pattern, giving us collections of songs, stories, and beliefs for a young audience. Joanna Galdone's *Tailypo: A Ghost Story* (1977) and James Still's *Jack and the Wonder Beans* (1977) and *The Wolfpen Rusties: Appalachian Riddles and Gee-Haw Whimmy-Diddles* (1975) set the stage for the continued retelling of Jack tales in the 1980s and 1990s by such notable writers as Gayle Haley (*Jack and the Bean Tree,* 1986; *Mountain Jack Tales* 1992), William Hooks (*Snowbear Whittington: An Appalachian Beauty and the Beast,* 1994; *Three Little Pigs and the Fox,* 1989), and Joanne Compton (*Ashpet: An Appalachian Tale,* 1994).

Another trend begun in the 1960s and 1970s was the impetus toward Native American material. Forrest Carter's now controversial *The Education of Little Tree* (1976), Electa Clark's *Cherokee Chief: The Life of John Ross* (1970), and Peter Collier's *When Shall They Rest? The Cherokees' Long Struggle with America* (1973) were followed in the 1980s by excellent fiction, such as Robert J. Conley's *Witch of Goingsnake* (1988), for which Wilma Mankiller wrote the foreword.

African Americans were largely ignored in the early decades of Appalachian children's fiction (except as a stereotypical backdrop) until Virginia Hamilton gave us *M. C. Higgins the Great* (1974), *Arilla Sundown* (1976), and *The Magical Adventures of Pretty Pearl* (1986). Following Hamilton, more attention has been given to such classics as the poetry of Nikki Giovanni, to the extent that her poem "Knoxville, Tennessee" was illustrated in picture book form in 1994. Michelle Greene's *Willie Pearl* (1990) has developed into a highly popular series about an African American family in a Kentucky coal-mining town.

Though every decade from the 1920s forward saw the proliferation of children's books about the region, the 1980s can truly be called its golden age. It saw the publication of nearly 20 percent of the children's titles identified as Appalachian. The authors most readily identified with the Appalachian children's market today all published their first titles in this decade: Jo Carson, Connie Jordan Green, Michelle Green, Gloria Houston, George Ella Lyon, and Cynthia Rylant. An important aspect of the work of these authors, and others in the 1990s, such as Jeff Daniel Marion, is that they are free to explore the past with the "re-vision" of the present, exploring new forms and new themes.

Carson's *Pulling My Leg* (1990) and *You Hold Me and I'll Hold You* (1992) are notable for their rich language. Connie Jordan Green has given us one of the few children's books about the development of the atomic bomb in *The War at Home* (1989). Gloria Houston has given us historical fiction about western North Carolina, notably, *The Year of the Perfect Christmas Tree* (1988) and *My Great Aunt Arizona* (1992). George Ella Lyon experiments with subject and form in her picture books (*A Regular Rolling Noah*, 1986; *Mama Is a Miner*, 1994) as well as her fiction for the middle grades (*Borrowed Children*, 1988; *Here and Then*, 1994). Cynthia Rylant, one of the most prolific writers, is best known for her picture books *When I Was Young in the Mountains* (1982) and *The Relatives Came* (1985) and for her Newbery Medal–winning *Missing May* (1992). Rylant is one of the few contemporary Appalachian writers to produce poetry for children as well (*Waiting to Waltz*, 1984).

Drama and Theater

In the 1930s, James Taylor Adams, a WPA writer and creator of Big Laurel Press, collected stories which have become a source for many contemporary Appalachian playwrights. In the 1950s, theater in Appalachia primarily took the form of outdoor dramas. Earl Hobson Smith (whose biography is included in the *National Playwright's Directory*) wrote two long-running outdoor dramas based on the novels of John Fox Jr.: *The Little Shepherd of Kingdom Come* ran in Whitesburg, Kentucky, until the late 1960s, and *The Trail of the Lonesome Pine* continues as an outdoor drama in Big Stone Gap, Virginia.

By the 1960s and 1970s, theater was influenced by the civil rights movement and alternative theater movements, as well as by the work of Frederick Koch, founder of the University of North Carolina Playmakers, who argued for every community to form its own theater group to speak to its own needs and dreams.

An arts organization of over two hundred members calling themselves Alternate ROOTS formed in Tennessee in 1976 at the Highlander Center, a place known for its commitment to social activism. According to North Carolinian Ruby Lerner, former director of Alternate ROOTS (from 1981 to 1986), the group is also "a grass roots cultural movement, peculiar to the South, whose aim is to be part of the transformation of the region—by acknowledging and critically assessing its past, particularly with regard to race, uncovering its buried history and untold stories, and celebrating its heroes."

In 1975, Roadside Theater began in Whitesburg, Kentucky, as a part of Appalshop, with a goal of discovering "a theatrical form and dramatic content that made sense to the rural people who live around the theater's home in the Appalachian mountains . . . a people for whom there was no written body of dramatic literature or tradition of attending the theater."[2] The ensemble company actors, all natives of the region, developed a theatrical form combining storytelling, acting, and music—"to vitalize its indigenous theatrical traditions for another generation of Appalachian people."[3] The form "includes the audience as a part of the show; there is no fourth wall, dense sets or effects. The actors and audience are free to improvise within the text and the moment."[4] Roadside's first original production was *Mountain Tales and Music.*

A founder of Roadside Theater, Don Baker is one of Appalachia's most prolific and important playwrights today. A freelance writer, director, and performer who grew up in Wise County, Virginia, Baker is generally credited with pioneering the multiple voice storytelling technique used in such plays as *Red Fox/Second Hangin',* which premiered in Whitesburg, Kentucky, in 1976 and toured regionally and nationally until 1988. The innovative technique involves one performer speaking the first part of a line, another voice continuing it, another sometimes joining in for a unison of voices before the end—and various other combinations of voices. Baker has written such ensemble dramatic presentations as *Pretty Polly; Cymbeline,* which he describes as a mountain tale "formerly a play by Shakespeare"; *Stonewall Country,* a musical drama with music by Robin and Linda Williams which examines "unresolved issues" concerning the Civil War and Stonewall Jackson's life; *Ear Rings; Backlife; Three Drops of Blood;* and others. In 1983, Baker cofounded Lime Kiln Arts in Lexington, Virginia, where he worked for a decade.

The Road Company, also founded in 1975, began in Johnson City, Tennessee. Directed by Robert H. Leonard, members of the company have included

Margaret Baker, John Fitzpatrick, Emily Green, Christine Murdock, Eugene Wolf, and Kelly Hill, who collaborated on *Blind Desire,* as well as other players.

Ecotheater of Hinton, West Virginia, is grass-roots theater organized by playwright Maryat Lee in the mid-1970s. Existing first as outdoor summer theater, performed from a farm wagon in open fields or shopping center parking lots (much like the medieval mystery and morality plays), Ecotheater has also taken plays to amphitheaters, hospitals, and other outdoor venues. Drawing material from local Summers County, West Virginia, sources and using local actors, the group, under the direction of Martha Asbury, has produced such plays as *Four Men and a Monster, Old Miz Dacey, John Henry,* and *A Double-Threaded Life: The Hinton Play.*

A number of playwrights from Appalachia also perform their works. Writer and performer Jo Carson from Johnson City, Tennessee, also a poet, has written thirty "community plays" developed from oral histories. Award winners include *Daytrips, A Preacher with a Horse to Ride,* and *The Bear Facts.* George Ella Lyon, also a poet and writer of children's books, has participated in her play *Braids,* directed by Ann Kilkelly. Angelyn deBord performs in her play *Stubborn Memories.*

Contemporary theater in Appalachia relies heavily on grass-roots efforts: playwrights who discover and explore local historical sources, local actors and stagecrafters who create for community audiences, and dramatic productions which combine storytelling, acting and music.

In his essay on education in Appalachia, "A Mirror for Appalachia," poet, essayist, and novelist Jim Wayne Miller wrote that, in order to ensure the best future for Appalachia, Appalachians must reject definitions of themselves and their region that have historically been imposed from outside the region.[5] They need, he wrote, "to see their lives and experiences mirrored in art, verified, corroborated, legitimized" and, ultimately, to define themselves.[6] By striving to present authentic characters, themes, and settings, Appalachian writers are creating a literature that is necessarily, though not overtly, political. The finest writing from and about Appalachia is both entertaining and provocative and explores lives that are at the same time unique and universal. Beyond the vicarious pleasure and pain that art is compelled to supply, the region's writing is moving us to become, as Loyal Jones argued that we must, "'aware of who we are and why, and be at ease with this knowledge.'"[7]

Emma Bell Miles, pioneer folklorist and writer from Walden's Ridge, Tennessee, c. 1901. From the collection of Grace Toney Edwards.

Jim Wayne Miller, poet, essayist, novelist, and teacher. By Ricky Cox.

Nikki Giovanni, poet, teacher, and activist. Courtesy of Nikki Giovanni; photograph by Barron Claiborne.

Robert Morgan, writer of fiction and poetry. By Ricky Cox.

Marilou Awiakta, Cherokee/Appalachian poet and philosopher. From the Collection of the Appalachian Regional Studies Center, Radford University.

Ron Short, Angelyn DeBord, and Tommy Bledsoe of Roadside Theater, Whitesburg, Kentucky. Courtesy of Roadside Theater; photo by Dan Carraco.

Notes

1. W. D. Weatherford and Wilma Dykeman, "Literature Since 1900," in *The Southern Appalachian Region: A Survey,* ed. Thomas R. Ford (Lexington: Univ. Press of Kentucky, 1962), 263.
2. Don Baker and Dudley Cooke, *Red Fox/Second Hangin',* stage play, premiered 1976.
3. Ibid.
4. Ibid.
5. Jim Wayne Miller, "A Mirror for Appalachia," in *Voices from the Hills,* ed. Robert J. Higgs and Ambrose N. Manning (New York: Frederick Ungar, 1978), 447–59.
6. Ibid., 455.
7. Ibid., 448.

Suggested Readings

Baker, Don, and Dudley Cooke. *Red Fox/Second Hangin'.* Stage play. Premiered 1976.

Miller, Jim Wayne. "A Mirror for Appalachia." In *Voices from the Hills,* edited by Robert J. Higgs and Ambrose N. Manning. New York: Frederick Ungar, 1975.

Weatherford, W. D., and Wilma Dykeman. "Literature Since 1900." In *The Southern Appalachian Region: A Survey,* edited by Thomas R. Ford. Lexington: Univ. Press of Kentucky, 1962.

Anthologies of Appalachian Literature

Baber, Bob Henry, George Ella Lyon, and Gurney Norman, eds. *Old Wounds, New Words: Poems from the Appalachian Poetry Project.* Ashland, Ky.: Jesse Stuart Foundation, 1994.

Chaffin, Lillie D., Glenn O. Carey, and Harry N. Brown. *God's Plenty: Modern Kentucky Writers.* Greenwood, Fla.: Penkevill, 1991.

Cuelho, Art, ed. *Harvest from the Hills.* Big Timber, Mont.: Seven Buffaloes Press, 1984.

deNobriga, Kathie, and Valetta Anderson. *Alternate ROOTS: Plays from the Southern Theater.* Portsmouth, N.H.: Heineman, 1994.

Giles, Ronald K., ed. *In Place: A Collection of Appalachian Writers.* Johnson City, Tenn.: Center for Appalachian Studies and Services, 1988.

Higgs, Robert J., Ambrose N. Manning, eds. *Voices from the Hills: Selected Readings of Southern Appalachia.* New York: Frederick Ungar, 1975.

Higgs, Robert J., Ambrose N. Manning, and Jim Wayne Miller, eds. *Appalachia Inside Out: A Sequel to Voices from the Hills.* 2 vols. Knoxville: Univ. of Tennessee Press, 1995.

Lee, Ernest, ed. *Discovering Place.* New York: McGraw-Hill, 1995.

Lyon, George Ella, Jim Wayne Miller, and Gurney Norman, eds. *A Gathering at the Forks: Fifteen Years of the Hindman Settlement School Appalachian Writers Workshop.* Wise, Va.: Vision Books, 1993.

McNeil, Nellie, and Joyce Squibb, eds. *A Southern Appalachian Reader.* Boone, N.C.: Appalachian Consortium Press, 1988.

Bibliographies

Caskey, Jefferson D. *Appalachian Authors: A Selective Bibliography.* Cornwall, Conn.: Locust Hill Press, 1990.

Collett, Dexter. *Bibliography of Theses and Dissertations on Appalachian Literature.* Berea, Ky.: Kentucky Imprints, 1995.

Farr, Sidney Saylor. *Appalachian Women: An Annotated Bibliography.* Lexington: Univ. Press of Kentucky, 1981.

Munn, Robert F. *The Southern Appalachians: A Bibliography and Guide to the Studies.* Morgantown: West Virginia Univ. Library, 1961.

Quillen, Rita. "Modern and Contemporary Mountain Poetry." *Appalachian Journal* 13, no. 1 (Fall 1985): 51–57.

Ross, Charlotte. *Bibliography of Southern Appalachia.* Boone, N.C.: Appalachian Consortium Press, 1976.

General Articles and Sources

Ballard, Sandra L., and Patricia L. Hudson. *Listen Here: Women Writing in Appalachia.* Lexington: Univ. Press of Kentucky, 2003.

Beattie, L. Elisabeth, ed. *Conversations with Kentucky Writers.* Lexington: Univ. Press of Kentucky, 1996.

Boger, Lorise. *The Southern Mountaineer in Literature: An Annotated Bibliography.* Morgantown: West Virginia Univ. Library, 1964.

Brake, Katherine Vande. *How They Shine: Melungeon Characters in the Fiction of Appalachia.* Macon, Ga.: Mercer Univ. Press, 2001.

Dyer, Joyce, ed. *Bloodroot: Reflections on Place by Appalachian Women Writers.* Lexington: Univ. Press of Kentucky, 2000.

Lanier, Parks, ed. *The Poetics of Appalachian Space.* Knoxville: Univ. of Tennessee Press, 1991.

Lyon, George Ella. "Contemporary Appalachian Poetry: Sources and Directions." *Kentucky Review* 2 (1981): 3–22.

Miller, Danny L., Sharon Hatfield, and Gurney Norman, eds. *An American Vein: Critical Readings in Appalachian Literature.* Athens, Ohio: Ohio Univ. Press, 2005.

Miller, Jim Wayne. "A People Waking Up: Appalachian Literature Since 1960." In *The Cratis Williams Symposium Proceedings.* Boone, N.C.: Appalachian Consortium Press, 1990.

———. "A Post-Agrarian Regionalism for Appalachia." *Appalachian Heritage* 5, no. 2 (Spring 1980): 58–71.

Mitchell, Felicia, ed. *Her Words: Diverse Voices in Contemporary Appalachian Women's Poetry.* Knoxville: Univ. of Tennessee Press, 2002.

Weatherford, W. D., and Wilma Dykeman. "Literature Since 1900." In *The Southern Appalachian Region: A Survey,* edited by Thomas R. Ford, 259–70. Lexington: Univ. Press of Kentucky, 1962.

Williams, Cratis. "Appalachian Fiction." *Appalachian Heritage* 4, no. 4 (Fall 1976): 45–56.

———. "The Southern Mountaineer in Fact and Fiction." *Appalachian Journal* 3, nos. 1–4 (Autumn 1975, Winter 1976, Spring 1976, and Summer 1976): 8–61, 100–162, 186–261, 334–92.

VISUAL ARTS IN APPALACHIA

M. ANNA FARIELLO

Appalachian Art in Context

If allowed to flourish in isolation, the arts of Appalachia would probably possess a distinctively rich flavor, something akin to the strong stock of turnip greens. But apart from its earliest history, Appalachia has not existed completely apart from the rest of the Western world, and hybridization has been particularly influential in the material culture of the region. Today, what might distinguish the arts in Appalachia from art making in the rest of the country are generalized factors, similar to what Appalachian scholars consider to be characteristics which distinguish the region across discipline-specific boundaries. A sense of place or connection to the land is expressed in many visual images, a tradition of storytelling is expressed in the region's wealth of narrative pictures, and an independent spirit keeps artists working in areas remote from available markets and contributes to a continual expansion of their repertoire beyond fashionable artistic trends.

Because of the need for an aesthetically critical audience and the more practical need for patronage, the arts have tended to flourish in places where a concentrated population might provide an audience or patron base. The issue of audience disadvantages the Appalachian artist, because in America, art is—and has been—judged by a number of factors that depend upon critical awareness of the aesthetic object and the artist who makes it. Like demographic statistics, this situation is continually changing; today, intellectual debate is less dependent upon a face-to-face meeting of the minds. As communication technologies change communities, so too do they change the relationship of the arts to those communities.

The arts are among the earliest of human activities, predating writing by fifty thousand years. What remains of the Western world's prehistoric legacy, in the form of surviving painted and sculpted images, has led scholars to believe that the role of the arts was once primarily ceremonial. It was through visual expression that humans explored the unknown, and to some extent, this remains true today. In order to fully understand and appreciate the arts of Appalachia, one must have some understanding of how the arts developed and functioned in human culture as a whole.

In the earliest Western population centers—be they Greek, Egyptian, or Mayan—the arts often assumed a narrative role. Through the rendering of images, cultures recorded stories, aspirations, and political history. The world's most enduring artistic monuments—such as the painted palace at Knossos in Crete, the temples of Ramesses and Nefertari in Egypt, or the Mayan temple group in Mexico—were not the result of individual artistic effort but products of the state, carried out by any number of makers with skills passed on from one generation to the next in a collective fashion. During the early Christian periods in Europe, the tradition of collective artistic expression continued. Anonymous artists in service to the church built and embellished the great cathedrals of the Middle Ages. For much of its history, art was expressive of religious teaching, and prior to the invention of the printing press, lessons were taught via artistic images, picture-stories that could be *read* and understood by common people. The importance of image making at this time cannot be overstated, as there were few other communication tools that had the capacity to bind cultures together over time.

During the Middle Ages, art began to play a new role, that of imparting status to the owner of, say, a work in silver and gems. The celebration of the elaborated individual art object, made apart from an ecclesiastical setting, would expand during the Renaissance, a time when individual wealth produced the first secular patrons in modern Europe. The Renaissance also radically altered the role art played since its beginnings, releasing it from its magical and religious purposes to isolate aesthetics and embrace the object as a measure of wealth, status, and sophistication. Art making changed from being communally produced and communally consumed to functioning as an individual act (or at least celebrated that way) made for an individual patron. Today's ideas concerning the arts have come to us from the Renaissance and the Enlightenment, periods in which the arts flourished as a result of increased trade and wealth.

Today the art world—including educators, critics, historians, curators, patrons, dealers, and art makers—continues to focus on the individuality of the artistic personality, talent, and expression.

Cultural forms that do not conform to the urbane model have been at a disadvantage in terms of art historical scholarship. Only in the late twentieth century did scholars begin to look again at the underlying assumptions upon which art was judged and begin to consider other methods worthy of inquiry and other groups worthy of research. Thus, only recently have scholarly studies been made of forms outside of the "fine" arts. New scholarship has explored forms such as folk art, popular culture, and crafts, as well as works by women and ethnic minorities and from outlying regions, such as Appalachia.

Native American Art

In North America, the arts developed in much the same manner as in the rest of the Western world. The earliest Appalachian artists were native to the region, primarily the Cherokee, who had lived in the southern Appalachians for more than two thousand years. Other tribes—Creeks, Chickasaws, Natchez, and Catawba—bordered the region, but Cherokees form the major population group in the southern highlands. Native Appalachian culture was transmitted through the hands of Cherokee craftspeople, from mother to daughter, from father to son. The skills necessary to produce a variety of objects—baskets, pottery, or weaving—remained integral to Native American life.

Images, be they representational or abstract, were derived from traditional beliefs and conveyed a sense of spiritual identity. While certain artifacts produced by native peoples may have functioned as a means of barter and others were used as a regular part of day-to-day life, each was imbued with a spiritual aura. Perhaps this is the most difficult concept for the twenty-first-century American to grasp, given our plethora of physical objects and their mundane status in our contemporary world. Today, a pot or a basket is just that, a pot or a basket. But to a traditional Cherokee, the use of such a container, even in the day to day, added a spiritual dimension to life. After European contact, the Cherokee arts increasingly became a mode of trade rather than objects of ceremonial significance.

While much has changed in the world today, surprisingly, the ceramic process employed by Cherokee potters some two thousand years ago is basically the same as that used today. Earthenware clay is dug from the earth, refined by removing debris and rock, formed into shape, and fired to hardness. Most Cherokee pottery is made by repeatedly circling a coil of clay around a slab base. This action, repeated again and again, results in raising the walls of a pot.

Cherokee pottery, like most Native American pottery, relied upon the vessel form and was finished with patterns impressed as a surface decoration.

Another art form characteristic of the Cherokee culture is basket making. Although pottery and baskets do not appear similar when finished, the process of their making has similarities. Like pottery, Cherokee baskets usually take the form of containers. Also like pottery, which depends upon the earth for its material, basket making materials are those commonly found in the region. Native Appalachian baskets are made of river cane, oak, and honeysuckle and constructed in the round by weaving a single strand of vine or cane in a circular motion. Because of dyes or color variations in the material, elaborate geometric shapes emerge within the basket walls during construction. Split-oak baskets, common to both native and non-native Appalachians, are made by splitting oak limbs into thinner and thinner strips until the result is sufficiently pliable. The Cherokee also use wood to carve ceremonial masks and figures.

While Cherokee pots and baskets were certainly used for day-to-day food preparation, their embellishment suggests they also were used for ceremonial and religious celebration, although in precontact America, the division between secular and religious life was not so distinct. The intricate carving and detailed patterning found on Native American art means that it was invested with time and skill, and thus expensive, even for a culture that depended upon barter and trade for economic exchange.

In 1838, the Cherokee, along with other Native Americans, were forced by the federal government to move from their traditional lands. They walked west on what has become known as the Trail of Tears. About one thousand Cherokee managed to evade the removal; their descendants form the core of the Eastern Band of the Cherokee today. For much of the nineteenth and twentieth centuries, the art of native peoples was relegated to ethnographic collections to serve as specimens or illustrate the anthropological aspects of native life. In today's climate of a growing appreciation of native cultures, there is an increasing effort to collect, study, and appreciate Native American art for its own merits rather than examine it as a means to understanding human development. The most concentrated site of Native American art in Appalachia is in Cherokee, North Carolina, located along the southern edge of the Great Smoky Mountains National Park. Behind the commercial glitter of this tourist town are several authentic Cherokee outlets, including the Qualla Arts and Crafts Mutual, the Museum of the Cherokee Indian, and the Cherokee Historical Association's Oconaluftee Indian Village.

Recording Nature in Antebellum Appalachia

The first European artists to record the North American landscape were those on exploratory expeditions in the sixteenth and seventeenth centuries. Before the advent of photography, skills of observation and rendering were valued as necessary to the documentation of the New World. Although many of the earliest renderings made in America and in Appalachia appear as amateur sketches in travel journals, professional artists were often part of exploratory teams traveling into new territories. As communities were settled, artists were employed as cartographers as well. The identities of many early artists remain unknown, although their work survives. Few in number, these known artists and their works form the basis for contemporary scholarship of this period.

In 1585, John White accompanied an expedition to the Roanoke colony in eastern Virginia, where he made images considered to be among the earliest renderings of life in the New World. White documented Native American life, albeit filtered through the distorted lens of European imperialism. His subsequently published work formed the basis for a European vision of the New World. The first systematic visual record of the New World came more than a century later, when Mark Catesby came to Virginia in the early 1700s. Born in London, Catesby was more field botanist than artist, but the publication of his many renderings in midcentury—*Natural History of Carolina, Florida, and the Bahama Islands* (1731)—has given him a firm footing in American art history. Catesby followed the James River upstream into the Appalachians and traveled south to the Carolinas, where he recorded the flora and fauna of the Appalachians. Catesby's work is admired not only for its faithful imitation of nature but also for its botanical content; he sketched birds and small animals in their natural habitat. John James Audubon's *Birds of North America* (1827) was published almost a century later. Although his work was produced in a limited edition of just a few hundred portfolios, Audubon would eclipse Catesby as America's premier wildlife illustrator. Both naturalists traveled the countryside, venturing into the remote wilderness outside of relatively populated areas.

Although works by Catesby and Audubon are considered for their aesthetic qualities today, prior to the nineteenth century, renderings of the natural world were considered documentary evidence rather than art per se. Others would continue the tradition of making a visual record of the natural environment. Thomas Addison Richards and Edward Beyer each made important contributions to the antebellum landscape tradition. Coincidentally, Richards and Beyer were born in the same year, in 1820, Richards in England and Beyer in Germany. Richards settled in Penfield, Georgia, in 1835, where his father was school principal. Together with his brother William, T. Addison Richards published a

volume titled *Georgia Illustrated* (1842), which celebrated the beauty of the
north Georgia mountains. "The upper part of the State abounds with romantic and picturesque views," he reported. "Mountains and vallies [*sic*], glens and
waterfalls, caverns and cliffs, with pastoral landscapes. . . . Nature has lavished
her beauties." German-born Edward Beyer may be the first professionally trained
artist to have traveled through Appalachia. In the mid-nineteenth century, he
immigrated to America, working first in Cincinnati and later in Virginia. Beyer
is best known for his impressive volume titled *Album of Virginia,* issued in
1857. James Cameron recorded the dramatic terrain of the lower Tennessee
Valley while working in Chattanooga; and later, Flavius Fisher, living in Lynch-
burg, Virginia, recorded the more open landscape of the Dismal Swamp.

In nineteenth-century America, there was a growing interest in establishing a distinct national identity, and the unique landscape features of the
American continent were gaining recognition as important to this idea. Far
from Appalachia, a group of artists working along the Hudson River in New York
painted the American landscape exclusively. Their depictions of awe-inspiring
epic landscapes were seen as evidence of the Divine in nature and set a standard
for landscape painting in America. In western Virginia, Natural Bridge was one
site frequently painted because of its unique features. William C. A. Frerichs
shared in the spirit of those nineteenth-century landscape painters who fashioned the image of America as an untamed and unending territory. Settling in
western North Carolina, Frerichs came to the region to teach at the Greensboro
Female College. He braved the wilderness of the Great Smoky Mountains at a
time when they were inaccessible, rugged, and sparsely populated. As far as we
know, Frerichs was the first painter to venture into this remote territory to capture the drama and magnificent beauty of the landscape. A three-time prisoner
during the Civil War, he eventually left North Carolina ill and penniless and
lived the rest of his life outside the region. Because of the popularity of landscape painting, examples by Frerichs and others can be found in virtually every
museum in the region.

Civil War and Cultural Expression

Like many in America, Frerichs's life was completely changed by the Civil War.
Deprivation, in the Confederate states in particular, reduced life to subsistence.
One avenue where artistic tradition continued during this period is illustration.
The first generation of professional American illustrators to illustrate popular
literature emerged just prior to the Civil War. The field was relatively new, gaining in popularity with the growth and availability of printed material and technological advantages that allowed for increased production and distribution.

Harper's Monthly emerged as America's first national magazine and employed graphic artists to illustrate articles, especially travelogues. David Hunter Strother, from West Virginia, produced one of the country's first illustrated, journalistic news stories when he covered John Brown's raid at Harpers Ferry. During the war, artists, including Winslow Homer, who is better known for genre scenes of a pastoral American life, were sent to the battlefield on behalf of *Harper's*. Another *Harper's* illustrator was Henry Mosler, who lived and worked in Nashville in the mid-1850s. Mosler would later be known for his poignant painting *The Lost Cause,* which depicted a soldier returning home to his mountain cabin.

At the close of the Civil War, many in the American South wanted to commemorate the heroism of fallen loved ones, and as a result, there was a movement to build commemorative monuments in many southern population centers. A commissioned portrait of Confederate general Robert E. Lee was made by Edward Virginius Valentine for the chapel at Washington and Lee University in Lexington, Virginia. Like most American sculptors of the nineteenth century, Valentine went abroad to learn technique and to be close to quarried marble. He returned to the United States and earned a reputation for his monuments to the Lost Cause. Sculptor Belle Kinney was awarded a contract for a monument to Confederate women that was planned for reproduction in each of the Confederate state capitols. Her design was criticized for portraying its subject as a "brawny Southern Amazon" rather than the accepted image of southern womanhood as acquiescent and quietly suffering. Consequently, Kinney's piece was installed at only two sites: Nashville, Tennessee, and Jackson, Mississippi. Her work stands apart from the standard Confederate soldier found on many a courthouse lawn. Carved on a mountainside in north Georgia is a commemoration on a grand scale. Begun in the last century and completed in 1970, the monument could be considered the Mount Rushmore of the South, with images of Lee, Davis, and Jackson carved onto an outcropping of rock face. Its comparison with Mount Rushmore is not accidental; both monuments were designed by sculptor Gutzon Borglum, who also created a bronze aviator as a World War I memorial on the campus of the University of Virginia.

Itinerant Artists and Portraiture

Demographics were a factor in the development of portraiture. Portrait likenesses of individual families flourished where there were enough people to commission them. Resident portrait artists were best able to sustain themselves in populated communities while itinerant portrait artists, many of whom remain anonymous, traveled from town to town making portraits for those who could afford them. Because a portrait was a visual document, perhaps the only one a family possessed, artists tended not to idealize their sitters. Thus, early American portraits, to modern eyes, look unflattering to their subjects. While family portraits were sometimes made, more often than not, artists were employed to render posthumous portraits of loved ones. Commonly, a memorial portrait was made at the bedside of the recently deceased, and in an age when infant mortality ran high, too often these portraits were made of young children.

A popular variation of the painted portrait was the paper silhouette, cut from black paper and mounted against a white background. Because such portraits did not entail a great deal of time, they were affordable and much more common than larger oil paintings. Also popular in the nineteenth century was the tradition of miniatures. Small and delicate, these portraits could be carried as personal mementos and passed onto succeeding generations. In the Shenandoah Valley, where Germanic influence was strong, a commemorative art form dating to the eighteenth century was the *fraktur*, a watercolor that looks much like a stitched "sampler" with motifs such as hearts and tulips surrounding calligraphy announcing a birth or baptism. While itinerant portraits, memorial portraits, silhouettes, and miniatures were common throughout Appalachia, most artists remained anonymous. The invention of photography would affect portraiture, extending the itinerant tradition to "picturemen" who traveled from town to town making family portraits and, thereby, documenting Appalachian life.

Photography Transforms the Arts

When photography was invented in the mid-nineteenth century, it had an immediate impact on the role art played in society; it soon eclipsed the documentary role of painting and drawing. By the turn of the new century, photography was practiced in all parts of the Western world, including Appalachia. Some of the earliest photographers in Appalachia, such as Michael Miley, Robert E. Lee's official photographer, made portraits of wealthy individuals in much the same way as anywhere else. But because photography was a new field, it was not historically bound to certain urban communities the way that painting and sculpture had been. This allowed photography to develop in more rural areas of the country and allowed for women and minorities to more easily enter the field.

American photographers shared an interest in documentation with painters of the American Scene; both groups attempted to portray the distinctiveness of the American landscape and its people. While many American Scene painters looked to the Midwest for rural subjects, many photographers worked in the rural South. Traveling from her Manhattan apartment by car, Doris Ulmann produced three thousand images of Appalachian people. In a style that is more pictorial than documentary, she carefully arranged her subjects with props to indicate their interests or station in life. Ulmann's photographs of Appalachian craftsmen were published posthumously in 1937 as part of Allen Eaton's *Handicrafts of the Southern Highlands*. Another female photographer to capture images of similar subjects was Bayard Wootten. Wootten's photographs of Appalachian subjects received criticism from their sitters after they were published in 1935 as part of Muriel Sheppard's book, *Cabins in the Laurel*, a text that presented an overly sentimental portrait of the region.

During the Great Depression, the Federal Arts Project provided funds for photographers to travel and work. Working for the Farm Security Administration, Dorothea Lange photographed sharecropper families. Walker Evans's photographs are known through their publication in James Agee's *Let Us Now Praise Famous Men*. The photographs by Lange and Evans captured the poverty of rural America during the hard times of the Depression. Their pictures were so compelling that the Appalachian region has found it difficult to escape their images of a "depressed" people, even though many of their photographs were made outside of the region.

During the 1950s, O. Winston Link photographed the last steam trains rolling through the Appalachians, capturing quiet, rural community life pierced by the drama of rolling steel giants. Link would set up a complicated array of lights and then wait for hours for a train to pass. His work reached a wider audience with the publication of *Ghost Trains*, a book of his photography.

Handcraft Revivals

Perhaps the most recognized art form to come out of Appalachia is handcraft. Evolving from indigenous traditions, the roots of handcraftsmanship were connected to the home. Textiles and pottery, once made for personal use, were produced for a national audience at the turn of the century, in a period that has come to be known as the Appalachian Craft Revival. The revival takes its place among a number of movements that evolved worldwide in reaction to the Industrial Revolution. In a rush to turn out large numbers of goods, newly mass-produced items were of questionable quality. Public reformers, craftsmen, and artists looked to earlier models of production to shore up craftsmanship and improve the deteriorating conditions governing factory work. First evident in England, the Arts and Crafts movement defined an aesthetic which embraced hand skill and craftsmanship and looked to the cottage industry to restore dignity to labor. As part of a strong spirit of service prevalent at the turn of the century, young educated women traveled into remote mountainous regions to "settle" among the poor, establishing settlement schools in remote areas similar to settlement houses in northern American cities. Within twenty years of the first log cabin settlement outside of Asheville, North Carolina, in 1895, there were dozens of such centers throughout Appalachia. Many turned to craft production to provide local people with a cash income. Admired by some and maligned by others, the movement was responsible for highlighting handcraft, especially weaving, and for somewhat stabilizing the population by marketing locally made goods to larger population centers, thus slowing rural-to-urban migration.

The most common object produced during the Appalachian craft revival was the woven coverlet. While many weavers remained anonymous, selling work under a production center's name, some achieved recognition in their day. Josephine Mast, from western North Carolina, and Emelda McHargue Walker, from East Tennessee, were two weavers whose work came to the attention of First Lady Ellen Axon Wilson. Subsequently, Mast and Walker were commissioned to create textiles for use in the White House in a bedroom that came to be known as the Blue Ridge Room. The fact that Appalachian craft was commissioned by the White House helped fuel the revival well into the 1920s. During the 1930s, a series of exhibitions helped propel the movement forward. Exhibitions at the Country Life convention in Blacksburg (1933), the World's Fair in Chicago (1934), and the Rural Arts Exhibition (1937) exposed America to the handwork of the region.

Pottery, baskets, wood carvings, pierced tin furniture, iron and silver work, instruments, walking canes, and, of course, quilts and coverlets were all produced in Appalachia. Many forms, especially quilts, baskets, and instruments, continue to be made by contemporary craftsmen. Handmade furniture, especially cane-bottom chairs, rockers, and pieces made from native woods were produced throughout the region. But because these were often too large or too heavy to deliver to distant markets, the revival favored smaller pieces, such as wood miniatures or woven textiles. Although pottery was produced in Appalachia, larger pottery centers are found in the lowlands, where there are more significant deposits of clay. While traditional weaving remained the hallmark of the craft revival, from the end of the 1890s up into the 1940s, nontraditional weaving was taught at Black Mountain College, east of Asheville. German émigré Anni Albers directed the weaving program at Black Mountain and significantly influenced subsequent generations of mainstream American craftsmen and women. But Albers and her colleagues worked apart from the craft traditions that surrounded them.

Today, there are several craft schools, founded during the craft revival, that continue to operate, offering courses to serious students as well as those who want an educational vacation. Most offer courses in short, workshop-type format. Arrowmont School (founded as the Pi Beta Phi Settlement School) continues to operate in Gatlinburg, Tennessee; the John C. Campbell Folk School and Penland School of Crafts are both in North Carolina. Established later, but operating on the same principles, are the Appalachian Center for Crafts in Tennessee and the Kentucky School of Craft in rural Kentucky.

Folk Art

Depending on who is asked, folk artists are naïve, outsiders, visionary, self-taught, rural, non-academic, primitive, and/or popular. Definitions of folk art have caused controversy within the art community because the "folk" tend not to fit neatly within academic categories. Folk art is sold through dealers and galleries but often written about by folklorists and cultural anthropologists who consider social factors apart from aesthetics. Folk art came to the attention of the art community via an important exhibition, "The Art of the Common Man: 1750–1900," at the Museum of Modern Art in 1932. This first flowering of folk art was prompted, in part, by a desire to establish an American cultural identity, the same desire which fueled the craft revival.

Regionalism affects the intellectual debate which has shaped our view of folk art. New England has long been recognized for its contributions to the genre, but as Charles Reagan Wilson points out in the *Encyclopedia of Southern Culture*, "[C]ollections of American Folk art have often included disproportionately large numbers of works by southerners without acknowledging the region's dominance." Scattered throughout Appalachia are many self-taught painters and sculptors whose work is labeled "visionary" or "outsider" art. Many use their talents in response to a divine calling, citing a higher power which compelled them to begin making art as adults after raising children or retiring. Their inner visions were realized using materials at hand, and as a result, their artwork assumes an eclectic form. Rather than making images on canvas, wood and tin are commonly used. Likewise, process grows from available tools. Tennessee artist Harold Green began his work with a chain saw, rough cutting timbers and applying layers of paint and colorful spots to his fantastical animal forms. Georgian artist Howard Finster may be America's best known folk artist, having appeared in national magazines and on television. Turning to art late in life after receiving a "call" from God, Finster's paintings reflect strong religious beliefs. Many are literal depictions of biblical quotations, some from the Book of Revelation. Finster was apt to add popular figures as well, such as Elvis or President Kennedy, who joined Jesus in heavenly conversation.

Like Finster, many contemporary folk artists have stepped outside of anonymity to become well known, their works selling in a network of galleries nationwide. Still, it is their tenacity to private vision which places them distinctly outside the art historical, Euro-American continuum. Finster and others have arranged their accumulated works into outdoor roadside museums of colorful display. Bessie Harvey was an African American folk artist known for her sculptures made from tree roots and branches transformed into fantastic creatures. Finster and Harvey, though one made paintings and the other sculpture, approached their work via an aesthetic which has come to define folk art. Each used nonspecialized materials—those at hand—such as house paint and natural and found objects, each responded to a spiritual calling that dictated subject mater, and each makes fantastical works, often called visionary, which incorporate religious, popular, and personal motifs.

The Twentieth Century and a Homogeneous American Identity

If one could say only one thing about the early twentieth century and its effect on American life, it would be that America developed a self-conscious identity. This identity departed from its European forebears but predated the concept of America as a "melting pot" of immigrant cultures. Artists looked homeward for imagery instead of referencing classical subjects. This visual self-examination paralleled ground-breaking ideas from the scientific community that were filtering into the public consciousness. Thus, discoveries of alternate ways of knowing the world—through the unconscious or on an atomic level—affected artists who attempted to portray layered realities of understanding. In many works made in the twentieth century, realistic observation gave way to non-objectivity, fantasy, and meditative introspection. Elliot Daingerfield, for example, was a painter whose work is known for its symbolic imagery. Like many turn-of-the-century artists, he was educated outside Appalachia. He maintained a studio in New York city but worked regularly from a summer studio in Blowing Rock, North Carolina. Daingerfield's landscapes reflected his belief that art was derived from divine inspiration. His work would be grouped with other symbolist painters of his generation.

Other artists would find positions within universities and wield influence over subsequent generations of regional artists. Catherine Wiley was an American impressionist from Appalachia. After studying at the University of Tennessee and briefly in New York, in 1905 Wiley returned to her home state to teach at her alma mater in Knoxville. Wiley painted women, usually in natural settings where light played an important part in her compositions. Will Henry Stevens taught at the Sophie Newcomb College in New Orleans and spent summers painting in the Blue Ridge Mountains. Much of his work is abstract, but from 1916 until his death in the 1940s, he produced a separate body of landscapes executed in chalk pastels. Aaron Douglas, an artist whose work received recognition as part of the Harlem Renaissance, came to Nashville in the 1930s to paint a series of murals focusing on the African American experience. Commissioned by Fisk University, Douglas subsequently became head of the Art Department there, where he remained until his retirement. Likewise, Lamar Dodd, a native of Georgia who trained at New York's Art Students League, returned to his home state in 1934 to establish the Art Department at the University of Georgia, which, like Fisk, provided an opportunity for young artists to study on their home turf. Dodd was active in the arts, holding national professional positions as well as being named an official artist for NASA.

While Douglass and Dodd worked at the outer edges of Appalachia, their work filtered into the region through their influential professional activities and their students. Historically, fine arts in Appalachia (and the lowland South) suffered from a lack of critical audience; there was just not enough of a population to support a thriving arts community. This situation was somewhat rectified in 1921 by the founding of the Southern States Art League, which until its demise in 1946, sponsored exhibitions and meetings that helped to solidify the art community. The subsequent establishment of the Southeastern College Art Association continued the tradition by providing a network for professionals working and teaching throughout Appalachia and the South.

The technological support to produce large-scale sculpture in bronze or marble was not available to artists in any part of America prior to the twentieth century. American artists who aspired to be sculptors generally emigrated to Europe to work. Still, there were those who made sculpture in spite of a lack of formal training and technical equipment. William Edmondson, whose parents were slaves, grew up in Nashville and began carving tombstones for the black community in the early 1930s. His work was recognized with a solo exhibition at the Museum of Modern Art in 1937. Other sculptors worked in rural Appalachia, taking advantage of space which was not at a premium the way that it was in larger cities. Because of a relative freedom from vandalism, contemporary public sculpture has thrived in Appalachia. Percent-for-art programs established in the 1980s made it possible for the public to enjoy sculpture in federal and corporate buildings, in airports, and in public plazas. In Appalachia, some college campuses—the University of Tennessee–Knoxville, Appalachian State University in North Carolina, and Radford University in Virginia, in particular—instituted outdoor sculpture programs during the 1980s. Cities such as Chattanooga have revitalized their urban centers, placing public works on permanent view.

Throughout the nineteenth century, American artists still trained in Europe, so that only an individual of significant means could pursue an art career. With the disruption of European cultural life brought about by two world wars, and the subsequent rise of American cultural identity and economic influence, the art world centered itself in Manhattan. The magic of modernism was enough to lure artists from more rural parts of the country to make lives for themselves in New York. Shedding their hometowns, many shed their regional identities as well, especially those who achieved fame through their assimilation into the American mainstream. As artists obliterated content from their work in favor of a universal voice, so, too, did they erase any remnant of the regional flavor left behind. Many artists originally from the region became completely assimilated into mainstream modernism. Well-known artists—such as Andy Warhol from Pittsburgh, Jasper Johns from South Carolina, Red Grooms from Nashville, and Cy Twomley from Lexington, Virginia—are included in mainstream art history texts, but they are hardly identified as Appalachian artists. Likewise, an important center for the arts was established in the Blue Ridge Mountains just east of Asheville. Although experimental and short-lived, Black Mountain College was an enormously influential school that functioned like a retreat where artists came together to focus on enhancing creativity. The roster of artists, architects, and critics who participated in the Black Mountain experiment reads like a *Who's Who* of the avant-garde. Thinkers and artists such as Walter Gropius, Clement Greenburg, and Josef Albers established their reputations as national, if not international, figures. While Black Mountain College strengthened the position of America as a serious player in the international arts community, it had little effect on the Appalachian culture in whose midst it was located.

Today, except for a prevalence of quilts, musical instruments, and visionary art forms, the visual arts in Appalachia are not much different from those in other parts of the country. Professional artists in Appalachia receive similar training and read the same professional periodicals as artists in the rest of the country. Likewise, they maintain studios, exhibit their work, enter competitions, approach galleries, meet collectors, give lectures, present demonstrations, read books, earn degrees, teach students, attend conferences, and discuss art. On the surface, their professional activity is similar to that of their peers, but then again, some differences are evident and welcome. To work in the studio to the rhythmic song of tree frogs on a summer evening is a truly Appalachian experience and one which is treasured by many an Appalachian artist. Yet there are other, conflicted differences, assumptions, and misconceptions that hum beneath the surface of professional life.

In 1926, an essay in the *Saturday Review* titled "The Artist as Southerner" attempted to analyze the conflict facing serious artists in the early twentieth century. Should one embrace innovation in pursuit of a more universal and progressive art, thereby abandoning one's roots? Or should one seek regional identity and subject matter and be exposed to accusations of provincialism? This dilemma, articulated during the 1920s, still faces artists today. As part of the South as a whole, Appalachia has been maligned by mainstream criticism published under the guise of academic objectivity. Wilber Cash in *Mind of the South,* reprinted as late as 1968, claimed that the region had "not a true culture at all." Bruce Chambers in *Art and Artists of the South* (1984) quotes another critic who issued the straightforward invective that the entire South was an "awe-inspiring blank" without "a single picture gallery worth going to." Still others concurred that the region was "almost totally devoid of any aesthetic achievement that can be recorded as a permanent contribution to the culture." With such definitive predispositions to their failure, is it any wonder that Appalachian artists find it difficult to achieve success with the region? For the same reasons, few scholars have braved the territorial waters. Thus, for the teacher, student, maker, and audience, the arts and material culture of Appalachian remains a challenging research topic to be explored.

Amateur photographer Orland Phillips. By Ricky Cox.

Cherokee basket maker Alice Walkingstick at Oconaluftee Indian Village, replica of a
Cherokee Indian Village of the 1750 period, Cherokee, North Carolina. Courtesy of Oconaluftee
Indian Village.

Pencil artist Willard Gayheart and author Donia Eley. By Lora L. Gordon, Radford University.

Skycastle, an enamel on aluminum sculpture by Dorothy Gillespie on the Radford University campus. Courtesy of Radford University Art Museum, Radford, Virginia.

234

Suggested Readings

Alvic, Philis. *Weavers of the Southern Highlands.* Lexington: Univ. Press of Kentucky, 2003.

Chambers, Bruce. *Art and Artists of the South.* Columbia: Univ. of South Carolina Press, 1984.

Dallas Museum of Art. *Black Art: Ancestral Legacy.* New York: Harry N. Abrams, 1989.

Driskell, David. *Two Centuries of Black American Art.* Los Angeles: Los Angeles County Museum of Art, 1976.

Duncan, Barbara. *The Cherokee Artist Director.* Cherokee, N.C.: Museum of the Cherokee Indian, 2001.

Dupuy, Edward L. *Artisans of the Appalachians.* Asheville, N.C.: Miller Printing, 1967.

Eaton, Alan. *Handicrafts of the Southern Highlands.* New York: Russell Sage, 1937.

Fariello, M. Anna, and Paula Owen. *Objects and Meaning.* Lanham, Md.: Scarecrow Press, 2003.

Fields, Jay, and Brad Campbell. *The Craft Heritage Trails of Western North Carolina.* Asheville, N.C.: Handmade in America, 1998.

Gayheart, Willard, and Donia S. Eley. *Willard Gayheart, Appalachian Artist.* Jefferson, N.C.: McFarland, 2003.

Gaynes, David. *Artisans/Appalachia/USA.* Boone, N.C.: Appalachian Consortium Press, 1977.

Hill, Sarah H. *Weaving New Worlds: Southeastern Cherokee Women and Their Basketry.* Chapel Hill: Univ. of North Carolina Press, 1997.

Jacobs, Philip Walker. *The Life and Photography of Doris Ulmann.* Lexington: Univ. Press of Kentucky, 2001.

Jargon Society. *Appalachian Photographs of Doris Ulmann.* Penland, N.C.: Jargon Society, 1971.

Lamprell, Ramona, and Millard Lamprell. *O, Appalachia: Artists of the Southern Mountains.* Huntington, W.Va.: Huntington Museum, 1989.

Mint Museum of Art. *Southern Arts and Crafts.* Charlotte, N.C.: Mint Museum of Art, 1996.

National Museum of American Art. *More than Land or Sky.* Washington D.C.: Smithsonian Institute, 1981.

Poesch, Jesse. *The Art of the Old South.* New York: Knopf, 1983.

Qualla Arts and Crafts Mutual, Inc. *Contemporary Artists and Craftsmen of the Eastern Band.* Cherokee, N.C.: Qualla, 1987.

Shapiro, Henry D. *Appalachia on Our Mind.* Chapel Hill: Univ. of North Carolina Press, 1978.

Virginia Museum of Fine Arts. *Painting in the South.* Richmond: Virginia Museum of Fine Arts, 1983.

Whisnant, David E. *All that Is Native and Fine: The Politics of Culture in an American Region.* Chapel Hill: Univ. of North Carolina Press, 1983.

Wigginton, Eliot, et al., eds. *The Foxfire Book* and *Foxfire 2–11*. New York: Anchor Press/Doubleday, 1972–2003.

Wilson, Charles Reagan, and William Ferris. *Encyclopedia of Southern Culture.* Chapel Hill: Univ. of North Carolina Press, 1989.

Wilson, Kathleen Curtis. *Textile Art from Southern Appalachia: The Quiet Work of Women.* Johnson City, Tenn.: Overmountain Press, 2001.

Other Resources

Art Museums in Appalachia

Asheville Museum of Art, Asheville, N.C.
Hunter Museum of Art, Chattanooga, Tenn.
Huntington Museum of Art, Huntington, W.Va.
Knoxville Museum of Art, Knoxville, Tenn.

Places to See Native American Art

McClung Museum, Knoxville, Tenn.
Museum of the Cherokee Indian, Cherokee, N.C.
Oconaluftee Indian Village, Cherokee, N.C.
Qualla Arts and Crafts Mutual, Inc., Cherokee, N.C.

Appalachian Folklife Museums/Interpretive Centers

Appalachian Culture Museum, Boone, N.C.
Blue Ridge Institute, Ferrum, Va.
Center for Appalachian Studies, East Tennessee State University, Jouhnson City, Tenn.
The Farm at Selu Conservancy, Radford, Va.
Mountain Heritage Center, Cullowhee, N.C.
Museum of Appalachia, Norris, Tenn.

Places to See or Study Crafts

Appalachian Center for Crafts, Smithville, Tenn.
Arrowmont School of Arts and Crafts, Gatlinburg, Tenn.
Berea College Archive, Berea, Ky.
Folk Art Center (Blue Ridge Parkway), Asheville, N.C.
John C. Campbell Folk School, Brasstown, N.C.
Kentucky School of Craft, Hindman, Ky.
Penland School of Crafts, Penland, N.C.

Places to See Outdoor Sculpture

Stone Mountain, Ga., public monument
University of Tennessee, Knoxville, outdoor sculpture throughout campus

M. ANNA FARIELLO

Sites outside the Region with Collections Relevant to Appalachian Art

Atlanta History Center and High Museum of Art, Atlanta, Ga.

Fisk University Galleries, Nashville, Tenn.

Georgia Museum of Art, Athens, Ga.

Museum of Early Southern Decorative Arts, Winston-Salem, N.C.

University of North Carolina, Southern Historical Collection, Chapel Hill, N.C.

APPALACHIANS OUTSIDE THE REGION

PHILLIP J. OBERMILLER, MICHAEL E. MALONEY, AND PAULETTA HANSEL

Early Out-Migrations

Throughout the history of Appalachia, people have moved into the region, traveled through the mountains, or left their mountain homes to settle in new places. The early settlers in the Ozark Mountains of Missouri and Arkansas came predominantly from migration out of the southern Appalachians between 1820 and 1840. A second wave of Appalachian migrants came to the Ozark-Ouachita mountain region following the Civil War. High rates of natural increase and subsequent overcrowding in the mountains between 1845 and 1880 brought families south and west out of the Appalachians into the Texas hill country. Jobs in the timber industry, along with the availability of large tracts of timber under the Federal Homestead Act, attracted migrants from the southern mountains to the states of Wisconsin, Washington, and Oregon.

Under Andrew Jackson's policy of Native American removal, some twenty thousand Cherokee were forced off of their mountain lands in eastern Tennessee, northern Georgia, and western North Carolina between 1838 and 1839. The Trail of Tears, a forced march from Tennessee to Oklahoma, covered only a few hundred miles, but the hunger, disease, and exposure involved in this involuntary migration from the Appalachians took four thousand Cherokee lives.

As early as 1847, mountaineers were seen as a potential source of factory hands, or "lint-heads" as textile workers were then known in the Carolinas. With the expansion of the cotton industry in the 1880s and 1890s, mountaineers were actively sought to work in the mill towns of the Piedmont. For many, these were the first steps in a migratory process that would last for many decades.

Families and Communities

Although most Appalachian migration has never been as organized or devastating as the removal of the Cherokee to Oklahoma reservations, it has displayed a definite pattern, generally following family and community lines. Members of a family would leave to scout employment opportunities and living conditions in other areas, then report their findings back to the base family. If the news was good, other family members would follow. If the news was bad, the "scouts" would have a safe haven to which they could return.

The Appalachian kinship system has been a highly effective means of relocation for literally millions of mountaineers. The extended family became a key survival mechanism, allowing Appalachian migrants to expand their economic opportunities in good times while reducing their risk during hard times. Moreover, it engendered frequent visits among relatives. This provided a social dimension beyond the purely functional aspects of reporting on employment opportunities or having an economic refuge: visits with kin were a form of cultural refreshment and social renewal that sustained Appalachian culture in urban areas.

Community also played an important role in channeling migration. Migrant families would typically move to cities and urban neighborhoods where some of their fellow townspeople had already settled. Some urban neighborhoods would eventually become known by the Appalachian county from which most of their new residents came. Moreover, mountain communities socialized their young to become migrants. Some Appalachian school teachers, for example, would routinely preface statements to their students with "When you grow up and move away from here . . ."

Flowing along family and community lines, the migration streams were often geographically discrete and highly focused. For example, families from the communities of eastern Tennessee most often went to Chicago; eastern Kentucky families favored Cincinnati, Dayton, and Detroit; West Virginians moved east to Baltimore or west to Columbus or Cleveland. Thus the cultural diversity of the mountains was replicated in the migration streams and in the urban neighborhoods into which they flowed.

Using the stem and branch system, many Appalachian migrants initially took temporary jobs before settling permanently outside of the region. Relying on a stable base in the Appalachians, the migrants became temporary laborers or, in more contemporary language, migrant workers. For instance, as early as 1907 onion growers in Ohio went into the mountains of Kentucky and West Virginia seeking seasonal labor. By the 1930s, many of these seasonal workers had become "stay-over" residents of northeastern Ohio; some stayed voluntarily to save the expense of transportation, while others simply could not afford to go back home between seasons. The situation in Indiana during the 1930s was similar; most of the five thousand out-of-state migrant workers who came to pick the tomato crop were from Kentucky. Some of these families were forced to sleep in barns, tent "jungles," and even straw stacks. After two or three seasons, many families stayed in Indiana and tried to find better, more permanent quarters.

Recruitment

The industrialization of the Appalachians after the Civil War attracted job seekers from the British Isles as well as numerous southern, central, and eastern European immigrant workers. The same economic opportunities drew newly emancipated black workers into the region from the Deep South. These groups, combined with white mountaineers, formed a labor pool experienced in railroad construction and coal mining.

Active recruitment of southern black and Appalachian workers grew after immigration restriction laws were passed in the wake of World War I. The expanding American economy required a larger work force at the same time as the flow of European immigrant labor to this country was being forcibly reduced. Company recruiters turned their attention to rural America, including the mountains and the Deep South. Using posters and newspaper ads along with enticements such as free, one-way train tickets, the recruiters got their message to the mountains, and mountain families responded. For example, the explosive growth of the rubber industry in Akron, Ohio, brought on an intensive recruitment campaign in West Virginia and a concomitant surge in migration to the Rubber City. In 1920, estimates of the mountaineer population in Akron ranged from 50,000 to 77,000 people, giving this Ohio city another title, the "Capital of West Virginia."

In addition to their availability, Appalachian workers were highly sought after for a variety of other reasons. Inured to the grueling labor of farming, timbering, and mining, Appalachians adapted quickly to the harsh circumstances of factory work. Moreover, they were perceived as "100 percent Americans" and therefore less susceptible to the call of bolshevism, an ideology employers greatly feared in their workers during the aftermath of World War I. For many employers of that era, the concrete expression of communism among their workers was the labor union. Perceived as fiercely independent workers, Appalachians were seen as being relatively immune to union organizing in the eyes of the companies that courted them.

In fact, urban employers seriously misjudged the Appalachian migrant worker's willingness to organize. The United Mine Workers of America was founded in 1890 and within four decades became one of the nation's strongest unions when Appalachian miners rallied to the calls of Mother Jones and John L. Lewis. In 1934, Appalachian migrant workers in Ohio formed the National Farm Laborers' Union, an affiliate of the American Federation of Labor. Walter Reuther, a migrant from West Virginia, organized Detroit's first sit-down strike in 1936 and went on to become president of the United Auto Workers.

Industrial work had its own seasons, and the mountaineers working in canneries, mills, and factories were regularly laid off according to cyclical fluctuations in the marketplace. During the Depression years of the 1930s, for example, the Ford factories in southeastern Michigan operated only from January to April. Having established an inventory of autos sufficient to carry through the rest of the year, the factory hands, many from the mountains, were laid off. Appalachian migrants went back to the mountains to work small "dog hole" mines or their family farms until they were called back to Detroit. This form of shuttle migration was familiar to many migrant families and continued until the outset of World War II.

Over time, Appalachian migration was augmented by improvements in transportation. In the late 1920s, the first surfaced highways and through-bus routes appeared in the mountains. More road-building programs came in the 1930s during the Roosevelt administration. North-south arteries such as Routes 23, 25, and 27, along with east-west corridors such as Routes 50 and 52, made the mountains and many outlying cities more accessible to each other.

Prewar and Postwar Migrations

World War II proved to be a watershed in Appalachian migration. Men and women left the mountains for military service or jobs in the war industries located in metropolitan areas along the eastern seaboard and in the Midwest. Prior to World War II, the first to leave the mountains were often those who had lived in the Appalachians the shortest period of time. Southern blacks and ethnic minorities who had found jobs in the mountains building railroads, mining coal, and cutting timber were readily attracted to the urban industrial labor force. Those who had resided in the mountains for generations were slower to leave but eventually joined the migration streams in growing numbers.

All migrants are influenced by both "push" factors that encourage them to leave their home place and "pull" factors that draw them toward a new location. Along with the pull factor of employment opportunities reinforced by active recruitment, population density became an important force pushing mountaineers out of the Appalachian region during the first half of the twentieth century. While birth rates in the country as a whole were falling, the rate of natural increase remained high in the Appalachian region. The resulting large families created another incentive for migration by putting a strain on basic local resources such as housing, education, and jobs.

After World War II, technological improvements caused fundamental changes in the region's economy that created a new push factor forcing workers and their families out of the mountains. Coal was displaced by electricity, diesel oil, and natural gas as the fuel of choice in steel mills, in marine and railroad engines, and in commercial and residential furnaces. Increased automation raised productivity in mining, timbering, and farming while shrinking the number of workers required to operate the machinery. The economic free fall in the mountains resulting from these structural changes was steep and painful. The relocation trends among mountaineers that had begun in the years prior to World War I and continued through World War II grew in the postwar era into a huge migration involving millions of Appalachian people.

In addition to the push factor of a devastated regional economy, industrialized urban areas outside of Appalachia had a great deal of allure. Postwar service, construction, and manufacturing jobs were abundant; a substantial housing stock became available as previous immigrant groups moved to the suburbs; and educational opportunities appeared to be plentiful.

Appalachian migration affected not only the future of the region but also the nature of the cities. Most of the major metropolitan areas surrounding the region soon had Appalachian populations in the range of 15 percent. In some highly favored destinations such as Cincinnati, the proportion was much higher. Like European immigrants, Appalachians formed enclaves or urban villages within cities. They replicated their rural community structures as best they could in their urban neighborhoods by, for example, establishing small, sectarian churches. In some cases, this desire for community resulted in large, densely populated Appalachian neighborhoods with more residents than some rural counties in the region.

Contemporary Out-Migration

After peaking in the late 1950s, Appalachian migration began to decline in sheer numbers. Although they have never stopped, the migration streams have changed direction. Earlier migrations clearly favored cities in the heavily industrialized areas of the Northeast and Midwest. Since 1980, a new trend has developed with the migration flows out of Appalachia going to economically thriving cities in the South and West.

A new component of today's Appalachian migration streams are the frail elderly. Without relatives or sufficient numbers of local care facilities in the mountains, some older Appalachians are forced to join urban family members or seek assisted living facilities outside of the region. There is also a stream of return migration as Appalachian retirees come back to the mountains. Some of those who are reappearing in Appalachia are in fact shuttle migrants—urban residents who maintain cabins and vacation homes in the mountain areas from which their families migrated. There is also evidence that the national efforts at welfare reform are affecting the composition of Appalachian migration. "Welfare to Work" programs assume jobs are available for able welfare recipients and place time restrictions on how long a person may receive payments. In those cases in which welfare payments are stopped and local jobs are unavailable in Appalachia, the region's poor have to move away in order to survive.

Urban Appalachians

The term "urban Appalachian" was coined in the early 1970s by Appalachians living outside the region after "Appalachian migrant" was no longer an accurate description. Today, most urban Appalachians are not members of the first generation of migrants but are the children, grandchildren, and great-grandchildren of those migrants. Although there are urban Appalachians living in cities within the region, this section focuses principally on those who live in urban areas outside of the Appalachian region.

Throughout the 1950s and 1960s, families left the mountains for the cities by the car full. The receiving cities did not quite know how to deal with these internal migrants, or even what to call them. Newspaper and magazine articles from this period refer to the mountain migrants variously as WASPs (white Appalachian southern Protestants), SAMs (southern Appalachian migrants), SANs (southern Appalachian newcomers), and "Oakies of the '60s." Street-level labels were more pernicious: redneck, swamp turkey, cracker, brier, ridgerunner, hillbilly.

The information that flowed through the migrants' stem and branch family networks enabled many of the newcomers to find jobs and to move out of urban port-of-entry areas into blue-collar neighborhoods near their work. Their moves were also prompted by the desire to be among family and friends and near familiar shops and services; these residential preferences soon created large Appalachian enclaves outside of the port-of-entry neighborhoods, which were often little more than central-city slums.

Accustomed to self-sufficiency and possessing a strong work ethic, the Appalachian migrant family put all available workers—men, women, and older children—into the urban labor force. Although frequently classified as unskilled labor by urban employers, the migrants in fact brought a tremendous inventory of knowledge, experience, and skills with them, which they soon adapted to the urban workplace. Former miners had experience in clearing roads, sinking shafts, shoring up tunnels, and illuminating and ventilating the mines. They put these skills to work in urban areas as heavy equipment operators, construction workers, carpenters, HVAC technicians, and electricians. Machine operators from mill towns made the transition to assembly-line workers in local plants. Sawmill workers found jobs in paper manufacturing and furniture factories. Women with no previous employment experience quickly adapted sewing skills to producing everything from mattresses to coffin liners, cooking skills took them into restaurants and commercial bakeries, and housekeeping skills brought them jobs in motels and hospitals. Appalachian migrants with more education found work as business managers, nurses, teachers, and social workers.

Black Appalachian Migrants

As many as one out of ten Appalachian migrants were black, reflecting the overall racial composition of the region. The industrialization of Appalachia resulted in a great loss of jobs, and blacks were often among the first to lose work. In some eastern Kentucky counties, the black population dropped by 67 percent between 1920 and 1960.

Black Appalachians in general identified and associated with urban blacks rather than their white counterparts from the region. This assimilation into the urban black community occurred despite the fact that black Appalachians as a group enjoy higher incomes and occupational status than their urban black counterparts. On the other hand, black Appalachians in the cities have less education, smaller incomes, and a lower occupational status than white Appalachians.

Black Appalachians are seldom recognized by others in the city, but they know who they are. The Eastern Kentucky Social Club (EKSC) was formed when a small group of black Appalachian migrants living in Cleveland decided in 1967 to hold a reunion of their friends from the Kentucky towns of Lynch and Benham. By 1971, there were local EKSC chapters in Cleveland, Chicago, Detroit, and Lynch. Currently, there are eleven local chapters attending the annual Memorial Day "down home" event in Lynch and coming to a reunion held on the Labor Day weekend each year. Today the EKSC continues to hold reunions in cities such as Long Beach, Milwaukee, Atlanta, Cleveland, Houston, Chicago, Detroit, and Lexington.

Stereotypes

The epithet "redneck" first appeared in the American lexicon in the 1830s, just about the time of the first migrations from the Appalachians to the rural West. "Hillbilly" came into common use at the beginning of the twentieth century, just as these migration flows were turning from the West to the urban North. The comic strip *Li'l Abner* appeared in the 1930s as Appalachian shuttle migration between the cities and the mountains was underway. *The Beverly Hillbillies* became a television sensation in the 1960s on the heels of Appalachia's great migration.

Stereotypes generally have a twofold nature: first, to ridicule the subject group because of its perceived difference from prevailing norms, and second, to provide the rationale for active discrimination against the group. The first phase belittles the group in what appears to be a humorous or benign manner: urban Appalachians were initially branded with the lazy, ignorant image of the barefoot hillbilly asleep under a tree with a jug under one arm and a hound dog under the other. Jokes about incest among mountaineers promote one of the most prevalent and pernicious misconceptions in urban society. As newcomers are perceived as a threat in the competition for jobs and housing, the stereotypes turn to depictions of a violent and menacing group. In the Appalachian case, the urban white community fabricated an image of mountaineers as combative, knife-wielding rednecks. In the urban black community, Appalachian newcomers were often mislabeled as members of the Ku Klux Klan.

The influx of mountain whites into urban areas affected the receiving communities in a variety of ways, not the least of which was in the area of race relations. The Detroit race riot of 1943 was popularly, and incorrectly, blamed on southern white migrants to that city. Racial tensions rose across the country in the wake of the riots. The image of urban Appalachians as extreme racists is one of the many negative stereotypes used to denigrate the group. In fact, there is no evidence that racism, incest, violence, or other antisocial behaviors are more prevalent among Appalachians than any other urban group. The stereotypes are most often political ploys to disadvantage a particular group in the urban competition for resources, opportunities, and power.

Urban Appalachian Organizations

Conventional thinking among urban leaders, social workers, educators, and other residents was that urban Appalachians either would not or could not

245

organize as did earlier immigrants to the cities. Nevertheless, Appalachian migrant organizations have been successfully established in several cities.

The West Virginia Society in Akron, Ohio, was founded in 1917 when more than eight hundred people gathered for a picnic. They elected officers and identified their mission as strengthening the friendship between the West Virginians now living in Ohio. The society's purpose was primarily social. Its annual picnic in 1937 attracted thirty thousand people, but today it does not hold regular meetings. Dayton's Our Common Heritage grew out of a picnic event as well. Lela Estes, president of the organization, remembers the group formed in 1972 following a "big homecoming type event" sponsored by the Kentucky Chamber of Commerce. The organization has gained in credibility over the years and celebrates its Appalachian heritage each year with one of the largest cultural festivals in Dayton.

In the Detroit area, the Kentuckians of Michigan organized in 1960. Formed as a "Kentucky organization, hoping to keep alive our family roots," the group owns its own park and continues to draw about fifteen hundred people to its annual picnics. In 1959, Stanley Dezarn, an elementary school principal in Hamilton, Ohio, founded an organization called the O'Tucks to hold annual "homecomings" for the area's Kentucky migrants. At the end of the 1970s, the O'Tucks started their current tradition of an annual dinner at the Hamiltonian Hotel. Today, about four hundred people gather each December at the O'Tucks banquet to celebrate their mountain heritage, listen to Renfro Valley musicians, and recognize scholarship recipients.

In Cincinnati, the first urban Appalachian street academies, the East End Adult Education Center and the Lower Price Hill Community School, were organized in 1972. The Appalachian Community Development Association, dedicated to promoting Appalachian culture, was founded in late 1973; the Urban Appalachian Council, an advocacy and social welfare organization, was incorporated in 1974. In 1989, the Appalachian political action group Appal-PAC was formed.

Arts, Music, and Literature in Urban Culture

More than a generation away from the great migration from the mountains to the city, urban Appalachian art has deep roots in both locales. Organized cultural programs in cities such as Cincinnati and Dayton focus not just on preserving Appalachian art forms but on chronicling the experiences of Appalachian migrants and their descendants and exploring the dynamic blend of rural traditions and city experiences in our families and communities.

One such program is the Urban Appalachian Council's (UAC) Cultural Program in Cincinnati, Ohio. From its beginning, the UAC has sought to

OBERMILLER, MALONEY, AND HANSEL

increase appreciation of and pride in Appalachian cultural heritage, both within the Appalachian community and throughout greater Cincinnati. In the fall of 1988, UAC formed the Cultural Task Force, the major focus of which is to encourage artistic expression by urban Appalachians through artist residencies, community arts projects, and other means. An example of such expression is *The Lower Price Hill Story,* a theater piece written and performed by a Lower Price Hill youth group with the assistance of local artists.

The UAC is not the only community organization to use the arts in reaching its goals. In Kentucky, Covington Community Center's *Jack in the City* developed and presented urban Jack Tales to look at life in that urban Appalachian community. In Ohio, Dayton's CityFolks engaged in a multiyear residency with Appalshop's Roadside Theater to create *The Dayton Story Project,* using storytelling, theater, and music. Ohio's Miami Valley, between Xenia and Cincinnati, has perhaps the world's largest concentration of bluegrass, country, and gospel groups. The Solid Rock Church near Middletown is one of the many large Appalachian-led congregations in Ohio. It has become a significant center for the presentation and celebration of bluegrass gospel music and in 2003 hosted Ralph Stanley. Appalachian cultural festivals continue to be major events in both Cincinnati and Dayton. With its Appalachian Outreach Program, Dayton's Sinclair Community College is a local leader in providing arts programming with a mountain theme.

Appalachian migration literature dates back to this country's early fascination with the Appalachian region. One of the earliest pieces is a short story by Elizabeth Haven Appleton published in *Atlantic Monthly* in 1864. The work of John Fox Jr. expands on the theme of Appalachian migrants as "strangers in a strange land." Best known is Harriette Arnow's novel *The Dollmaker,* published in 1954, which chronicles the journey of a fictional Kentucky family to the Detroit of World War II.

Even now, most urban Appalachian literature deals with migratory themes. Most urban writers identified with the Appalachian region are mountain-born. Many, for example poet and essayist Richard Hague, an Appalachian from Steubenville, Ohio, living in Cincinnati since the 1960s, produce writing with a stronger connection to the Appalachian region than to the communities where Appalachian migrants settled. Others, such as poet Brenda Saylor, explore through their writing a sense of displacement or a bifurcated sense of place. A few writers, notably novelist Mike Henson, have created very graphic descriptions of urban life as seen through the eyes of young Appalachian migrants. To date, a self-identified second-generation urban Appalachian writer (city born and raised) has yet to emerge.

"Perceptions of Home: The Urban Appalachian Spirit" is a traveling exhibit of photography and oral history produced by the Urban Appalachian Council in collaboration with Appalachian photographer Malcolm J. Wilson and writer Don Corathers. This exhibit of twenty-four rough lumber and cedar panels tells the tale of Appalachian migration through the stories of twenty-two families and individuals who through choice or circumstances made the urban environment of greater Cincinnati their home. Photographic portraits of these individuals and families are presented with short biographies on each cedar exhibit panel. The exhibit also includes a brief history of the Appalachian migration and photographs of rural and urban communities. An exhibit guide includes selected photographs from the exhibit, essays by noted Appalachian scholars Ronald Eller and Michael Maloney, and selections from the interviews with these individuals and families who once called Appalachia home. A recorded audio track of interviews and music, housed in a kiosk, travels with the exhibit. The Urban Appalachian Council has also sponsored visual-arts residencies. A collaboration between urban Appalachian artist Lisa Schare and community youth groups has resulted in mural projects in two Cincinnati neighborhoods, Lower Price Hill and East Price Hill.

Cincinnati's Annual Appalachian Festival, sponsored by the Appalachian Community Development Association, has been since 1969 one of the most visible indications of an Appalachian presence in that city. Featuring music, crafts, storytelling, and demonstrations by artisans, the three-day festival (held over Mother's Day weekend) draws nearly fifty thousand people annually. Our Common Heritage in Dayton sponsors an annual Mountain Days Festival. The southwestern Ohio community of Hamilton held an annual Down Home Festival well into the 1990s.

The predominantly Appalachian Cincinnati neighborhood of Lower Price Hill holds an annual Mini-Appalachian Festival featuring bluegrass music, crafts, and traditional food on the weekend prior to the citywide festival. Summer festivals in Cincinnati's other Appalachian communities are not specifically Appalachian but are reflective of the culture through arts, food, and other folkways.

Urban Appalachians Today

Urban Appalachians now encompass the entire migration spectrum, from recent arrivals to families that have lived outside the region for several generations. Although large-scale approaches such as survey research and census data necessarily lose some of the flavor of individual experiences, they nonetheless give a sense of contemporary urban Appalachian life. In our research, we used survey information gathered from individual respondents in Hamilton County,

Ohio, in 2001 as well as information from the 2000 census on neighborhoods in the county's principal city, Cincinnati. While Appalachians are not identified as such in the census, the census findings in the city's predominantly Appalachian neighborhoods do produce useful insights. Moreover, the social and demographic characteristics of urban Appalachians in southwestern Ohio can be used as an effective template for understanding similar communities in other cities.

At least one in five people in Hamilton County is Appalachian. As the migration streams slow and change direction, actual migrants are outnumbered by Appalachians who are lifelong residents of the county. One in six of the county's residents is both Appalachian and African American.

Appalachian women outnumber their male counterparts three to two. This can be attributed to the natural mortality rate among an aging population in which women frequently outlive men and to a divorce rate among Appalachians which is higher than that for non-Appalachian whites and African Americans. (Divorced males tend to be more mobile than their former spouses.) Although previous surveys have attested to the stability of the urban Appalachian family, the 2001 survey indicates this circumstance may be changing.

Aging is also an important demographic factor in the urban Appalachian population. In Hamilton County, the average age of white Appalachians is forty-nine, for non-Appalachian whites forty-three, and forty-two for black residents. The aging factor may also explain the relatively large number of adults in Appalachian households when compared with the other two resident groups. The age factor does not affect time of residence in the county, however. All three comparison groups have lived in Hamilton County for an average of thirty-three years.

Nearly one in four Appalachians in the county does not have a high school diploma; at the other end of the educational spectrum, more than one in five Appalachians has a college degree or some postcollege education. Appalachians in Hamilton County's labor force had a very high employment rate (95 percent) in 2001, but 15 percent of these were involved in part-time work. Just over half of Appalachians reported total family incomes in the range between twenty thousand and fifty thousand dollars, a proportion significantly higher than that reported by non-Appalachian white families and African American families. High employment rates and large numbers of adults per household have translated into higher incomes for Appalachians than for the comparison groups.

Although they are predominantly Protestant (66 percent), nearly one in five Appalachians in the county is Catholic, and about one in seven responded "other/none" to the religion question on the survey. At the time of the survey, Appalachians were concentrated in suburban areas of the county outside of the city of Cincinnati at a nearly two-to-one ratio.

We can summarize the survey data on urban Appalachians in Hamilton County by noting that they are a major population group in the area. In Cincinnati, Appalachians make up a major component of the work force, as they do in many cities throughout the Midwest. Many have risen to leadership positions in the labor movement, education, social services, health care, medicine, business, the arts, and government. Covington, Kentucky, as well as Cincinnati and Dayton in Ohio, have had Appalachian mayors. The racial composition of urban Appalachians is similar to that of the Appalachian region as a whole. Appalachian women outnumber men as the typical nuclear family fades due to death and divorce. Urban Appalachians are aging, and they are aging in place because their residency times are on a par with other groups. Urban Appalachians do not appear to be returning to the region in large numbers during their retirement years. The county's urban Appalachians have reasonable educational attainment but are still not on a par with non-Appalachian whites in terms of schooling. Appalachian workers in Hamilton County have high employment rates and commensurately high incomes. Signs of assimilation for urban Appalachians appear in their high rates of suburban residency and election of alternatives to Protestantism.

The rosy picture of urban Appalachians painted by the county-level data—for instance, their high employment and incomes as well as their concentration in the suburbs—is tempered by the community-level analysis. There are pockets of deep Appalachian poverty in the county and other communities living at the margins of success. Some blue-collar Appalachians—their numbers are not insignificant—live just one serious health problem or pink slip from poverty.

As we have noted, Appalachians in the greater Cincinnati area are widely dispersed throughout the metropolitan area. However, blue-collar Appalachians are more likely than the affluent to live in ethnic enclaves. Specific neighborhoods in Cincinnati and the adjacent cities of Covington, Newport, Norwood, and Elmwood Place have long been identified as Appalachian communities. Predominantly Appalachian neighborhoods within Cincinnati include Lower Price Hill, East Price Hill, South Fairmount, Camp Washington, East End, Sedamsville-Riverside, Linwood, Carthage, and Northside. By using data from four U.S. censuses (1970, 1980, 1990, 2000), it is possible to measure socioeconomic trends in these neighborhoods to see what socioeconomic changes are affecting urban Appalachians.

The first conclusion from examining the census data is that all of Cincinnati's Appalachian neighborhoods are declining in population. This is similar to population trends for the city of Cincinnati overall: between 1970 and 2000, Cincinnati lost 121,862 residents, or 26.9 percent of its population. The rate of loss in its Appalachian neighborhoods between 1980 and 1990 ranged from

−6 percent in East Price Hill to −50 percent in the East End. Between 1990 and 2000, on the other hand, these losses were much less dramatic.

In the most recent edition of the report, *The Social Areas of Cincinnati: An Analysis of Social Needs,* socioeconomic status (SES) is measured by an index consisting of income level, educational attainment, family status, housing (over-crowding), and occupational status. In terms of overall socioeconomic status, five of the nine Appalachian neighborhoods improved between 1990 and 2000 while the other four declined. Neither the improvements nor the declines in socioeconomic status were dramatic, however, except in the East End, where large-scale gentrification was accompanied by serious depopulation. Between 1980 and 1990, four Appalachian neighborhoods were among the twelve Cincinnati neighborhoods experiencing the greatest decline in socioeconomic status. In the period between 1990 and 2000, no Appalachian and only two African American neighborhoods were on the list of the twelve fastest declining neighborhoods.

During the 1980s, poverty levels increased dramatically in all of Ohio's central cities, deeply affecting their African American and urban Appalachian residents. In the case of Cincinnati's Appalachian neighborhoods, 28 percent of the people in South Fairmount were living in poverty, 36 percent of Camp Washington's residents were in poverty, and the poverty rate in Lower Price Hill was 56 percent. The numbers of those in poverty dropped in all of Cincinnati's Appalachian neighborhoods during the 1990s. This, as well as some improvement in overall socioeconomic status, is consistent with the general boom in the local and national economies during the decade.

Poverty levels are accompanied and compounded by lack of education. At the beginning of the twenty-first century, high school dropout rates are at disastrous levels in some of Cincinnati's Appalachian neighborhoods. For instance, the rates of sixteen to twenty-one year olds not in school and not high school graduates in 2000 were 58 percent (the city's highest) in Lower Price Hill and over 33 percent in both Camp Washington and Carthage.

In the 2000 census, unemployment rates ranged from 6 percent in the blue-collar Appalachian neighborhood of Carthage to 14 percent in South Fairmount and Camp Washington, 16 percent in Lower Price Hill, and 18 percent in Linwood. The jobless rates in the Cincinnati's Appalachian neighborhoods are comparable to those of the city's most impoverished African American neighborhoods.

Historically, Appalachian migration has been an important component of American urbanization, and it remains so to this day. Urban Appalachians in cities and towns across the nation are contributors to the economic development and cultural vitality of their adopted homes. Along the way, they have established social organizations that help them celebrate their heritage and defend against stereotypes. While some live at the socioeconomic margins of urban society, the majority have established productive and culturally rich lives in the city.

Out-migrants at home for a family funeral, c. 1940. From the collection of Ricky Cox.

Protesters in Over the Rhine, an Appalachian neighborhood in Cincinnati, Ohio, 1996. By Jimmy Heath.

Military service in Iraq, 2003. From the collection of Grace Toney Edwards.

Suggested Readings

Berry, Chad. *Southern Migrants, Northern Exiles.* Urbana: Univ. of Illinois Press, 2000.

Borman, Kathryn M., and Phillip J. Obermiller, eds. *From Mountain to Metropolis: Appalachian Migrants in American Cities.* Westport, Conn.: Bergin & Garvey, 1994.

Obermiller, Phillip J., and Michael E. Maloney. "'We Ain't Agoin' Back': A Retrospective Look at Urban Appalachians in Greater Cincinnati." In *Appalachia: Social Context Past and Present,* edited by Phillip J. Obermiller and Michael E. Maloney. 4th ed. Dubuque, Iowa: Kendall/Hunt, 2002.

Obermiller, Phillip J., and Steven R. Howe. "New Paths and Patterns of Appalachian Migration, 1975–1990." In *Appalachia: Social Context Past and Present,* edited by Phillip J. Obermiller and Michael E. Maloney. 4th ed. Dubuque, Iowa: Kendall/Hunt, 2002.

Obermiller, Phillip J., Thomas E. Wagner, and E. Bruce Tucker, eds. *Appalachian Odyssey: Historical Perspectives on the Great Migration.* Westport, Conn.: Praeger, 2000.

Philliber, William W. *Appalachian Migrants in Urban America: Cultural Conflict or Ethnic Group Formation?* New York: Praeger, 1981.

Schwarzweller, Harry K., James S. Brown, and J. J. Mangalam. *Mountain Families in Transition: A Case Study of Appalachian Migration.* University Park: Pennsylvania State Univ. Press, 1971.

Wagner, Thomas E., and Phillip J. Obermiller. *African American Miners and Migrants: The Eastern Kentucky Social Club.* Urbana: Univ. of Illinois Press, 2004.

CONTRIBUTORS

ANNE B. BLAKENEY is an associate professor of Occupational Therapy at Eastern Kentucky University in Richmond, Kentucky. She is also a member of the Advisory Board for the Center for Appalachian Studies. Her dissertation research examined teenage motherhood in the political economy of an economically distressed central Appalachian county. Her previous publications in the area of Appalachian studies include the 1987 article "Appalachian Values: Implications for Occupational Therapy," in *Sociocultural Implications in Treatment in Occupational Therapy* (Haworth Press) and "The Impact of Culturally Bound Behaviors on Health Care Delivery in Appalachia," in *Health in Appalachia: Proceedings from the 1988 Conference on Appalachia* (Appalachian Center, Univ. of Kentucky, 1988).

SANDRA L. BALLARD is editor of *Appalachian Journal* and co-editor of *Listen Here: Women Writing in Appalachia* (Univ. Press of Kentucky, 2003). She is professor of English at Appalachian State University in Boone, North Carolina.

PATTI PAGE CHURCH, ESQ. is a practicing attorney concentrating on criminal defense in Lee County, Virginia. She holds a juris doctorate from the Appalachian School of Law in Grundy, Virginia, and is a member of the Virginia State Bar. She was employed for several years by the United Mine Workers International Union in Washington, D.C., before moving to the coalfields of Virginia. She characterizes herself as a community organizer/activist and a labor supporter/activist.

CHRISTINE WEISS DAUGHERTY is the founder of Rural Strategies, which has provided assistance to small nonprofit organizations in community and economic development since 1988. In 1996, she left the United States to run a rural development program in Slovakia, using community development tools developed in West Virginia, where she lived for twenty-five years. She now assists nonprofit organizations with fundraising, strategic planning, organizational management, and executive coaching and splits her time between West Virginia and California, with short-term contracts in both places as well as occasional overseas assignments. She serves on the Board of Directors of the Association of Enterprise Opportunity, a national trade association of microenterprise programs, and CAMEO, the California Association of Micro Enterprise Organizations.

M. ANNA FARIELLO is adjunct associate professor in the Interdisciplinary Studies Department at Virginia Tech in Blacksburg, Virginia. A former research fellow with the Smithsonian American Art Museum and field researcher for the Smithsonian

254

Center for Folklife, she has served as a section editor for the *Encyclopedia of Appalachia* and for ten years as director of the Radford University Art Museum. Currently director of *Curatorial InSight,* Fariello is author of *Objects and Meaning* (Scarecrow Press, 2003) and *Movers and Makers: Doris Ulmann's Portrait of the Craft Revival in Appalachia* (History Museum of Western Virginia, 2003).

STEPHEN L. FISHER is Hawthorne Professor of Political Science and director of the Appalachian Center for Community Service at Emory & Henry College. He has written extensively on political economy and citizen resistance in Appalachia and is the editor of *Fighting Back in Appalachia: Traditions of Resistance and Change* (Temple Univ. Press, 1993).

L. SUE GREER-PITT is a sociologist at Southeast Community College in Whitesburg, Kentucky. She earned her M.A. and Ph.D. degrees in sociology from the University of Kentucky. Major publications include "Marriage and the Family," in *Everyday Sociology* (2002); "The United States Forest Service and the Post-War Commodification of Outdoor Recreation," in *For Fun and Profit: Transforming Leisure into a Commercial Product* (1990); and with John B. Stephenson, "Ethnographers in Their Own Cultures: Two Appalachian Cases," in *Human Organization* (1981).

PAULETTA HANSEL is an eastern Kentucky native who has lived in Cincinnati, Ohio, since 1979. Her collection of poetry, *Divining,* was published in 2002 by WovenWord Press. Beginning in the 1970s, Pauletta helped establish early networks of Appalachian writers, including the Soupbean Poets and the Southern Appalachian Writers Cooperative. She is past assistant director of community development at the Urban Appalachian Council, where her work included directing community arts programming. Pauletta now works as teacher and administrator at Women Writing for (a) Change, a feminist creative writing center, and as a free-lance writer and consultant.

ROBERTA T. HERRIN is a native Appalachian who earned the B.S. and the Master of Arts in English from East Tennessee State University and the Ph.D. in English from the University of Tennessee. She has taught a wide range of courses, including Appalachian literature and children's literature, with a research emphasis in Appalachian children's literature. She is past president of the Appalachian Studies Association and past chair of the Board of Directors of the Appalachian Consortium. From 1995 to 2004, she served as Associate Dean of the Graduate School at ETSU, and she is currently director of the Center for Appalachian Studies and Services at ETSU. In 1998, she won the Cratis Williams/James Brown Service Award of the Appalachian Studies Association.

STEVAN R. JACKSON teaches anthropology in the Sociology and Anthropology Department at Radford University, as well as Appalachian Studies at Virginia Tech and Radford University, where he is an associate in the Appalachian Regional Studies Center. He has published numerous articles on Appalachian and Celtic subjects and ethnomusicology. His latest book, *Tartan and Strings: Ethnography of a Musical Culture,* was published in October 2004 by Kendall-Hunt Publishers. He is a professional performing musician in the folk, classical, and jazz genres.

BENNETT M. JUDKINS is Vice-President for Academic Affaris at Greensboro College. He was born and raised in the Appalachian Mountains of southwest Virginia and completed his doctorate at the University of Tennessee. His first book, *We Offer Ourselves as Evidence: Toward Workers' Control of Occupational Health* (Greenwood Press, 1986), was about the occupational health movements of coal miners and textile workers as they struggled with black lung and brown lung, respectively. He is currently doing research on cultural diversity in Appalachia and in the United States.

AJAY KALRA, a doctoral student in ethnomusicology at the University of Texas at Austin, honed his editorial and writing skills while working as an assistant editor with the *Encyclopedia of Appalachia* at the Center for Appalachian Studies and Services at East Tennessee State University. In an earlier phase of his life, Kalra was diagnostic radiologist, an artist, and a rock music trivia champion in Delhi, India. He is also a bassist and a collector of country rock, folk rock, jazz rock, early world jazz, and 1970s disco, soft rock, and Euro-pop music.

MICHAEL E. MALONEY is a native of Breathitt County, Kentucky, and the son of a coal miner. He applied his academic background in social and regional planning as the founding director of the Urban Appalachian Council. Since 1984 he has been a planning and management consultant for nonprofit, church, and governmental organizations. He is the editor of a monthly newspaper, the *Appalachian Connection,* and has produced four editions of the needs analysis *The Social Areas of Cincinnati.*

DANNY MILLER is chair of the Department of Literature and Language at Northern Kentucky University. He is the author of *Wingless Flights: Appalachian Women in Fiction* (Bowling Green State Univ. Popular Press, 1996). With Gurney Norman and Sharon Hatfield he is the editor of *An American Vein: Critical Readings in Appalachian Literature* (Ohio Univ. Press, 2005).

STEPHEN D. MOONEY teaches English and Appalachian Studies at Virginia Tech. He has published articles and reviews or has pieces forthcoming in *Appalachian Journal, Appalachian Heritage,* the *Journal of Kentucky Studies,* the *Journal of Appalachian Studies, CrossRoads: A Journal of Southern Culture, Iron Mountain Review, Now and Then,* the *Encyclopedia of Appalachia,* and the *West Virginia Encyclopedia.* He is also the author of longer studies, including *Mountain Voices* and *Coal Dust in Our Blood.*

IRENE MOSER is professor emeritus, Mountain State University, Beckley, West Virginia, where she taught literature, folklore, and Appalachian studies and founded the university's Appalachian Visions public program series with funding from the West Virginia Humanities Council and Christine Hatfield Lilly. In retirement, she teaches courses in folklore and anthropology as an adjunct in the Sociology Department at Warren Wilson College, Swannanoa, North Carolina, and at Western Carolina University in Cullowhee, North Carolina. Her publications include "Native American Imaginative Spaces," in *American Indian Studies* (Peter Lang, 1997), and "Entering the World of American Literature Through the [Cherokee] Discourse of Harmony," in *The Canon in the Classroom* (Garland, 1995).

PHILLIP J. OBERMILLER is a founding member of the Urban Appalachian Council and serves on the council's research committee. He is a Center fellow at the University of Kentucky's Appalachian Center and a Senior Visiting Scholar in the School of Planning at the University of Cincinnati. He coedited the fourth edition of *Appalachia: Social Context Past and Present* (Kendall/Hunt, 2002) and *Appalachian Odyssey: Perspectives on the Great Migration* (Praeger, 2000).

TED OLSON teaches Appalachian studies and English courses at East Tennessee State University. He is the author of *Blue Ridge Folklife* (1998), the editor of James Still's *From the Mountain, From the Valley: New and Collected Poems* (2001), the coeditor (with Charles K. Wolfe) of *The Bristol Sessions: Writings About the Big Bang of Country Music* (2005), the "Music" section editor for the *Encyclopedia of Appalachia* (2005), and the editor for Mercer University Press's *CrossRoads: A Southern Culture Annual.*

DAVID L. ROUSE is professor of philosophy at the University of Virginia's College at Wise. He has taught a variety of courses on environmental ethics as well as a course in Appalachian history. He has presented several papers on environmental and economic issues of the Appalachian region. His publications include essays in the *Radical Philosophy Review of Books.* His current research is on the political economy of coal.

SHAUNNA L. SCOTT is associate professor of sociology at the University of Kentucky, where she also serves as the director of Appalachian studies and is a faculty associate of the Appalachian Center. Her major works on Appalachia include *Two Sides to Everything: Community and Class Consciousness in Harlan County, Kentucky* (SUNY Press, 1995) and journal articles published in *American Ethnologist, Rural Sociology, Qualitative Sociology, Appalachian Journal,* and the *Journal of Appalachian Studies.*

THOMAS R. SHANNON is professor of sociology at Radford University. In the early 1980s, he was one of the founding members of the Appalachian Studies Committee at Radford. He has written a number of conference papers on economic and demographic trends in Appalachia. In the mid-1980s, he was coauthor (with William Hrezo) of *An Appalachian Atlas,* which is used in courses in Appalachian Studies at Radford University and elsewhere. He also has published two undergraduate sociology textbooks in the areas of world-system theory and urban sociology.

RICHARD STRAW is professor of history at Radford University, where he teaches courses on American history, Appalachia, and the American South. He has written on topics as diverse as coal mining, Appalachian music, historical photography, and Appalachian foodways. He is the coeditor, with Tyler Blethen, of *High Mountains Rising: Appalachia in Time and Place* (Univ. of Illinois Press, 2004) and *Images of America: Blacksburg* (Arcadia Press, 2004). Professor Straw's degrees are from Ohio University and the University of Missouri–Columbia, where he earned the Ph.D. in history in 1980.

SHARON TEETS is professor of education at Carson-Newman College. Publications relevant to education in Appalachia include editing the 1994 issue of *Hands On: A Journal for Teachers* (Foxfire publication) and the *Foxfire Course Book,* with Cynthia Paris and Bobby Starnes, in 1997. She was the senior author on two articles, "Foxfire:

Lighting the Way for Collaboration in Teacher Education," published in *Partnerships in Teacher Education: Schools and Colleges Working Together* (a monograph of the Association of Liberal Arts Colleges for Teacher Education, 1996), and "Foxfire: Constructivism for Teachers and Learners," published in *Action in Teacher Education,* in 1996.

DEBORAH THOMPSON is former director of the Appalachian Semester at Union College in Kentucky. She holds an M.A. degree from Appalachian State University and is currently a doctoral student in Geography at the University of Kentucky. She is coauthor of *Transylvania: The Architectural History of a Mountain County,* and is coeditor of the "Families and Communities" section of the *Encyclopedia of Appalachia.*

SUSAN O'DELL UNDERWOOD recently completed a novel, *Genesis Road.* She teaches creative writing and Appalachian literature courses at Carson-Newman College. Besides an MFA in Creative Writing from the University of North Carolina at Greensboro, she earned the Ph.D. in English from Florida State University; her dissertation concerns the poetry and fiction of Fred Chappell. She is currently coediting an anthology of Appalachian poetry with Jim Clark.

MELINDA BOLLAR WAGNER is professor of anthropology at Radford University, associate chair of the Appalachian Studies Program, and faculty advisor to the Appalachian Events Committee. She was president of the Appalachian Studies Association in 2004–5. Her publications include numerous book chapters and journal articles as well as *Metaphysics in Midwestern America* (Ohio State Univ. Press, 1980) and *God's Schools* (Rutgers Univ. Press, 1990). She received her Ph.D. in anthropology from the University of Michigan.

JACK WRIGHT is an artist whose work is strongly informed by the culture of the Appalachian Mountains. A founding member of the Appalship media collective in Kentucky, he is an actor, documentary filmmaker, and musician whose work has appeared on National Public Radio, PBS, June Appal Recordings, and in Hollywood films. His articles about Appalachian art and artists, particularly film and video, have appeared in *Independent Spirit, Iron Mountain Review, Appalachian Journal, Riverwind,* and other publications. Wright has twice received individual artist fellowships from the Ohio Arts Council for his writing. In 2002–3, he taught at Berea College, where he was the National Endowment for the Humanities Chair of Appalachian Studies. He lives in Athens, Ohio, and works at Ohio University in the MFA program in the School of Film, where he teaches personal documentary filmmaking and manages student film production.

Editors

GRACE TONEY EDWARDS directs the Appalachian Regional Studies Center at Radford University and is a Dalton Distinguished Professor of Appalachian Studies and English. Among her numerous articles, reviews, and book chapters are "Marilou Awiakta: Poet for the People" in *Her Words: Diverse Voices in Contemporary Appalachian*

Women's Poetry (2002), a critical essay about Corra Harris in the foreword to Harris's *A Circuit Rider's Wife* (1998), and "Emma Bell Miles: Feminist Crusader in Appalachia" in *Appalachia Inside Out*. She also served as coeditor for the "Literature" section of the *Encyclopedia of Appalachia*. She earned B.S. and M.A. degrees from Appalachian State University and her Ph.D. in English from the University of Virginia.

JoAnn Aust Asbury is a member of the English Department at Radford University, associate of the Appalachian Regional Studies Center, and assistant director of the Highland Summer Conference. She has published articles, poems, and essays in *Virginia English Bulletin, Bluefield Daily Telegraph, New River Historical Society Journal,* and *ERIC: Clearinghouse on Rural Education and Small Schools*. She is past editor of *ALCA-Lines: the Journal of the Assembly on the Literature and Culture of Appalachia,* an affiliate of the National Council of Teachers of English, and current editor of *Stitches,* the Appalachian Teachers' Network Newsletter.

Ricky L. Cox is a member of the English Department at Radford University, where he teaches composition, American literature, and Appalachian folklore. He has published essays, literary criticism, and photographs in regional journals and anthologies and has written several entries for the forthcoming *Encyclopedia of Appalachia*. As an associate of RU's Appalachian Regional Studies Center, he is currently coordinating development of the Farm at Selu: The C. E. Richardson Appalachian Heritage Education Park.

INDEX

272

New York: art, artists, 222, 228, 230;
forests, 53–54; health services, 104,
108; immigrants, 13, 19, 29, 39–40;
music recordings, 167–68; urban
legend, 153
newspaper, 18, 38, 57, 187, 239, 242
nineteenth century: agrarianism, 67; art in,
221–24, 229; distilling in, 145; economy of, 67–68, 70, 204; education,
122; forests, 14; immigrants in, 39;
isolation in, 5; mixed marriages, 33;
music in, 150–51, 163, 168–69, 173
Nixon, Richard, 18
Norman, Gurney, 45–47, 203–5
Norris, Tenn., 156
North Carolina: chestnut, 53–54; Civil
War, 8; conservation, 87; cultural
expressions, 10, 151, 155–56, 168,
170–71, 201–2, 209, 222, 227–29;
economic development, 63, 79, 226;
education, 122, 125–26, 130–31, **136**;
forests, 54; Great Smoky Mountains,
51; health, 105; Indians, 33–34, 220,
232; industry, 72; labor, 94; Lost
Colony, 34; migration, 35–36, 79,
237; minerals, 57; Melungeons,
34–35; national forests, 55–56; pulp
and paper, 55; settlement, 23, 34, **42**;
textiles, 20; Ulster Scots, 34. *See also*
western North Carolina.
North Carolina Piedmont, 33. *See also*
Piedmont, N.C.
North Dakota, 59
Northeast, 10, 14, 123–24, 242
northern Appalachia, 31, 104
Northwest Ordinance, 121
novel: in health care training, 110–11;
local color, 9–10. *See also Appalachian
Literature*
Now and Then, 132
nuclear family, 6, 249
nuclear power, 76
nursing, 10, 92, 106–7, 243

"O Death," 172
Oak Ridge, Tenn., 63, 87
Ocmulgee River, 51
Oconaluftee Indian Village, **42**, 220, **232**
Oconaluftee River, 144
Oconee River, 51
Office of Economic Opportunity
(OEO), 19
Offutt, Chris, 203
Ohio: environmental issues, 87–88;
migrant workers, 239–40; preserva-
tion of Appalachian traditions, 245–49;
protest, **252**; union activities, 13, 92.
*See also Appalachians Outside the
Region*
Ohio River, 3, 51
Ohio Valley Environmental Coalition, 88
Oklahoma, 34, 237–38
Old Christmas, 146
Old Dominion, 123
old-time music, 168
Olympic Games, 52
oral history, 204, 247
Oriskany Church, **190**
Osborne Brothers, 173
Otto, John Solomon, 178
Our Common Heritage, 245
outdoor dramas, 209
out-migration, 17, 75–77, 79, 202, 237,
241. *See also Appalachians Outside
the Region*
Over the Rhine (Cincinnati, Ohio), 252
Owl, Freeman, 144
Ozark Mountains, 168, 237

Palatinate, 36
paper manufacturing, 243
paper mill towns, 13
paper pulp mills, 55
Pardo, Juan, 37
Park Service, National, 52
Parton, Dolly, 166
paternalism, 71

INDEX

quilts, 147–48, **158**, 226, 230
Quinn, Carolyn, 193

Rabun County, Ga., 133
racism, 32, 85, 88, 244
Radford University, **43**, 131, **177**, 193,
    214; Appalachian Studies minor, 132;
    Art Museum, **233**; health care, 107,
    114; sculpture program, 229; teacher-
    training program, 131
Radford, Va., 63, **113–14**, **233**
Radical Reconstruction, 8
radio, 150, 154, 163–64, 166–67, 169–70,
    187
railroads, 11, 13, 38, 70, 152, 239, 241;
    building, 12, 54, 57, 240; and coal 75;
    coming of, 5; immigrants, 29, 40
Raitz, Karl B., 34, 46, 47
Raleigh, Sir Walter, 34
Rappahannock River, 51
Rasmussen, Donald, 91
Reagan, Ronald, 129
Reconstruction, 7, 29–30
recording industry, 166–67, 169
recreation, 37, 55–56, 87, 102, 124, 169
recreational facilities, 13, 52, 71
Red baiting, 85
Redemption Democrats, 9
Reece, Byron Herbert, 205
Reece, Florence, 173
Reed, Blind Alfred, 174
Reese, Nat, **177**
reform, 87, 91, 103, 201; education,
    94–95, 129–30, 133, 135; efforts, 91,
    130; health, 95; social, 188; tax, 87;
    welfare, 242. *See also* Kentucky
    Education Reform Act; Welfare
    Reform Act
Reformed-Presbyterian Church, 182
regional identity, 20, 169, 230–31
Regular Baptists, 183
religion. *See Religion in Appalachia*

Renfro Valley, Ky., 245
Republicans, 8–9, 18
retirement, 77, 79–80, 90, 92, 102, 249
return migration, 242
revival meetings, 183
rhythm and blues, 165, 174
Richards, Thomas Addison, 221
Ridge, Major, 33
Ritchie, Jean, 173
rivers: flooding, 17; navigation, 74; river
    bottoms, 52; valleys, 3, 6, 53, 62, 69.
    *See also Natural Resources and Envi-
    ronment of Appalachia*
road building, 6, 77, 240
Road Company, The, 210
Roadless Area Review and Evaluation
    (RARE II), 56
Roadside Theater, 210, **214**, 246
Roanoke Island, N.C., 34
Roanoke, Va., **244**
Roanoke (Staunton) River, 51
Roberts, Elizabeth Madox, 206
Robertson, Eck, 167
Robertson, James, 3
Romania(n), 28, 31
roof falls, 13, 60
Roosevelt, Franklin, 16
Roosevelt, Theodore, 55
roots music, 164–65
Ross, John, 33, 208
rubber industry, 239
Rural Arts Exhibition, 226
Russia(n), 31, 41, 153
Rylant, Cynthia, 209

Sacred Harp singing, 152
salt, 5, 7, 68
salvation, 120–21, 183–86, 188–89
sanitation, 13, 104
Savannah, Ga., 51
Save our Cumberland Mountains
    (SOCM), 88–89, 95

sawmills, 54, 68, **82**
Saylor, Brenda, 246
Schare, Lisa, 247
schools, 127, 131–32; arts, 155; attendance, 127; craft schools, 226; college preparatory, 120; company owned, 71; consolidation, 126, 128, 132, **136**; dame schools, 120; folk schools, 10, 125, 155; funding, 121, 123, 127; grammar, 123, 130, 131; high schools, 121, 125; home, 120; Latin grammar, 120; medical, 107; middle, 129, 134; missionary, 130; New England, 120; normal 131; one room, 15; private, 120, 127; public improvements, 7; public 9; settlement 10, 123–24, 225. *See also Education in Appalachia*
Scotch-Irish/Scots-Irish, 3–4, 32, 36, 46–47, 143, 145, 147, 154, 183, 193
Scotland, 27, 31, 33, 35–36, 43, 46, 151, 165, 193–94
Scott, Darrell, 173–74
Scottish Piper, **43**
Scruggs, Earl, 151, 172
sculpture(s), 149, 224, 228–29; aluminum, **233**
Secretary of Labor, 93
self-sufficiency, 5, 7, 21, 72, 243
Sellers, Bettie, 205
senior citizens, 77, 110, 242, 248–49
Sequoyah, 33, 207
serpent handling, 38
Settle, Mary Lee, 203–4
settlement, 67; frontier, 2, 122; English, 34; European, 167; Melungeon, 34; patterns of, 122; Ulster Scots, 35
settlement schools, 10, 123–24, 225
Seventh Day Adventist Church, 123
sexism, 85, 88
shaped notes (musical style), 152
Sharp, Cecil, 10, 151, 165
Shenandoah National Park, 56

Sheppard, Muriel, 225
"shivanee," **147**
Short, Ron, **214**
short stories, 9, 110–11, 200, 203, 205, 246. *See also Appalachian Literature*
Shull, Margaret Wise, 208
Shultz, Arnold, 171
shuttle migrants, 242
Silver, Roy, **65**, **98**
Simon, Charlie May, 207
Sinclair Community College, 246
singing school, **175**
Skaggs, Ricky, 166
Skidmore, Hubert, 207
Skycastle, **233**
slash-and-burn farming, 33
slavery, 3, 6–8, 37–38, 123, 150, 208, 229
Slavic, 13, 29, 31, 40, 143
small farm, 4, 7–8, 67, 70, 205
Smith, Bessie, 174
Smith, Earl Hobson, 209
Smith, Lee, 111, 164, 178
Smoky Mountains, 51
snake-handling, 184
Sneedville, Tenn., 63
Social Security Act, 16, 77
social welfare, 9, 245
Solid Rock Church, 246
Sophie Newcomb College, 228
Soupbean Poets, 205
South Africa(n), 93
South Carolina: artist, 230; automobile manufacturers, 103; forests, 53–55; gold, 57; gospel music, 172; textile mills, 72
Southern Appalachian Migrants (SAMs), 242
Southern Appalachian Newcomers (SANs), 242
Southern Baptists, 123, 182
Southern Empowerment Project, 96
Southern States Art League, 229

southwest Virginia: baptizing, **206**; coal, 11, 70; Dungannon Development Commission, 90; farming, 62; furniture factories, 72; Little River, **64**; Melungeons, 34; minerals, 57; outreach activities, 132; Pittson strike, 93; railroad building, 11; settlers, 3; topography, 51; VOP, 88. *See also* Virginia

Spanish, 27–28, 37

Spanish American War, 151

speech patterns, 108, 153, 154

square dancing, 149–50

Stanley Brothers, 172

Stanley, Doug, 153

Stanley, Ralph, 172–73, 246

Steele, William O., 207

steelworkers, 93

Stein, Conrad, 208

Steinbeck, John, 201

stem and branch system, 238

stereotype: early, 9; hillbilly, 168–70; homogeneity, 31–32, 41; region's culture, 163

Steubenville, Ohio, 246

stick-ball game, 144

Still, James, 201, 204–5, 208

stonemasons, 148

storyteller, 144, 153

storytelling: festivals and clubs, 154; forms of, 154; mountain culture, 143; multiple voice, 210; sessions, 153; social bond, 153; subject, 153; theatrical forms, 210–11; traditions, 151, 155. *See also Appalachian Folklife*

string bands, 150, 170

strip mining, 18, 80, 87, 110; competing, 75; destruction, 17, 76; fiction, 208; protests, 20; reclamation, 62; SOCM, 88, 94; surface, 17

Strother, David Hunter, 223

Stuart, Jesse, 194, 201, 207

subscription schools, 121

subsistence farming, 16

Summers County, W.Va., 211

Surface Mine Control and Reclamation Act (SMCRA), 60–61

surface mining, 58, 60, 61

Susquehanna River, 51

sustainable agriculture, 62

Swan Silvertones, The, 172

Swannanoa, N.C., 144

Swedish immigrants, 31

Swiss culture, 40

Syrian immigrants, 31

Szakos, Joe, 99

Taft-Hartley Amendment, 58

Tall Woman, The, 203

Tayal, Sudesh, **113**

Taylor, Emma, 144

teachers, 127–28, 243; channeling migration, 238; learner-centered approach, 133–35; migrants, 243; need for, 131; non-mountain, 127; post-Civil War, 9–10; preparation, 129; quality, 133–34; singing, 152; sources, 206. *See also Education in Appalachia*

Tennessee: African Americans, 12; agriculture, 62; arts, 210–11, **212**, 222–23, 226–29; Cherokees, 33, 144, 206, 237; Civil War, 7–8; coal mining, 11–12, 67, 70; development, 63; early settlers, 3; education, 96, 125–26, 131–32; English immigrants, 36; explorers, 28; dulcimer, 151; fiction, 200, 202, 206–7, 209; forests, 53–56; Germans, 39; health, 104, 107; Highlander Center, 96, 119, 174, 210; Melungeons, 34; minerals, 57; Museum of Appalachia, 156; music, 166, 170, 172–74; out migration, 237–38; protests, 87–88, 92, 96, 174; railroads, 11; river systems, 51; river valleys, 6–7; snake handling, 184; slavery, 7, 38; storytelling, 154; topography, 51; tourism, 17; Trail of

A Handbook to Appalachia was designed and typeset on a Macintosh computer system using QuarkXPress software. The body text is set in 10/13 Minion and display type is set in Novarese. This book was designed and typeset by Kelly Gray and manufactured by Thomson-Shore, Inc.